FERGIE
THE GREATEST

FERGIE
THE GREATEST

MANCHESTER UNITED 1986–2013

THE BIOGRAPHY OF SIR ALEX FERGUSON

FRANK WORRALL

JOHN BLAKE

Published by John Blake Publishing Ltd,
3 Bramber Court, 2 Bramber Road,
London W14 9PB, England

www.johnblakepublishing.co.uk

www.facebook.com/Johnblakepub facebook
twitter.com/johnblakepub twitter

First published as *Walking in a Fergie Wonderland* in 2010
This edition published in 2013

ISBN: 978-1-78219-730-0

British Library Cataloguing-in-Publication Data:

A catalogue record for this book is available from the British Library.

Design by www.envydesign.co.uk

Printed in Great Britain by CPI Group (UK) Ltd

3 5 7 9 10 8 6 4

Papers used by John Blake Publishing are natural, recyclable products made
from wood grown in sustainable forests. The manufacturing processes conform
to the environmental regulations of the country of origin.

Every attempt has been made to contact the relevant copyright-holders,
but some were unobtainable. We would be grateful if the
appropriate people could contact us.

This book is dedicated to my wife Angela, my sons Frankie Lennon and Jude Cantona, and my great friend Danny Bottono at the *Sun*.

CONTENTS

'Mourinho, are you listening?
You'd better keep the trophy glistening.
We'll be back here in May
To take it away
Walking in a Fergie wonderland!'

Manchester United fans taunted José Mourinho, then Chelsea manager, with this terrace chant in 2006.

ACKNOWLEDGEMENTS

SPECIAL THANKS: Allie Collins and all at John Blake Publishing. Alan Feltham and the boys at *SunSport*, Dave Morgan at the *Sun*, Ben Felsenburg at the *Daily Mail*, Alex Butler at *The Sunday Times*, Kit Tomlinson at *Unveiled*, and Mark Maddock at lastminute.com.

THANKS: Jon and Theo Simpson, Mike Gould, Duncan Williams, Ian Rondeau, Colin Forshaw, Ash Hussein, Gary Edwards, Adrian Baker, Clive Martin, Steven Gordon, Lee Clayton, Darren O'Driscoll, Martin Creasy, Lee Hassall, John Fitzpatrick, Roy Stone, Russell Forgham, Paul Hazeldine, Nigel Wareing and Tom Henderson Smith.

Not forgetting: Natalie, Barbara, Frank, Bob and Stephen, Gill, Lucy, Alex, Suzanne, Michael and William.

FRANK WORRALL is the author of 15 biographies on British and Irish sporting heroes – including the bestselling *Roy Keane: Red Man Walking*, *Rory McIlroy: The Biography* and *Lewis Hamilton: The Biography*. For more details about the author and his bestselling books with John Blake Publishing, visit www.frankworrall.com. Follow Frank Worrall on Twitter @frankworrall

CHAPTER 1
THE GOVAN-ER

'I'D NEVER BEEN AFRAID OF ANYONE BUT FERGUSON
WAS A FRIGHTENING BASTARD FROM THE START.'
Bobby McCulley, East Stirlingshire forward, June 1974

When Alex Ferguson arrived at Old Trafford in November 1986, he was largely unknown to fans of English football. In itself that is quite remarkable, given the way he had turned the Scottish game on its head by transforming Aberdeen into the No. 1 side at the expense of the 'Old Firm', Celtic and Rangers. But just as stunning is the way he worked his way from humble beginnings in Govan, Glasgow, to the very top of world football to become arguably the greatest manager ever.

There must be something special in the air up on the banks of the Clyde and in the coalmines of Lanarkshire – something that provides an inherent set of necessary traits, psyche and character for certain of its sons to become world-class football managers. Sir Alex is one of a breed steeped in the proud ideals and culture of the region that would also produce fellow legends Sir Matt Busby and Jock Stein.

1

Alexander Chapman Ferguson was born in Govan on 31 December 1941 to a Protestant, working-class family. He remembers his childhood as a happy one, a warm one, and says he felt secure, even though life on the edge of southwest Glasgow's rough-and-tumble shipyards could be exacting and challenging at times. He was to admit, 'there was never a shade of menace over my boyhood.'

Fergie was named after his father, Alexander Beaton Ferguson, a shipyard worker. Young Alex's brother Martin would also turn to the shipyard for work – indeed, he was to work with their father at the Fairfield yard. Years later, Sir Alex would pay tribute to them both by naming his luxury home in Wilmslow, Cheshire, after the yard in which they toiled – Fairfields. His mother Elizabeth had given birth to him at his grandmother Janet's home in Shieldhall Road, Govan, just yards from the River Clyde but he was to grow up in a tenement at 667 Govan Road (which has since been demolished), where he lived with his parents as well as Martin, who was born almost a year after him.

Money was tight and the brothers shared a bedroom but Alex had a sunny, optimistic outlook on life. He was a bright boy and attended Broomloan Road Primary School and later Govan High School – although he initially failed the qualifying exam for the secondary school after a period of ill health. At the age of 16 he knew he wanted to be a professional footballer. He was football mad – and had been since he first kicked a ball as a toddler. While his father Alex senior supported Celtic, both Alex junior and Martin were Rangers-crazy and Alex's ambition, as he grew up in Govan, was one day to play for the Ibrox giants.

Fergie explained his childhood obsession in this way: 'It was only football, football, football. That was it. My house [in

Govan] was one up from the back court and there were clothes poles on either side and it was all walled-in, so you could play there all the time. It was an absolute football arena – housewives wouldn't hang the washing on clotheslines; it was too dangerous – boys were playing football all the time. It was fantastic. The competitions were going on all summer. Boys were coming from all over Govan to play. Football was a release, it was what you loved, it was your enjoyment.'

Yet while his dream was to play for Rangers – and he would do everything in his power to achieve that ambition – he knew that he had to be realistic, too. He needed a job that he could fit his football around, one that would also provide a trade, so he became a toolmaking apprentice, even though he was convinced he had what it took to become a professional footballer. The job would one day provide him with an opportunity to show off his leadership qualities – instinctively, a proud, working-class man, he became interested in union activities while working in the Clyde shipyards. One day, as a shop steward, he would lead an unofficial walk-out over a pay dispute.

But football remained his main love. Of course, he had played his way up from youth teams to schoolboy level and local amateur outfits, but his career as a player began in earnest at the age of 17, with Queen's Park in 1958. He stayed there two years – fitting his toolmaking work around the football – and scored 20 goals in his 31 games, but he could not hold down a regular place in the side and moved to St Johnstone in 1960.

A bustling centre-forward, he would spend four years at McDiarmid Park before finally turning professional and joining Dunfermline in 1964. The highlight of his spell at St Johnstone had, ironically, come when he was called on to play against Rangers and duly grabbed a hat-trick. It was the first time St Johnstone had ever won at Ibrox – and it was the first time a player had scored a hat-trick against Rangers at their home fortress.

Fergie amassed a total of 19 goals in 37 games for Saints and easily bettered that with 66 in 89 at Dunfermline. Yet in the 64/65 season he was to experience the lows that invariably walk side by side with those joyous highs when he was dropped for the 1965 Scottish Cup final an hour before the game.

Willie Cunningham explained it was because of a poor performance in a league game against St Johnstone but Fergie was incandescent with rage and screamed 'You bastard!' at the Dunfermline boss. Eventually, Dunfermline lost the final 3-2 to Celtic and then failed to win the League by one point.

The following season (65/66), Fergie hit 45 goals in 51 games for Dunfermline – a feat that would earn him the accolade of joint top scorer in the Scottish League with Celtic's Joe McBride. Thirty-one of the 45 goals had come in the League. It was an astonishing goal record at a club not viewed as big-timers – and it would certainly have played a major part in bringing the big man's lifetime dream to fruition.

Yes, almost 10 years after he had set out on the trail to the top with Queen's Park, he eventually arrived there with his beloved Rangers. In 1967, the Ibrox outfit splashed out a fee of £65,000 for his signature – at the time a record between Scottish clubs.

But what should have been a joyful peak as a player ended with an acrimonious split after he was fingered for his team's 4-0 thrashing by Celtic in the 1969 Scottish Cup final. Fergie was blamed for one of the goals and forced to play for the club's junior side instead of the first team. According to his brother, Fergie was so upset by the experience that he threw his runners-up medal away. There were claims that he left Ibrox over racial discrimination because he married Cathy, a Catholic, but in his autobiography, *Managing My Life*, he stressed this was not the case; that the club knew of his wife's religion when he joined and that he quit Ibrox because of the bitterness over the Cup final.

The following October, Nottingham Forest wanted to sign him but Cathy was not keen on a move to England at the time, so he went to Falkirk. He was promoted to player-coach there, but when John Prentice became manager he removed Ferguson's coaching responsibilities. Fergie responded by requesting a transfer and moved to Ayr United in 1973, where he finished his playing career.

As a manager, Fergie started out as part-time boss of East Stirling in 1974, at the age of 32. He was paid the grand total of £40 a week but quickly earned the respect of his players with his disciplinarian attitude. It was there that the famous 'frightening bastard' quote would originate. Striker Bobby McCulley would say of Ferguson: 'He terrified us. I'd never been afraid of anyone before but he was such a frightening bastard from the start. Everything was focused towards his goals. Time didn't matter to him; he never wore a watch. If he wanted something done he'd stay as late as it took, or come in early. He always joined in with us in training and would have us playing in the dark until his five-a-side team won. He was ferocious, elbowing and kicking.'

I tracked down journalist John Fitzpatrick, who was one of the first to interview Fergie in his first managerial post. Fitzpatrick worked for the *Falkirk Herald* and would, like Fergie, go on to greater things himself, eventually ended up at the *London Evening Standard* and the *Mail on Sunday*. He told me that even back in 1974 it was clear that Fergie was clearly someone going places; that he had all the attributes needed to be a success. Fitzpatrick said: 'It might have been a case of very humble beginnings, but Alex Ferguson struck me as a person who knew exactly what he wanted, where he wanted to be and how he would get there – however long it took.

'He was a determined man, passionate about his football and full of integrity. East Stirling was simply a stepping stone, an early staging post on a journey to the top. No doubt about that. In any conversations I had with him he was always very pleasant and courteous. I felt sad when he moved on so quickly, but knew that I would be hearing a lot about Alex Ferguson over the years – and I wasn't wrong on that score!'

Six months after joining East Stirling, Fergie moved to St Mirren on the advice of Jock Stein. Many years later Tony Fitzpatrick, the then St Mirren captain, would say of his new boss: 'He made me captain at just 17 and was always fantastic with me. I've heard all about his reputation now but he never threw teacups at me or anyone else, but he had a very young team and it wasn't necessary. He is one of those people with an aura about him – you could just feel it. I think he's one of those great figures we see running through history; he's definitely got the gift of leadership.'

That strand – a leader among men – would also be taken up when Fergie quit Love Street for Aberdeen in 1978. His four years at St Mirren transformed an ailing club – turning them from Second Division strugglers when he arrived into First Division champions the year before he departed for the Dons.

In the Granite City his similarly rock-hard, rock-solid, hands-on approach was also a winner. While at Pittodrie, Ferguson won three championships, four Scottish FA Cups, one Scottish League Cup, the European Cup Winners' Cup (beating Real Madrid 2-1 in Gothenburg) and the European Super Cup in a remarkable eight and a half years. It was an incredible haul, given the traditional gulf in resources between the Dons and Celtic and Rangers.

His centre-half at Pittodrie was current Birmingham boss Alex McLeish and he would say: 'Alex is a leader of men. That's what he does best, and it wouldn't have mattered where or when he managed a club like United, he would have been successful. He just gave players so much belief and even when we played Real Madrid in that Cup Winners' Cup final he wasn't fazed at all and made sure we weren't either. His enormous mental strength is unquestionable.'

The triumphs at Aberdeen would also prove some sort of revenge on Rangers for their ill treatment of him. In those eight and a half years at the bleakest, most northern of outposts of British football Ferguson broke the Old Firm monopoly of Rangers and Celtic. Pre-Fergie, the club had not won the title since 1955, but he changed all that when they lifted the League trophy in 1980. It was the first time in 15 years that the title had not been won by either Rangers or Celtic and Ferguson now felt he had the respect of his players, later saying: 'That was the achievement which united us. I finally had the players believing in me.'

Aberdeen then followed up with back-to-back titles in 1984 and 1985. They also lifted the Scottish Cup three seasons in a row: 1982, 1983 and 1984, but their greatest success came when they beat Real Madrid to lift the European Cup Winners' Cup in 1983.

Fergie was also to briefly manage the Scotland national team after the tragic death of Jock Stein before becoming manager of United. He would admit to being devastated by the death of Big Jock, whom many view as his mentor. Fergie was in the Scotland dug-out as assistant to the former Celtic manager for the World Cup qualifying draw against Wales on 10 September 1985.

Stein suffered a heart attack and collapsed before the end of the match, which the Scots drew 1-1 to earn a play-off place against Australia. The first man to lead a British team to European Cup glory – with the Hoops in 1967 – passed away in the dressing room at Ninian Park.

Ferguson expressed his agony 20 years later. He said: 'To this day, I still miss those night sessions we would have in the team's hotel when he was manager of Scotland and I was his assistant. He hardly slept, of course, and would sit up all night talking, if you let him. At about 3am, I'd say, "Jock, it's all right for you, but I'm taking training in the morning and I'll have to get to my bed."

'He would say, "Ach, you can have a nap in the afternoon." Then he'd turn to Jimmy Steel, the masseur and a wonderful character, and say: "Steely, order another pot of tea."

'But it was inspiring, listening to him talk. With some men who get a bit of success there is a bit of me, me, me, in their conversation – telling you what they did, and how they did it. Whenever I asked Jock about his great Celtic teams and how they did what they did, especially in specific matches like, say, the European Cup final, he never once mentioned his own part.'

He would dearly miss Big Jock, both as a friend and a footballing sounding board, whom he could trust implicitly.

Fergie's tenure as Scottish boss started on 16 October 1985 and ended on 13 June 1986 – taking in that year's World Cup in Mexico. Of his 10 matches in total, he won three, drew four and lost three – the side scoring eight goals and conceding five. The World Cup campaign was hardly a success: Fergie got it off to a controversial start by ignoring the claims of one Alan Hansen for inclusion in his squad and the results in Mexico were unsatisfactory; Scotland lost their first game 1-0 against Denmark, their second 2-1 against West Germany (Gordon

Strachan giving Fergie hope with a consolation goal) and drew their third and final game 0-0 against the Uruguayans.

The World Cup may have been a disappointment, but when he returned to Aberdeen after the World Cup, Fergie found he was much in demand. He was approached by Barcelona, Arsenal, Rangers and Tottenham and Manchester United. The Spurs job appealed and he was tempted, but when United came in there was only one destination for the much-travelled Scot.

The legend of Alex Ferguson and Manchester United was about to be written...

CHAPTER 2

UNITED HE STANDS

'I WANT TO KNOCK LIVERPOOL RIGHT
OFF THEIR FUCKIN' PERCH.'
Alex Ferguson, 1986

Alex Ferguson walked into Old Trafford on 6 November 1986, surveyed the wreckage that was the legacy of the Ron Atkinson era, smiled at the crowd of United employees gathered to welcome him and shared a joke with one of his groundsmen. He started as he meant to go on: he was a man of the people from humble beginnings, who felt it was important to treat all the staff the same, whether MD or a cleaner.

Fergie, then 44, knew he had his work cut out – but so what? What was new? It had always been that way, hadn't it, from clawing his way through an upbringing that was warm in family love though hardly privileged to battling through the echelons and challenges of football, first as a player and then as a manager.

But the size of the task at United was gigantic. He might have been taking over the biggest football club in the world, but they were in a bad state: United were helping to prop up the table, second from bottom in the old First Division, and relegation was a frightening possibility. Fergie quickly instilled a discipline in the squad that had been lacking – and warned that their drinking would have to stop and their levels of fitness increase or they would be on their bikes. The iron fist worked: United climbed up the table to finish the season in 11th place.

In that first season, Fergie would also set out his ambition to the media. It was simple: as at Aberdeen, he wanted to win everything even though United, like the Dons, were considered outsiders when it came to the glory stakes. Also like Aberdeen, he would have to break up a monopoly of the established order to do that. This was the man who, at Pittodrie, had shaken up the Glasgow stranglehold on Scottish football with his exciting young side. Now his aim was to do a similar job in England in targeting Liverpool's hold on the English top-flight title.

His one superstar player at Old Trafford, club skipper and lionheart Bryan Robson, confirmed that that was what his new boss wanted more than anything at the start of his reign. Robbo said: 'His aim was to knock Liverpool and Everton off their perch and make United number one again.'

And Fergie was to succeed – he would turn the club upside down after surviving an uneasy initial three years and achieve his ambition of overwhelming Liverpool within seven years. But it meant revolution at Old Trafford: many unpalatable changes, in personnel, mindset and attitude, would need to be rushed through. He would have to sort out the rabble and the rubble bequeathed him by his predecessor, Ron Atkinson.

Atkinson's five-year reign had been a festival of glitter and bling for the United faithful. He took the club to the very brink of the Promised Land but could not gain the visa allowing unlimited access to the whole dream. Unlike Fergie, he let things get out of hand when, with a little more of the boot camp rather than the holiday camp, he maybe could have won the League. But to be fair, Big Ron's reign did coincide with the particularly dominant years of Liverpool.

A Scouser himself, Atkinson worked on the 'Mars bar' premise – that if you worked hard, you deserved to play hard – but he failed to instil the third tenet of that manifesto into his players: that they also needed to rest and look after themselves. When Fergie took over he was stunned by the poor levels of fitness and the lack of respect some of the players had for the manager and the club.

There's a saying often associated with Atkinson and his time at Old Trafford – and I think it is an apt one – that the United fans loved him, until it all started to go wrong. Then they questioned whether he was tough enough ever to bring the major honours (the League title and the European Cup) back to the club.

It is a criticism with foundation. Atkinson, always a bon viveur, would, to his credit, answer back with the line, 'Well, it was bloody good while it lasted...' He would also point out that he won the FA Cup twice – in 1983 and 1985.

A journeyman wing-half as a player, he trod similar ground as a boss before taking over at United in 1981. Big Ron had begun his managerial career in 1972 when, at the age of 32, he took up the reins at non-league Kettering Town. In December 1974, he stepped up into League management with Cambridge United. By 1978, he had been appointed in the hot seat at West Bromwich Albion, taking them to the top reaches of the old First Division and twice into the UEFA Cup, in 1978/79 and 1979/80.

United's board decided he was the perfect antidote to the dour, dull years of his predecessor Dave Sexton and he rewarded them with the entertaining football the fans demanded. Along the way, he also signed some quality players – men who would ensure the team performed with bravado, imagination and gusto. Chief among them were Frank Stapleton, Gordon Strachan, Arnold Muhren, and 'Captain Marvel' himself, Bryan Robson. The latter was his best buy, and one of United's greatest-ever purchases. A British record transfer of £1.5 million saw 'Robbo' arrive at Old Trafford in October 1981 and he would be the man around whom Atkinson would build his team of musketeers.

Robson would certainly prove worthy of the fee: he was to go on to become the top British midfielder of his generation, earning his place in the annals of United legends with his all-action displays and inspirational captaincy skills.

In his 12 years at Old Trafford, the legendary No. 7 would make 437 appearances and score 74 goals for the club he loved. Famed for his superb tackling and driving runs, he would also captain his country, winning 90 caps and scoring 26 times in the process. Robson appeared in the 1982, 1986, and 1990 World Cup finals and his goal against France in 1982 is the second fastest-ever scored in the World Cup finals.

Twelve years as United skipper made him the club's longest-serving captain. Under Fergie's guidance he would win the FA Cup in 1990, the Cup-Winners' Cup in 1991 and finally won the League title in 1993 and 1994. His number of appearances for club and country and achievements are all the more remarkable given the injuries he would suffer along the way (including three broken legs).

Fergie would build his dream around Robbo in those early years after convincing him that they had to eliminate the excesses of the Atkinson era if they were to achieve top-table success. Big Ron finally ran out of steam in 1986: the wheels had started to come off his wagon the previous campaign after United had started like a train, winning their first 10 League matches and remaining unbeaten for 15. But they finished fourth, 14 points behind the team who, at the time, painfully appeared champions in perpetuity: Liverpool.

Early the following season Atkinson paid the price for a poor start when he was dismissed in the November. The departure of Mark Hughes to Barcelona for £2.5 million and Ray Wilkins to AC Milan for £1.5 million only added to Big Ron's woes: it left a feeling around Old Trafford of futility and hopelessness; that they would never win the League. At any other English club Atkinson's legacy – the two FA Cup wins and League finishes of third, third, fourth, fourth, fourth – would probably have been seen as an acceptable return. Not so at United.

Under Fergie, the days of wine and roses were finally over for United's pampered stars, used to easy, relaxed smiles and a holiday camp atmosphere. In their place came an altogether more serious, tougher regime. A regime designed to turn United from a successful cup competition side into a successful side full stop.

The days of Alexander Chapman Ferguson would bring to an end that agonising holy-grail search as United finally returned to the top of the pile, once again winning the top-flight title and the European Cup.

On that cold, dreary day in November 1986 when the abrasive Scot became United's eighth postwar manager he made it clear he was no champagne Charlie, unlike Big Ron. Fergie would be at his office at 8am, five days a week – the first to arrive and the last to leave, setting the example that he expected his players and management team to emulate.

His first match came two days after his appointment and he quickly realised the size of the task as his new team crashed 2-0 to Oxford United in the old First Division. As we have noted, he did go on to steady the ship that first season, however, bringing the Red Devils home in a respectable eleventh position.

He also set about the task of instilling some much-needed discipline among the ranks. And that meant dealing with three of the most naturally gifted players on the books – including his skipper. Yes, Robbo's love of 'his pint' was almost as legendary as his playing prowess back then. Along with Paul McGrath and Norman Whiteside, he was known as one of the club's 'Three Musketeers'. It is to his credit – for his footballing dedication and application – that, out of the trio, only he would survive the cull under Ferguson's tougher regime. The two Irishmen were brilliant players but could not control their boozing and they would pay a heavy price as both were sent packing early on in the Fergie years. Whiteside was to end up at Everton; McGrath at Aston Villa.

The fact that Fergie would gamble by confronting his captain, the man he most needed on his side to bring about the necessary revolution, was an early indicator of his managerial skills, mental strength and belief that discipline is essential if you are to succeed in top-class sport – even if that meant alienating your club captain. Robbo could easily have taken the 'advice' the wrong way and flounced out of the club in a strop, which would have left Fergie in an almost impossible position with the fans who adored their on-pitch leader, but he realised from the boss's hard-line stance that the new manager was only confronting him because he shared the same dream as himself: total success for United. If that meant changing his 'refuelling' habits, then he would have to stay in line and Fergie's gamble was to pay mighty dividends.

In 1987 the boss also began his transfer marker revolution – signing Steve Bruce, Viv Anderson, Brian McClair and Jim

Leighton. United were flying and they would finish runners-up to Liverpool, nine points adrift of the Scousers.

Yet it would not be until 1990 that Fergie would lift the first trophy of his reign – the FA Cup, the competition United had won five years earlier under Atkinson. Robbo scored United's first goal in the final against Crystal Palace, which ended in a 3-3 draw. United won the replay 1-0 with a goal from Lee Martin – and Robson became the first player to lift the FA Cup three times at Wembley as captain.

The FA Cup triumph proved a job saver for Fergie and provided him with a much-needed lifeline and platform from which to build. By now Robson was 'working on the same wavelength as the boss': he had become a close confidant of the United manager in the four years that Fergie had been at the club.

Indeed, Robbo looks back on that 1990 win over Palace with pride, but also admits relief because it meant Fergie would survive at the club. He had grown to believe in the man who put such emphasis on personal discipline, on and off the field. Robbo said: 'I have great memories of FA Cup finals, especially as I never lost one as a player – but that 1990 final is the one I treasure most of all. Not many people gave Palace a chance, but it showed how good players in smaller clubs can be. Ian Wright and Mark Bright were in their team, so it was no wonder they gave us such a tough one with those two against us.

'We had to go to a replay, but I was just so pleased for all the youngsters in the team who had been given a tough time in the media. There was a lot of stick going around and people were saying the team was underachieving, and so on; people like Paul Ince and Gary Pallister were having to put up with all sorts of criticism.

'There was also talk along the way that Sir Alex Ferguson

would have been sacked if we hadn't won the competition, although I found out later that it wasn't the case. The victory was the launching pad for the club to go on to become the powerhouse it is now. It gave us a lot of confidence to go on, and the following year we won the European Cup Winners' Cup and it snowballed from there.'

Fergie had certainly been under immense pressure from the fans and the press as he entered the Christmas of 1989 – with a 5-1 Division One defeat at Manchester City a few months earlier hardly helping his cause. In January 1990 many pundits were predicting Fergie would be sacked – with legendary Liverpool skipper, the late Emlyn Hughes, leading the chorus of disapproval. In the *Daily Mirror* that winter Hughes wrote a piece attacking Ferguson's management under the headline FERGIE – OBE. But it did prove one thing: while the much-missed Hughes was a giant out on the pitch, he did not possess the same skills as a professional writer or clairvoyant.

Fergie approached what will go down as one of the defining games of his reign confidently in January 1990. His critics argued that defeat to Nottingham Forest in the third round of the FA Cup that month would spell the end for the Scot but he survived, thanks to a goal from reserve striker Mark Robins in the 1-0 win at the City Ground on 7 January 1990 and the die was cast for what would become an unprecedented haul of domestic trophies in the following decade.

During the next season injury would limit Fergie's talisman Bryan Robson to 17 League appearances, but he was fit for that legendary Cup Winners Cup final, in which United beat Barcelona 2-1 – thanks to his driving force and Mark Hughes' brilliant brace.

It had been a wonderful achievement in Rotterdam, yet the nagging doubts about Fergie's ability remained – chiefly, of course, because the club had still not won the League for a demoralising 23 years. In 1992 it looked as though the nightmare might finally come to an end, but bitter rivals Leeds pipped United at the post for the title. The 1-0 League Cup final victory over Nottingham Forest the previous March did not feel much of a consolation prize – although it was, of course, another trophy along the road.

As the fans despaired their team might never again win the League, providence smiled on Fergie in the shape of a remarkable Frenchman. Yes, the great Eric Cantona was about to arrive at Old Trafford with a confident swagger. He would walk in as if he owned the place, but his arrogance would prove well founded: his influence was to blow away the cobwebs surrounding the club for 26 agonising years – and help ease Fergie on the road to legend at Old Trafford.

CHAPTER 3

KING ERIC – HIS GREATEST BUY

'ALEX FERGUSON LOVES THE GAME AND WILL DIE
ON THE UNITED BENCH, I AM SURE OF THAT.'
Eric Cantona, 2003

'WE'LL DRINK A DRINK, A DRINK TO ERIC THE
KING, THE KING, THE KING, HE'S THE LEADER OF
OUR FOOTBALL TEAM. HE'S THE GREATEST CENTRE
FORWARD THAT THE WORLD HAS EVER SEEN.'
Terrace chant, 1996

When Fergie finally passes on to Heaven's version of the Theatre of Dreams there will be all kinds of debate about his legacy, his place in the pecking order of all-time managerial greats, his credits and debits at Old Trafford over the years. You can be sure that one heated topic of discussion will centre round his dealings in the transfer market: his best buys – and his worst.

My view remains that Ryan Giggs is the greatest player of the Ferguson era at United. You can argue the odds, but his unrivalled honours, influence on young players and outstanding ambassadorial skills perch him right at the top of the tree.

But there is little doubt about the man who stands just behind him at No. 2. Yes, the King – Eric Cantona – is the genius who spurred on the likes of Giggs and the other Fergie Fledglings to greatness. He was the catalyst who would end an excruciating 26-year period for the club and fans; who would finally bring the League title back to Old Trafford after that spell in purgatory. And at just £1.2 million he is surely Fergie's greatest-ever signing, given that he led United out of the wilderness to that elusive League crown.

OK, there were other great buys by the boss during his tenure. In defence, I think of the brilliant Peter Schmeichel, a mere snip at £530,000 in 1991, a price Fergie himself later described as the 'bargain of the century'. The Dane was voted the World's Best Goalkeeper in 1992 and 1993, and still holds the record for the greatest clean-sheets-to-games ratio in the Premier League – with 42 per cent of his league outings ending without his team conceding.

In 2001 Peter was voted Best Goalkeeper in the World in a public poll held by Reuters and two years later, he was inducted into the Football Hall of Fame.

The man who skippered United to their first Champions League triumph in 1999 was also named one of the 125 greatest living footballers at the FIFA 100 celebrations. For eight years, Schmeichel was a superb servant for Fergie, culminating in that farewell appearance at the Camp Nou. In that time, he won five FA Premier League titles, three FA Cups, one League Cup and the UEFA Champions League.

Other defensive stalwarts who could be classed in almost the same league as Eric the King were Rio Ferdinand, Jaap Stam, Denis Irwin and Steve Bruce. Again, their contribution to the club was immense, though not so powerful as the King. Rio and Brucey became club skippers and while Rio has class and skill beyond the range of your usual defenders, Brucey was an outstanding warrior and leader – and cost a fraction of Rio's £29 million, at just £850,000. Similarly, Stam was a wonderful centre-back and repaid the faith Fergie showed in him (and his £10.8 million fee) by helping United to that first Champions League win under the boss.

Midfield, you could argue the case for the overall contribution of Roy Keane to United's (and Fergie's) cause. After Cantona, he was the second most important signing of the early Ferguson era. At the time, his £3.75 million fee was a British transfer record, but this was certainly money well spent as the Irishman would eventually step in and plug the gap left by the departures of Bryan Robson and Paul Ince in the centre of the park.

Like Robbo and Brucey, he was another braveheart – a skipper who would lay himself on the line for the red cause (and frequently did). Again, he was someone who would build on the foundations of success laid by the great Cantona.

Finally, two men in the modern era who would certainly be among Fergie's top buys: Wayne Rooney and Cristiano Ronaldo. The cornerstone of the team that lifted the Champions League in 2008, are they really above Eric in the pecking order? More on the two attacking geniuses in later chapters, but I have to say now that I firmly believe they are behind the King in the Greatest Buys league.

So, what of Cantona? What made him tick and why did he succeed in such a wonderful fashion at Old Trafford when behind him trailed a mass of broken dreams in an earlier career that promised so much, yet delivered so little. The answer is simple: he found at United what he had never experienced before.

A club and a manager who embraced and adored him – and a club big enough to achieve the major ambitions that he himself demanded. In Sir Alex, a manager who would stand by him and praise him; a manager who knew the best way to deal with a man like Cantona was with respect and friendship. The big stick had never worked before with Eric, so why should it fare any better at Old Trafford?

He arrived in November 1992 and soon got to work, showing the kids in the team how it was done and bringing a huge confidence lift to the club. Fergie had joked that United could do with Superman to take them to the next level – well, he didn't get the man from Krypton, but he certainly got the next best thing in his own footballing superman.

Indeed, United had been crying out for a superman to lift them from the depths for 26 years. Twenty-six long, miserable years since they had last won the League title. Within six months of Eric's arrival, the wait that had lasted from 1967 had finally ended. The nightmare was over: Cantona was the final piece of the jigsaw, the catalyst for what would become known as 'The Ferguson Years': three decades of non-stop glory. With Eric in the team for five of them, there was half a decade of non-stop cabaret too.

He strutted into Old Trafford like he owned the place: 26 years old, but with more baggage than a regular team might pick up in two lifetimes. Thanks to several well-documented run-ins with the football authorities in his native France he had picked up the tag 'Le Brat'. In 1988, he was left out of the French national squad and responded by saying on TV that the manager, Henri Michel, was 'a shitbag'. That earned him a one-year ban. In 1989, while on loan at Montpellier, he threw his boots in the face of a team-mate who had criticised him. And in 1990, he threw the ball at the ref while playing for

Marseille and was banned for a month at a French FA disciplinary meeting. He responded by telling each member of the committee to his face that they were idiots, and had his sentence doubled.

Cantona had managed to fall out with Howard Wilkinson at Leeds within nine months of arriving in the UK. But it was to be that very temperament that would endear him to Manchester United's vast army of fans – indeed, most of us can relate to the rebel, usually we just don't have the guts, or if you look at it another way, the foolhardiness, to act like one. Eric did what he wanted, how he wanted and when he wanted: he remains the ultimate rebel without a pause, in the process earning himself a permanent place in the heart of the fans.

At Old Trafford, he was to forge a partnership with Fergie that would win four Premiership titles in five years, including two League and FA Cup 'doubles', and in 2001 he was voted Manchester United's Player of the Century. To this day, United fans still refer to him as Eric the King, the Frenchman taking up the mantle that once belonged to the also-legendary Denis Law – and this is how the equally-loved Bobby Charlton described Cantona's qualities in the mid-1990s: 'We're just very grateful he's here. He's such a great player; I'm still pinching myself. A player like that only comes along once or twice in a lifetime, and you don't leave him out or put him in the reserves. You respect his skill. Eric is the brainiest player I've ever seen – he sees such a lot when he has the ball. The big thing he has given United is the ability to make attacks count, not waste good positions until the right option appears, and we now finish almost every move with an effort on goal. The other thing is his ability to release players, even when the pass doesn't look on. If you make the run, Eric will probably get you the ball.'

Cantona was born on 24 May 1966 in Marseille, in the South

of France – his parents named him Eric Daniel Pierre – just two months before England's greatest footballing triumph, when Bobby Moore lifted the World Cup at Wembley. His father's family originated from Sardinia, his mother's were from Spain and that production line perhaps helps to explain the volatility of his mixed-Latin temperament. Yet from an early age, Eric was no 'brat' – indeed, he much preferred painting and reading in the cave high above the city of Marseille that his family called home.

His father Albert loved painting and hunting. He worked as a psychiatric nurse, but he also loved to play football, earning a reputation as a fine amateur goalkeeper. Albert would tell Eric: 'There is nothing more simple than football. Look before you receive the ball and then give it, and always remember that the ball goes quicker than you can carry it.'

Eric's mother Eleonore would spend her time bringing up the man who would become known as the King, along with his older brother Jean-Marie and Joel, 17 months younger than Eric. They were poor, but Eric loved his young life, later claiming he was the 'son of rich people' because of the variety of cultural and artistic activities open to him with his family.

By the age of five he was playing football in the streets and fell in love with the game, saying: 'You start wanting to play [it] when you are three, four or five... you know you have a passion when you can't stop playing the game, when you play it in the streets, in the playground, after school, and when you spend your time at school swapping photographs of footballers... playing football in the streets gave us a tremendous need for freedom.'

But Cantona's career in France was littered with run-ins with authority and suspensions. By the age of 25, he had quit his homeland and joined Leeds United in February 1992, initially on a loan deal that would see the Yorkshire club pay Nîmes £100,000, plus Eric's wages until the end of the 1991/92 season.

That season he would take Leeds to the old First Division championship at the expense of Manchester United and the move to Leeds was made permanent, with an extra £1 million leaving the Elland Road coffers.

Howard Wilkinson and Eric Cantona? Even in the same sentence the names hardly gel; in fact, they grate – one, an English footballing pragmatist and a dull, dour Yorkshireman, the other a French romantic, a dreamer, a painter, a poet, a motorcyclist philosopher – a footballer who believed the beautiful game was just that: an opportunity for expression and joyful highs. It would always be a marriage of convenience that would not last, though thanks to Cantona, Sgt. Wilko would notch up the one major success of his career.

To this day, Wilko remains the only Englishman to have led a team to the Premiership title – and it was Leeds' first top-flight triumph in 18 long years. But that would never be enough to assuage the demands and ambitions of the King for years later, he would say that Leeds, as far as he was concerned, had only been a shop window, a showcase that would ultimately lead to his dream move to the club he was always destined to grace and to lead: Manchester United.

Legend has it that Fergie signed Cantona as a spur-of-the-moment act. That Leeds MD Bill Fotherby rang to ask United chairman Martin Edwards if Denis Irwin would be available for a move and that, sitting across from him, Ferguson had scrawled on a piece of paper: 'Ask him if Cantona is for sale'. The piece of paper bit is true, as is the fact that Fotherby rang back later that day to confirm Eric was, indeed, available. But a source close to Sir Alex told me Fergie had been on the case for months, that this was hardly a last-minute move dreamed up out of nowhere; that the United manager had been interested when Cantona turned up in England for an initial loan spell at Sheffield Wednesday; that he knew all about the man who had been a nightmare to manage in France. What's more, he had already earmarked Eric Cantona for a starring role at Old Trafford – he wanted to pit his managerial skills up against the man who would play the George Best role to his Busby. This would be the ultimate test and naturally, Fergie was keen to bring it on when Fotherby gave the all-clear.

The wheels had actually been put in motion, I am told, weeks before when the then France boss Gerard Houllier telephoned to say all was not well with Cantona at Leeds and that a bid to Howard Wilkinson might prove fruitful. Fergie bided his time – he did not want to pay over the odds and he knew that Cantona was perceived as the perennial problem boy.

At the end of the day, Wilko was simply relieved to get his £1 million back.

So it was that on Friday, 26 November 1992 Eric Cantona finally came home – for the ridiculously small fee of £1.2 million. Fergie will never forget that day: it would be the day that would go a long way to transforming him from being just another manager at United into a legend. At that time, the signing of Cantona was the last piece in his jigsaw; he would later comment on how Cantona had thrilled him by 'walking in as though he owned the bloody place' and that while some players found Old Trafford and the United aura too much, Cantona was at the very head of the queue of those who 'simply belonged' from day one.

Fergie needed his latest signing to settle in quickly if he was to have any hope of winning that first crown for 26 years in 1993. United's season had been a letdown – they were sixth in the table, behind the likes of big-spending Aston Villa and

Blackburn Rovers and surprise challengers, including Norwich City and QPR.

Goals had been a problem and Fergie prayed Cantona would put that right. Never one for low-level publicity, Eric made his competitive debut as a second-half sub in the derby against Manchester City at Old Trafford on 12 December 1992. United won 2-1, but Eric had only a bit-part role that day. Not something you would normally associate with Fergie's Gallic genius, and a role he would never again fulfil.

Cantona soon settled down, scoring goals and creating them. His first goal for United came in the 1-1 draw at Chelsea on 19 December 1992; his second, a week later on Boxing Day, as United claimed a point at Sheffield Wednesday after being 3-0 down at the interval.

The next couple of weeks saw a 5-0 win over Coventry and a 4-1 thrashing of Tottenham – Cantona scored one and made one against Spurs. He had taken United to the top of the table, a slot that would generally be theirs throughout his five years apart from a period during his ban.

The shadow that Cantona cast over Old Trafford can be seen by the fact that the 1994/95 campaign – which took the brunt of his ban for the infamous kung-fu kick – was the only one of the player's five seasons in which United failed to win the Premiership, or indeed, any other trophy. There had been an inkling of the Frenchman's dark side that first season when he spat at a fan on his return to Leeds; an indiscretion that would land him a £1,000 fine from the FA.

In Eric's first two seasons at Old Trafford United went on an amazing run, winning the inaugural Premier League in 1993 by 10 points and let's not forget they had been six points behind Norwich when Cantona strolled into Old Trafford! That title breakthrough was vital to Fergie's ambition of becoming a

United great like Sir Matt Busby himself, but it was also extra-sweet for Eric because it meant that he had already written himself into English football's history books by becoming the first – and as this book went to the printers – *still* the only player ever to win back-to-back English top-flight titles with different clubs.

That first season, Cantona hit nine goals in 22 Premiership games and he would lead United to even greater glory in his second, scoring 25 goals in 48 matches, and bringing United their first 'double'. There had even been hopes of a first Treble in the English game but Aston Villa outplayed the Reds at Wembley in the 1994 League Cup final to win 3-1.

Cantona's successful brace of penalties against Chelsea helped United to a comfortable 4-0 triumph in the FA Cup final to secure the 'double'. Then came the icing on the cake when he was named Footballer of the Year by the PFA and, after being an outcast from his national side for many years, captain of France by the new manager, Aime Jacquet.

In the words of the legendary movie star James Cagney, Eric was certainly 'on top of the world, Ma' – and so too was his boss Fergie. The two were on a winning streak that would seemingly never end: Fergie's gamble on the Frenchman had turned the club round and transformed United into a major footballing force.

But there would be trouble in Cantona's third season at Old Trafford – big, big trouble. As a boy, he had adorned his bedroom wall with pictures of the one and only Bruce Lee. Years later, Manchester United fans would guffaw when the news of the Frenchman's idol was relayed to them; guffaw and nod sagely. Now it all made sense: exactly why the man who was now their ultimate hero, because of his rebellious and winning ways, had kicked out that dark midwinter night in 1995.

Eric will invariably be linked to that night of kung fu fighting at Crystal Palace on 25 January 1995. This was the turning point, the defining moment of his career: his nine-month ban undoubtedly cost United the League and the Cup – indeed, it left them trophy-less at a time when the team was arguably strong enough to win everything, perhaps the strongest in Ferguson's entire reign at Old Trafford. Yet it brought an unlikely bonus: for the first time in his career Cantona found a man who would back him when most others pronounced: 'Sack him'.

Arguably, this was also the defining moment of Sir Alex's own managerial career at United. The boss put his reputation on the line for the mercurial Frenchman and showed what an outstanding manager he had become by somehow managing to retain Cantona's services. Whereas Sir Matt struggled and ultimately failed to 'save' Georgie Best from himself, Fergie did prevent Cantona from imploding. If Eric had left United during the ban for Italy's Inter Milan, who is to say what might have happened?

Would he have knuckled down and changed at the San Siro; or would he suddenly have lost the edge that made him the player he was? More likely his indiscretion at Selhurst Park would have been followed by further speedy black marks at Inter – and he might have been cast out of the game for good.

Fergie saved Eric – and his own developing team – by showing him amazing love and loyalty. In Alex Ferguson, Cantona finally found the only manager he had ever played under who would hunt him down and plead with him to remain a part of his football club.

Four minutes into the second half of United's Premiership match against Palace – which ended 1-1 – Cantona had been sent off at Palace for kicking out at defender Richard Shaw. As he made his way from the pitch, 20-year-old Palace fan Matthew Simmons rushed down the stands to taunt him. Enraged, Cantona responded with his kung fu kick and then exchanged punches with Simmons.

Looking back on the incident, there is of course no defence for the fact that Cantona finally took his Bruce Lee obsession one kick too far. Sure, Simmons was out of order, but verbal abuse happens all the time in football.

One Palace insider assures me that Simmons, a 20-year-old self-employed glazier and 'victim' of Cantona's attack, was not the loyal fan of the club he was usually portrayed as. Indeed, I am told his 'first love' was not Palace, but Fulham and that he returned to Craven Cottage after he was given a life ban from Selhurst for his part in the run-in.

Simmons would claim that all he said to Cantona – was along the lines of: 'Off, off, off! Go on, Cantona, that's an early bath for you.' Cantona was to insist it was far more racist, more: 'Fuck off back to France, you French motherfucker.' Simmons remains adamant, insisting in an interview with the *Observer* in 2004: 'For God's sake, you can't say a worse thing about anyone [than what he alleges I said], can you? What he did in saying that was totally unjustified. The man is filth. How can he accuse me of saying such a thing? Where has this allegation against me come from? From him! It ruined my life and that is why it is inexcusable.'

Simmons subsequently became one of the most recognisable and hated men in Britain: the episode cost him his job and family members ignored him while reporters pursued him.

Most commentators would range against Cantona, describing his assault as 'shameful'. There were a couple of notable dissenters, however: Jimmy Greaves in the *Sun* and Richard Williams in the *Independent on Sunday*. Greavsie wrote: 'We've heard a lot about Cantona's responsibilities. What about analysing the responsibility of Simmons and every foul-mouthed yob who thinks his £10 admission gives him the right to say what he likes to a man, to abuse, taunt, spit and behave in a way that would get you locked up if you repeated it in the high street?'

And Williams believed 'Cantona had the excuse of genuine provocation.' – 'You didn't have to look very long and hard at Matthew Simmons of Thornton Heath to conclude that Eric Cantona's only mistake was to stop hitting him. The more we discovered about Mr Simmons, the more Cantona's assault looks like the instinctive expression of a flawless moral judgement.'

Martin Creasy, a United fanatic since the Seventies, told me he feared this would be the end of Cantona at Old Trafford – and that he believed the Frenchman got a bad deal from the English press precisely because he was from abroad. Creasy observed: 'When Eric launched his assault on that Palace moron, I must have been the only United fan still in my seat in stunned disbelief, wondering if this would be the last we would ever see of the greatest United genius since George Best. United fans all around me were too busy jumping up and celebrating Eric's revenge in an incident some in the press would sneeringly label "The Shit Hits The Fan" to share my immediate concerns. People go on about cutting out racism in football. Total hypocrisy. If Eric had been English, would he have taken the level of crap he did – especially from the press? Of course not.'

As well as the nine-month ban, Cantona was sentenced to two weeks in prison, reduced on appeal to 120 hours' community service for the attack. He was also fined £20,000. It was during a news conference after the appeal that he would cryptically refer to the British press as 'a flock of seagulls following the trawler.'

Fergie's work in travelling to Paris to track down the King in exile and to persuade him his future was still at Old Trafford was one of the key moves of his time as manager. It is also the stuff of legend – including the tale of how he jumped incognito onto the back of a motorcycle for a showdown in a café.

He certainly had his work cut out when he arrived in the French capital. It is not always remembered that Cantona actually put in a transfer request in the summer of 1995, the reaction to uproar when it was disclosed that he had taken part in a practice match against Rochdale. Although the game was held behind closed doors at United's training ground, it appeared to breach the terms of the suspension and the FA opened an inquiry. The boss convinced him all would turn out well if they both stayed solid to their belief in Manchester United – that the club was once again on its way to becoming the best in the world.

Richard Williams explained it in typically elegant style: 'By asking for a move, he was making a stand not against the club but against English football. He went off to Paris, apparently intending to talk to the representatives of other clubs. That spring he had received a £4.2m offer from Massimo Moratti, then recently installed as president of Internazionale. Instead he signed a new contract to stay at Old Trafford, worth £3m over three years. But it was assumed Moratti's offer was on his mind when, in exasperation, he put in his request.

'Sir Alex Ferguson flew to Paris, where he sweet-talked Cantona back to the club. In truth, however, Cantona knew that in England he had found a place where his talent could find its fullest expression. In Italy, it would all have been very different. In the Premiership, Cantona's touch and vision shone. In Serie A, he would not have stood out to such a degree, if at all. The directness of his play would have gone down well there, but his low boiling point would have betrayed him, perhaps fatally.'

It is an interesting point of view – basically that while Cantona was the cream in England, he could not cut it in Europe and he knew that, so he stayed for reasons of self-preservation.

What is beyond doubt is that Fergie made the summer trip to France in 1995 out of self-preservation and admiration for the man on the brink of implosion. The boss was naturally upset and bewildered by the events of that crazy night at Selhurst Park. He would admit that he had not seen the incident – and the fact only dawned on him when he watched the video over and over again when he got home to Manchester at 4am the following morning.

It was a Burns Night the proud Scot would never forget. Many years later Fergie would later admit that what he saw on the video was 'pretty appalling' and say: 'Over the years since then I have never been able to elicit an explanation of the episode from Eric, but my own feeling is that anger at himself over the ordering-off and resentment of the referee's earlier inaction [at the way Palace players were getting away with fouling him] combined to take him over the brink.'

But he never had the slightest doubt that he and United should move heaven and earth to keep the Frenchman. Eric was his talisman, the man who had made all the difference and now it was payback time, time to stand by the footballer extraordinaire who had made Fergie's dream come true. And his efforts would pay dividends for Cantona would serve his ban and stay at United for almost another two years; he would later admit his love of United and the fans had played a key role in his decision to stay, saying: 'I feel close to the rebelliousness and vigour of the youth here. Perhaps time will separate us, but nobody can deny that here, behind the windows of Manchester, there is an insane love of football, of celebration and of music.'

The boss was in no doubt that he did right to fight for Cantona – he only had to look to see how United suffered as a consequence of the fall-out from that traumatic incident.

At the start of 1995 things were looking good for Fergie. He had just been awarded the CBE in the New Year's Honours List, he had bought Andy Cole for £7 million from Newcastle United and United looked on their way to a third Premier League title. But the Red Devils would lose the plot after 25 January and failure to win at West Ham on the last day of the season and falling to Everton in the FA Cup final meant that the trophy cabinet at Old Trafford was empty for the first time in five years.

Fergie would grind his teeth on the *Cantona Speaks* video and complain: 'I think it's summed up in the three games we had in a row at home [between 15 March and 17 April]. We drew 0-0 with Chelsea, 0-0 with Tottenham and 0-0 with Leeds United. Having only lost the League by one point, no one's going to tell me or even attempt to convince me that he would not have made one goal or scored a goal in one of those three games.'

But the King would be back at the top table – and so too would Fergie and United. Typically, he would return to the side with the spotlight beaming on him. No comeback against some lower-level opposition – no, the big man was welcomed back in what was traditionally recognised as one of United's two greatest games of the League campaign – the home match with Liverpool (the other being the away game at Anfield).

It was 1 October 1995 when Cantona walked out, chest puffed out and collar up, smiling and saluting the fans who had stood by him. The Reds were second in the League and Fergie voiced the opinion that Eric's return was just the boost they needed to propel themselves back to the summit they believed was their rightful place.

Against the revved-up rivals Cantona clearly felt the pace, but still managed to set up a goal for Nicky Butt two minutes into the game and then scored a penalty after Ryan Giggs was upended to salvage a valuable point in a 2-2 draw. A brace from Robbie Fowler had looked like giving the visitors the edge.

Despite Cantona's return, United struggled to keep pace with Kevin Keegan's Newcastle at the top of the table. But Eric – and a Keegan blow-out – came to the rescue. The Frenchman scored the only goal at West Ham on 23 January 1996 and triggered a six-match winning run in the League, culminating in the vital 1-0 triumph at Newcastle on 4 March. Almost inevitably, Eric was the goalscorer and Fergie was quick to rush out and hug him at full-time. The boss knew the debt he owed to this wonderful footballer.

Nine days later, United finally overtook Newcastle with a 1-1 draw at QPR; now they would not look back. It was an amazing outcome when you consider that at one point they were actually 13 points behind the Toon. A combination of sheer guts, Cantona brilliance and mind games by Fergie on nervy Newcastle boss Kevin Keegan meant they turned around a massive deficit to win the title.

During the run-in, Fergie destabilised the man known in his playing days as 'Mighty Mouse'. Newcastle had just beaten Leeds 1-0 and Keegan famously claimed Fergie had implied Leeds would roll over against Newcastle – a catalyst for his rant on Sky TV: 'Things which have been said over the last few days have been almost slanderous. I think you will have to send a tape of the game to Alex Ferguson, don't you? Isn't that what he wants? You just don't say what he said about Leeds. I would love it if we could beat them, love it. He's gone down in my estimation. Manchester United haven't won this yet; I'd love it if we beat them.'

Keegan's disastrous loss of composure that night and over the previous couple of months as the pressure got to him certainly seemed to filter through to his team. From a position of major strength, they were eventually overwhelmed, with the Red Devils winning nine of their last ten League games of the season to take the title.

The Fergie/Cantona duet still had one more act to run that remarkable comeback season for the Frenchman: at Wembley against bitterest rivals Liverpool, in the FA Cup final.

After clinching the League crown, United had headed off for a celebration at the Four Seasons Hotel, near Manchester Airport. Everyone had sore heads, but Fergie was happy enough: he knew they still had a week to go before the Cup final.

By the day of the game, Liverpool provided the talking point as they paraded around Wembley in white suits ('John Travolta suits', as Ryan Giggs would have it), but United did all the talking on the field.

Fergie's boy provided him with a 'double double' – as the Reds became the first club to do so, and the first to win the FA Cup nine times. It was Ferguson and his team's third FA Cup final in as many seasons and Cantona helped them wipe away the bitter taste of the defeat by Everton the previous May. The match itself was a bit of a damp squib until five minutes from time when Eric slotted the ball home after David James punched it straight to him from a corner.

The newly-crowned Footballer of the Year was swamped by his grateful team-mates. Once again he had produced a miracle for United: his legend was now assured at the Theatre of Dreams and in Fergie's heart. Cantona had become the first foreign player to lift the FA Cup as captain (regular skipper Steve Bruce missed the game). He had paid back Fergie and the loyal fans that had stood by him. Afterwards, he said: 'You know, that's life – up and down.'

Well, life with the King was certainly that during his memorable reign. The start of the next season would see Fergie confirm him as the new skipper, following the departure of Steve Bruce to Birmingham – and his exit from United and football for good by the end of it. It was an incredible emotional roller coaster for the boss, the club and the fans.

One of Cantona's lasting legacies would be seen on the pitch in that final season as the brilliant youngsters from the youth academy stepped up to the plate and prospered under his tutelage. The likes of Ryan Giggs, David Beckham, Paul Scholes, Nicky Butt and Gary Neville played like seasoned pros as Eric helped United retain their League crown in the 1996/97 season: more of Fergie's babes and their impact in the next chapter.

Eric had won four League titles in five years with United, but admitted that he had lost his love for the game. He was particularly anguished to have failed yet again in Europe – United were eliminated by Borussia Dortmund in the semi-finals of the Champions League – and felt that he had become a marketing tool at Old Trafford.

Fergie would later reveal that Cantona told him of his decision to retire within 24 hours of United's European exit – confirming just how badly the legendary Frenchman had taken the defeat. But it would be another month before he left for good, his last competitive game the 2-0 home win over West Ham on 11 May 1997.

Later, he would explain his exit from football in this way: 'When you quit football it is not easy, your life becomes difficult.

I should know because sometimes I feel I quit too young. I loved the game, but I no longer had the passion to go to bed early, not to go out with my friends, not to drink and not to do a lot of other things – the things I like in life.'

In five marvellous years, he had scored a total of 82 goals in 185 appearances for United. Fergie knew he would be missed and he would certainly miss Cantona – his professionalism, his genius and the way he inspired those around him.

In his autobiography, *Hughsie*, United legend Mark Hughes would later sum up the unique relationship between the boss and his star player in this way: 'Alex Ferguson didn't exactly rewrite the rule book but he treated him differently and explained to the rest of us that he was a special player requiring special treatment.'

That grey day in 1997 when Cantona quit was a sad day indeed, but Fergie knew he could not afford to mope or have public regrets. There was still unfinished business in Europe. He knew his kids were ready to take the Continent by storm, that with a few tweaks in the team here and there, they would soon not be far off becoming major contenders. Now let's take a look at how Fergie brought his 'fledglings' through into the first team, ushering in the greatest era since the halcyon days of Sir Matt Busby's own babes.

CHAPTER 4
THE FERGIE BABES

Looking back on his reign after 20-odd years, Sir Alex Ferguson was asked what had been his most important move in those first few months at Old Trafford in 1986. Was it identifying the problem drinkers and making plans to get rid of them? Maybe it was working out who should be shown the door because they were simply not good enough? Or was it putting into place a more stringent fitness regime than the one that had existed under the laidback 'Big Ron' Atkinson.

Fergie smiled and shook his head. 'No, it was none of them,' he would say, 'It was sorting out the youth set-up so that one day soon we would have great kids coming through the ranks.'

The new boss swiftly set about streamlining the system, ensuring there were scouts at all ends of the country and encouraging youngsters to come to the club. The youth team and reserves would become a key component at Old Trafford and by 1992, the results would be clear for all to see as the kids stormed to glory in the FA Youth Cup final.

Ryan Giggs would skipper the boys to a 6-3 triumph over Crystal Palace (he played in the second leg, which United won

3-2). It was the first time the club had won the trophy since 1964, when they beat Swindon 5-2. The triumphant team of 1992 included some other youngsters who would go on to join Giggs in United's senior side at the very top of the game – namely David Beckham, Gary Neville, Paul Scholes and Nicky Butt.

It had been 28 years since United had last won the trophy – two years more than they would take to win the senior top-flight league again a year later! This only emphasised how bringing their own players through had taken a back seat at the club. It needed Fergie to arrive and build on the simple premise that Sir Matt always believed in: that your own kids can win you titles; the fact that so many years had passed by without proper youth facilities at the club and that managers like Atkinson had simply not bothered to big up the youth set-up was a disgrace.

Mark Robins, who scored that vital goal for Ferguson at Nottingham Forest in the FA Cup in 1990, was one of the first to come through the new set-up. He explained Fergie's impact and influence in this way: 'I had just arrived at the club myself, aged 16, and from day one I felt included – it was just a knack he had. He learnt your names really quickly. That counts for a lot when you are a young lad at a club like that – and he was excellent. He looked out for the young players and always had time for you, and you can imagine how busy he was. City had a cracking youth policy at the time and Sir Alex wanted United's to be the best. He tried to change things and he was proved successful.

'You know what he is like – you cross him and you are finished. But he has had to be like he is, he was trying to make players. He was manager and he had our respect. If you stepped out of line, in no uncertain terms you were hammered. It kept everyone on their toes. He put you under pressure, but it was not about fear. It was a good learning environment and the way it had to be if you were going to end up playing for United.'

Robins had made an admirable, vital contribution to Fergie's fortunes at United, but he would not be the biggest success story of the new youth set-up – not by a long chalk.

That accolade would go to the Welsh boy that the boss signed up at the age of 14. Yes, the wonderful Ryan Giggs – in my mind, as I have already argued, surely the greatest player of the Ferguson era. A home-grown legend, United's most decorated player ever and a true gent to boot – a modern-day Bobby Charlton.

Giggs had moved from his native Cardiff to Swinton, a town a few miles north of Manchester and Old Trafford, when he was six. The Welsh wonderboy, his mother Lynne and brother Rhodri upped sticks after Ryan's rugby-playing father Danny had been offered the chance to switch codes – to swap from Union to League – by Swinton RL.

Ryan would himself excel at rugby, but his first love was always football and at the age of 13, he was offered a trial at Manchester City. Giggsy went out of courtesy, but he knew he could never sign for the Sky Blues. A Red through and through, he used to watch United from the Stretford End when he wasn't playing rugby or football – and he hardly endeared himself to the City youth team bosses by wearing a red United top for training!

Nevertheless, he did play one game for City youth when he was 13. But for Ryan, it was a game too many – his heart lay across the city, at Old Trafford, and he still dreamed of the chance of making it at United. His dream became reality, thanks to another man who had his interests at heart: a newsagent by the name of Harry Wood.

Wood was a steward at Old Trafford and he persuaded Fergie

to take a look at the boy. Ryan headed to Old Trafford for a week-long trial but the boss caught a glimpse of his genius in advance and is said to have made up his mind that he would sign the boy right then.

Playing in a match for Salford Boys against a United Under-15s side at The Cliff Giggsy scored a hat-trick and as he played, he spotted the United boss watching with interest from his office window. Though Ryan believed he had done enough there and then, he still attended the trial.

He knew for sure that he had done enough on his 14th birthday when the dream became reality. Returning home from school, he saw a golden Mercedes parked outside the house. Anxiously, Giggsy hurried inside, where he saw Alex Ferguson sitting in an armchair, sipping at a cup of tea out of some of the best china mum Lynne could find. Fergie did not beat about the bush, instead quickly offering the prodigy a two-year deal as an associate schoolboy with Manchester United.

Ryan was 14, captain of England Schoolboys, and he had signed for Manchester United.

Key to it all was the attitude of the United boss: he had acted swiftly and decisively to bring the young lad to Old Trafford, even putting in a personal appearance at his home. It showed the importance he placed on youth development – and how he treated the kids he believed would guarantee a bright future for them both and Manchester United.

Later, Fergie would rhapsodise about Giggs' obvious talent, saying: 'I shall always remember my first sight of him, floating over the pitch at the Cliff so effortlessly that you would have sworn his feet weren't touching the ground.'

Ryan signed schoolboy forms and officially joined United on 9 July 1990, when he was 16. He turned professional on 29 November 1990, his 17th birthday.

The boss knew he was already capable of holding his own in the first team, but he didn't want to push him in too deep. For Fergie, Giggsy would be the prototype for the other boy wonders eventually following him through the ranks. At Aberdeen, he had encouraged youth and decided the best way to avoid any problems was to embrace and cosset the talented kids who were coming through the production line that he had put in place four years earlier. Now he would wrap Ryan in cotton wool, using him sparingly and keeping him well away from the wolves of the media, whom he eyed suspiciously. Fergie would tell the pack to back off; that no, Ryan was not available for a chat after a particularly inspiring showing and no, he would not be doing columns, adverts or promotions until he, the manager, decided the time was right.

Nearly three decades earlier, United had been the focus of national attention when the original celtic wonderkid came through the ranks. And Fergie, to his credit, knew all about that, and how the press would try to turn Ryan into Georgie Best Mark II. He also knew that Sir Matt Busby had tried his damnedest to help Georgie, to 'sort him out', but Matt was hardly a psychologist. The two managers shared a similar Glaswegian upbringing – the idea that 'we're all big boys who don't cry' – but to his credit, Fergie matured and moved on, professionally and personally, as the years rolled by.

He knew that Ryan Giggs would need his attention – and his protection. Of course there would be comparisons with Best and some pundits would sniff out Ryan's background – that he was from a broken home – and suggest he could easily go the same way as the late, great Georgie Boy. So, he looked out for him, shielded him and became almost a surrogate father.

Paul Parker, the former United fullback who played in the team of Ryan's early career, confirmed this was the case: 'The boss brought Ryan through from a troubled childhood and always saw him as one of his own.'

Giggs made his League debut at the tender age of 17 in the old Division One against Everton at Old Trafford on 2 March 1991 as a substitute for Denis Irwin. I was fortunate to be at the match, along with *Sunday Times* sports editor Alex Butler.

On the way up to Old Trafford Alex had told me to watch out for a young lad who Fergie had been grooming for stardom. Name of Giggs...

It was a bitterly cold afternoon and the match was not particularly memorable. United were already trailing 2-0 when Denis Irwin fell awkwardly and was taken off. This was the cue for Ryan's arrival. Butler nudged me in the arm and said: 'This is it – he'll bring on the lad Giggs.' The big man of Fleet Street wasn't wrong: a gawky, skinny boy with dark hair took off his tracksuit and headed towards the touchline.

He looked as if he might be blown over by the wind from the nearby Ship Canal, but he was stronger than he seemed. Fergie had patted him on the back and whispered in his ear: it was that sort of moment, history defining, epoch making. 'Good luck, Ryan,' I am told the boss said affectionately. 'And give 'em hell!'

It would later emerge that Fergie hadn't been just wrapping Giggs up in cotton wool and protecting him from the press. He had been encouraging him to build up his strength and physique and had told the backroom staff to work on that side of the boy's development. That work had clearly paid off – he danced around defenders and had not been overwhelmed and buffeted when they used their dark arts tricks to bundle him off the ball.

As Ryan trooped off, Fergie threw a protective arm round him and told him he had done well.

His first full start for the club came at Old Trafford almost exactly two months later when he scored the only goal against Manchester City (although this was disputed as it did take a deflection off Blues centre-back Colin Hendry).

Fergie showed his managerial skills again in pulling the boy out of the spotlight. He did not even include Giggsy in the squad of 16 that defeated Barcelona in the European Cup Winners' Cup final in Rotterdam on 15 May 1991. Without Ryan, United would beat the Spanish giants 2-1 to celebrate the re-admission of English clubs to Europe after a five-year absence in the wake of the Heysel disaster. Mark Hughes grabbed the brace to bring home a European trophy to Old Trafford for the first time since 1968.

'I shall never forget the whole day,' Sir Alex later said. 'The goals were obviously memorable and important, but for me the lasting impression was the atmosphere in the Feyenoord Stadium and watching the jubilation of our supporters in the pouring rain.'

The 30,000-plus Reds fans had celebrated United's first European final victory for 23 years by whistling and chanting, 'Always look on the bright side of life'. Things were certainly looking up at the club: Fergie had now brought home the FA Cup and the European Cup Winners' Cup – and with kids like Giggsy coming through the production line, the future looked even brighter.

And so it would prove for the boss.

Two more trophies were collected the following season. First, the Reds beat Red Star Belgrade 1-0 in the European Super Cup final, thanks to a winner from Brian McClair. And just five months after that United overcame Nottingham Forest by the same margin in the League Cup final (known then as the Rumbelows Cup). Again Scottish centre forward McClair was the goalscoring hero.

It was the first time that the Reds lifted the League Cup and McClair, who had joined from Celtic for £850,000 in July 1987, proved to be another of the boss's shrewd signings. The Scot would also become another solid influence on Giggsy and the kids, who would go on to lift the Youth Cup just months after the League Cup win.

Despite the accolades coming Fergie's way, some assessed the season as a failure – because they exited at an early stage from both the Cup Winners' Cup and FA Cup. More crucially, they did not win the League title when it appeared to be theirs for the taking.

After leading the race for much of the season the Red Devils lost out to Leeds United. The collapse that cost them so dearly began at Easter 1992, with three defeats in their final four games ending the dream. It led to major inquests in the press and in the pubs around Old Trafford – and even Fergie conceded that 'many in the media felt that [his] mistakes had contributed to the misery.'

The boss admitted his side needed an 'extra dimension' if they were to go one step further the following season and end 26 years of darkness by lifting the crown. He had tried to sign Mick Harford from Luton Town to bring that spark and said he believed United would have won the title with the big striker in tow. I am not sure about that – and many other pundits (and United fans) felt the same. Did the big bluff Harford really have the wow factor needed to turn United into champions?

The man who would finally arrive at Old Trafford the following Christmas certainly did, as we have noted: yes, Cantona, and nothing would ever be the same again at the Theatre of Dreams.

By now Fergie was introducing more of his wonderkids into the team, specifically Paul Scholes, David Beckham and the

Neville brothers – and all would benefit from the arrival of Cantona. He would cajole and encourage them – and Sir Alex openly encouraged the Frenchman to help them. He knew the footballing education they would receive, with his dedication to training and skills, was priceless.

If Becks was the headline star over the following years, then Scholes was the unsung hero: the true star. I do not think I am out of order in saying that, after Giggsy, he was the most naturally gifted of the boys. Certainly, Fergie knew he had a real gem on his hands with the shy Oldham-born youngster. Over the years, he had been receiving regular updates and glowing reports on him from youth team boss Eric Harrison and reserve team supremos, Brian Kidd and Jim Ryan.

Surprisingly, Scholes would not make his senior debut for Manchester United until September 1994. To put it another way: he would be kept on the sidelines for a full season on the boss's say-so after careful consultation with Eric Harrison and Brian Kidd. This was Fergie at his perceptive best; already he knew that Scholes had what it took to make an immediate impact in the first team, but he wanted to protect his star pupil. The United manager had blooded David Beckham and Nicky Butt at senior level, but Harrison and Kidd told him that Scholes was a different case; that he needed to be treated very carefully for a while longer because there were still question marks over his physical well-being.

Yes, Scholes had it all, but on occasions he could tire towards the end of matches. They warned that his breathing problems – he suffered from asthma and used an inhaler – meant patience was the key: that his time would come, but that it might be better to build up his strength a little more.

It meant that for the 1993/94 season Paul Scholes would spend his time training with the A team and the reserves, and that he would build a steady reputation in second-tier matches. In fact, in some games he was quite brilliant, the outstanding player on the pitch. Harrison agreed that, at the peak of his game, Scholes was undoubtedly the pick of the crop; the one with the greatest star quality of all the brilliant youngsters at Old Trafford that season. He recalls that in one game against Liverpool A, Scholes ran past half the opposition to score a typical wonder goal and received a resounding ovation for his efforts. By the middle of 1994, Eric knew the youngster was ready and would nag Ferguson to now let him – and the other kids – loose on a regular basis in the Premiership.

Harrison said: 'I could not contain my excitement at watching these young stars train and play, and I was always telling the boss how good they were.' He revealed that every time he urged Fergie to give them a sustained run of action in the first team, the boss's answer would be: 'Trust me, I will give them their chance.'

Of course Fergie was eventually as good as his word: one of his former stalwarts believes the United manager was spot-on in his 'softly-softly' treatment of Scholes. In the famous 1992 Youth Cup triumph George Switzer would play a key role as United's left-back. Initially, Scholes was tried out in the position but he had been uncomfortable and it was only when Switzer made the left-back slot his own that Scholes was drafted into his favoured attacking midfield role.

Switzer, now a van driver after being shown the door at United the season after that Youth Cup win, said: 'Paul Scholes had a few health problems when he was growing up. He had breathing problems and he was quite short. They tried playing him at left-back for a while, but it didn't work out so I ended up playing there.

'In one game he got a bang on the head and they moved me

into the left-back spot, even though I'd never played there before. I was quite small then, but Scholesy was even smaller. And after he got that bang they didn't fancy him as a left-back any more; they moved him into midfield and he hasn't looked back since.'

Switzer believes Fergie deserves praise for the way he waited patiently for Scholes to come through: 'Obviously Alex Ferguson saw something in him and they persevered with him. It was the right decision because he filled out, got stronger and developed into an amazing player.'

By the start of the 1994/95 season Scholes was raring to go – United had been waiting for him to come into full bloom and now they could hold him back no longer. The boss introduced him gently into the first team, before throwing him and the other wonder boys in en masse at the start of the following season. Scholes would make his United senior debut away from Old Trafford on 21 September 1994, when he scored both goals for the Red Devils in the 2-1 victory over Port Vale in the League Cup. He said: 'It was a great feeling to make my United debut and then to score two goals as well, it was just brilliant. I was walking on air for days.'

Fergie recalled the breakthrough of Scholes and his young team-mates that night in this way: 'In all my managerial career I have never been so positive about a group of young footballers as I was about those who were coming through as teenagers at the beginning of the 1994/95 season. As early as January 1993 I had awarded eight professional contracts and what was really exciting was the way the best of them had progressed to the point where they were competing for places in the first team. That was certainly true of Nicky Butt, Paul Scholes and Gary Neville. I relied mainly on graduates from the youth team for a League Cup tie at Port Vale and was rewarded with a 2-1 victory, with Paul scoring both goals. I knew he had the talent to make it to the very top.'

That double goal-scoring feat would not be enough to earn him a regular starting spot in the side, although he would make his full debut three days later and score another goal in the 3-2 loss away at Ipswich. That season Paul would make a total of 17 League appearances and score five goals.

One man's misfortune is another's opportunity and Scholes' came at the end of January 1995. He would take his chance to impress after Cantona was banned for eight months following his infamous kung fu kick on a Crystal Palace fan – even playing a minor role in the FA Cup final at the end of the campaign.

Scholes came on as a substitute in the 50th FA Cup final as United went down 1-0 to Everton, a Paul Rideout goal separating the teams. United started without three key players: the suspended Cantona, Andrei Kanchelskis (injured) and Andy Cole, who was cup-tied. Between them, they scored 41 goals during the season.

With 17 minutes to go, Scholes replaced Lee Sharpe but was unable to unlock a resolute Toffees defence, superbly marshalled on the day by the two Daves, Watson and Unsworth. I was at the match and witnessed the blossoming skills of Scholes; indeed, he would have equalised after being put through by Giggsy (another sub on the day), but for a breathtaking double save by Neville Southall towards the end of the match. Typical of Scholesy that he would afterwards be ultra-critical of himself for missing that opportunity. He would say: 'I got on late, as a substitute for Lee Sharpe. I missed a good chance to make it 1-1.' Interesting to note that two of Paul's cohorts from the Youth Cup glory days, Gary Neville and Nicky Butt, had beaten him to the first team: both played 90 minutes in that final clash.

Another worthy aside is that Paul and United would almost

enter the record books that day, thanks to a blunder by Prince Charles. The hapless Royal had started to present the FA Cup and the winners' medals to United, rather than Everton! Only the quick-thinking of the then FA secretary Graham Kelly saved the Prince's embarrassment making the public records. In his book *Sweet FA*, Kelly told how the Prince tried to give the FA Cup to the losing captain, Steve Bruce of United, instead of Everton's Dave Watson: 'Bruce led his team up first as the losers and the Prince of Wales immediately reached out for the trophy to give to the losing captain, despite the blue-and-white ribbons and the instructions on the procedure given to him beforehand.

'For a moment we wrestled with the famous trophy – as I held firmly onto the top of the Cup to stop him giving it to Bruce – before he realised what I was about.'

For Scholes, Beckham and Phil Neville, their time was almost nigh. United and Scholes ended the campaign empty-handed in his first season in the big-time A week before the FA Cup final when it had looked as if they would clinch the Premiership title, but they fell at the final hurdle.

That setback, allied with the FA Cup final defeat the following Saturday, would set alarm bells ringing at Old Trafford. Fergie knew the game was up for some of his stars; he believed they had let success go to their heads, that they were living on past glories. Sitting in his office overlooking the Theatre of Dreams on the Monday after the Everton setback, he decided tough action was needed: he was about to make one of his bravest calls, even though some of his most ardent supporters at the time would question its wisdom and his sanity – and the kids were about to win him titles.

CHAPTER 5

KIDS DID WIN TITLES

In the summer of 1995 Alex Ferguson took the biggest gamble with youth at Old Trafford since Sir Matt Busby's wonderful introduction of his Babes in the Fifties. After a disappointing campaign that ended without a trophy, Fergie decided he would jettison three of the biggest names at the club and replace them with the youngsters that Eric Harrison was now demanding be given first-team roles.

Out would go striker Mark Hughes, midfield enforcer Paul Ince and dazzling right-winger Andrei Kanchelskis. In came Paul Scholes, Nicky Butt and David Beckham.

The fans were not impressed: they found the sale of Ince to Inter Milan for £8 million, Kanchelskis to Everton (£6 million) and Hughes to Chelsea (£1.5 million) a particularly bitter pill to swallow. They could not understand why the manager wanted to dismantle the backbone of a successful team and they were particularly upset and mystified by the sale of their warrior striker Mark Hughes. Yet, with the benefit of hindsight, it is easy to see that far from being a gamble, Fergie's decision was one of the crowning, defining moments of his reign. None of the three would go on to better themselves as players and their performances at the new clubs would prove that they had indeed seen better days.

The condemnatory proof for Ferguson had been their inability to bring glory to United at the end of what would prove to be their final season at the club, especially in that demoralising defeat against Everton in the FA Cup and the lacklustre draw against West Ham in the League.

For Scholes, the decision to sell Ince would pave the way for his eventual brilliant partnership with Roy Keane in the heart of United's midfield; the link-up that would for a decade see the eventual skipper inspire and drive on United, while Scholes used his visionary talent to create openings and set up goals for himself and the front two of any given era.

By May 1995, United had finished second in the Premiership after a 42-game season, amassing 88 points. They lost six League games, including one at home, scoring 77 League goals and conceding 28 – they had won nothing. By the end of the kids' first full seasons in the Premiership, a year later, United had lifted the double of the Premiership and the FA Cup. In their 38-game league programme, they lost six games, but none at home, scoring 73 goals and conceding 35.

It was the season that saw the group of players from the Youth Cup glory days finally make their mark as a unit at the very top of the footballing pile: Scholes, Beckham, Butt and the Nevilles – collectively known as 'Fergie's Fledglings'. Their skill, commitment and precocious talents soon won over those fans still pessimistic after the departure of Hughes and Co – their play also brought the odd tear to the eyes of veteran fans reminded of the glory days of the legendary Busby Babes.

In 1958, the Munich air disaster had ripped a hole in the very fabric of the club, but now a new generation of 'Babes' was following in the hallowed footsteps of Duncan Edwards and his mighty boys. At the very vanguard of the revolution was Paul Scholes, who quickly become known as the 'Ginger Prince' to Cantona's 'King Eric'.

Ferguson would talk publicly about Scholes, saying he had one of the finest footballing brains that he had ever come across and adding: 'We might as well all go home if Paul doesn't make it.' It would make the little man blush, for even in those early days it was clear that United had found a true gem – a great player in the making, but a boy who was also well grounded, who would never let any success or plaudits go to his head.

Long-time United fan Steven Haywood put it this way: 'From his very first appearances for United you could see that Paul was different class. He could run a game at the age of 18, but while he was aggressive and fully committed on the field, it was clear that off it he was an altogether different commodity. He was quiet and kept his own counsel. In that way, he reminded me – both on and off the field – of Bobby Charlton in his formative years at Old Trafford. He was a fabulous, intelligent player, but he also did not want to bask in the limelight away from football. The game and his family meant everything to him; it was exactly the same with young Paul Scholes.

'It was terrific to see how Fergie dealt with him and all the youngsters, looking after them and encouraging them. He was like a second father to them – they knew he believed in them, that was why they had no fear.'

At the start of the 1995/96 campaign, Scholes himself would say: 'I am very grateful to be given the chance to prove myself in the first team by the boss. I will do my best not to let him and the fans down. It is good to be starting with the other boys I have played with in the youth team. It makes it easier – we know each other's games and I think we can do really well.'

Surely he could never have guessed how well in that first full year. Certainly the knives were out after an opening-day defeat at Villa Park. United went down 3-1 on 18 August, their goal coming from substitute David Beckham. The Reds' team read: Schmeichel, Parker, Irwin, Neville G, Sharpe, Pallister, Keane, Butt, McClair, Scholes, Neville P.

Later that night, on the BBC's *Match of the Day*, former Liverpool defender Alan Hansen would once again prove his punditry skills did not match the silky, intelligent ones he had shown on the pitch at Anfield a decade earlier. He came up with a soundbite that would haunt him to the present day, dismissing Ferguson's new-shaped team with the words: 'You'll never win anything with kids.'

United's kids responded by going unbeaten in their next 10 Premiership fixtures, the run only ending with a 1-0 defeat at Arsenal, courtesy of Dennis Bergkamp's fourth goal since signing for the Gunners. The run started with a 2-1 home win over West Ham on 23 August – with Scholes grabbing the opener in a victory that helped avenge that distressing 1-1 draw at the end of the previous season – and continued up until the 2-0 win over Middlesbrough on 28 October.

Sandwiched between that terrific run was the return of the man that the kids looked up to more than anyone as a footballer of genuine class: the incomparable Cantona. Eric was always the first and last away from the training ground and, as Scholes and Beckham got closer to making the first team, would think nothing of also spending time helping them work on their skills. Scholes said: 'Eric Cantona was a major influence on me and the way I play football. He taught me that however naturally talented you are, you still need to put in the hard work in training. You need to be dedicated and committed and professional if you want to reach the top and stay there.'

The 1996/97 season was the one in which David Beckham made his name – scoring from his own half against Wimbledon on the opening day. The squad was also strengthened by the signing of the young Norwegian striker Ole Gunnar Solskjaer. Now the kids were hungry to show they could cut it in Europe as well as England, but in May 1997 they were faced with the stark realisation that if they were to win the Champions League, it would be without their inspirational guru and leader Cantona.

For Paul Scholes, the exit of Cantona at least raised the hope that he would now become a fixture in the side yet the boss then brought in Teddy Sheringham as the King's replacement. But Fergie had big plans for the Ginger Prince: he wanted him to become a king in midfield with Keane.

Both Scholes and Sheringham started the season in the team, but Paul was dropped to substitute in the third match at Leicester. He would worry that there would come a time when it would be either him or Teddy, but that time never came.

On 27 September 1997, the club's new skipper Roy Keane damaged cruciate ligaments against Leeds – and was ruled out for the remainder of the 97/98 season. Scholes would now step in to fill the void – and eventually end up as Keane's ally in the centre of the park.

Typically with Keano, it would be an exit marred by controversy – circumstances that would linger and reverberate. In a tangle with Leeds United's Alf Inge Haaland, Keane suffered a dreaded cruciate knee injury. The Irishman would not forget how his Norwegian opponent labelled him a cheat as he lay there, injured, while Haaland believed Keane was feigning injury to get him in trouble – in fact, Keane's absence for the rest of the season would prove how wrong he had been in that regard. The United captain spent a frustrating season in rehabilitation and four years later, would finally gain retribution on Haaland, who was by then playing for Manchester City. After being fouled in the Manchester derby of April 2001, Haaland was left with damaged knee ligaments.

For Fergie's kids the 1997/98 season would end in tears as fierce rivals Arsenal snatched the Double they themselves had so proudly claimed in the May of 1996. Their only consolation was lifting the FA Charity Shield at the start of the campaign. OK, it was only minor silverware, but it was still something to put on the mantelpiece in what was to be a barren season. In the traditional season opener at Wembley, United beat Chelsea. The match ended 1-1 after extra-time, with goals from Ronny Johnsen for the Reds and Mark Hughes for Chelsea, but United won the penalty shoot-out 4-2.

Fergie had made two new signings to bolster United's challenge for the campaign: Teddy Sheringham was the first, from Spurs, and defender Henning Berg was also brought in, from Blackburn, for £5 million.

In the first match after Keane's injury, Fergie plotted the downfall of Italian giants Juventus in a memorable encounter. The teams met in a European Champions league group clash at Old Trafford on 1 October 1998 and United won 3-2.

The result provided the Reds with their first win over Italian opposition for 18 years and helped dismantle the bogeyman belief that the club could never win the European Cup again if they were drawn with clubs from Italy. Even Sir Alex had been caught up in the mood of anxiety instilled by the Italians – in the 1996/97 season United were twice beaten by Juve and after the Turin leg of the tie, he conceded: 'I stood in the tunnel before kick-off and the Juventus players made ours look small.'

The boss's band of Babes would help dispel that atmosphere

of fear forever – beginning that cold, wet October night in the Manchester of 1997. Without the injured Keane, United got off to a terrible start, falling behind within 20 seconds to a goal from Alessandro del Piero. Fergie had left Scholes out for Ronny Johnsen in the hope that the defender and the tigerish Nicky Butt would be able to tame Zinedine Zidane.

Scholes' chance came when Butt was withdrawn with concussion. Teddy Sheringham had equalised for United with a header and the Red Devils' good luck continued as Didier Deschamps was sent off. Ryan Giggs made it 3-1 with a fine shot past a hapless Angelo Peruzzi, and although Zidane's injury-time free-kick had nerves jangling, United held on for a famous win. The bulk of the Babes had come through their first major test of nerves together in the first team. Fergie's famous five of Beckham, Butt, Scholes and the Neville brothers all featured at some stage in a United team reading: Schmeichel, Neville G, Irwin, Johnsen, Pallister, Beckham, Butt (Scholes), Sheringham, Giggs, Solskjaer (Neville P) and Berg.

After the Juve match a delighted Fergie would almost purr while talking about the impact his very own Babes had made. He would also admit for the first time that one of the reasons why he had not worried as much as he might have done when Cantona quit was the knowledge that, in Scholes, he had a long-term replacement waiting in the ranks. Privately, he had already likened the boy to Kenny Dalglish because of his footballing intelligence – now he also conceded that Scholes could go on to have as illustrious a career as King Eric – indeed, it might be even more glittering if he could lead United to European glory.

Fergie said: 'I am very proud of the way my boys performed against world-class opposition – and to finally end our poor run against Italian teams made it all the sweeter, especially as they had to do it without the skipper [Keane]. And these kids of ours will get better and better – be sure of that. The best is yet to come.'

I once asked Cantona what he thought of Paul Scholes the man and the footballer: his response was illuminating. Eric, a man who could easily sense bullshit and falseness, said: 'Paul is a good man; a real man. He is not plastic like so many people you meet. What you see is what you get. He is simple in his needs and tastes and soulful; he loves life and his family. He is like me in that he does not appreciate hangers-on. I like his company and I like his philosophy.

'As for Paul the footballer... Well, I have played with many great players but Paul Scholes is certainly one of the best I have ever worked with. When I first came across him he was a youngster, but he was a youngster who was keen and who wanted to learn. He had that hunger you need if you are to be a success at anything in life; he worked hard and he was lucky in that he had the natural talent and skill at the base of it all. It was a joy and a pleasure to play alongside him at Manchester United. I consider Paul Scholes to be one of the all-time greats of world football.'

Yet the season that promised so much – and looked as if it might deliver when the Reds beat Juventus that magical night in Manchester – would end in despair for Fergie and co. By the end of it the boss realised he had a new serious rival to contend with. Yes, Arsène Wenger would cap his own brilliant first full season as the new man in charge at Arsenal by stealing the Double from the Reds.

Over the next decade he would rival Sir Alex with a series of honours, turning Arsenal into United's biggest worry. That first season, his Gunners equalled United's record of two League Championships and FA Cups as they overhauled Fergie's men in the Premiership title race and beat Kenny Dalglish's Newcastle in the FA Cup final.

Arsenal pipped United to the title by a single point, their win at Old Trafford in March courtesy of a lone Marc Overmars' goal merely piling on the agony. Credit where credit is due, the Gunners trailed United by 11 points at the beginning of March but had the nerve and ability to overwhelm that massive lead as they won their games in hand and gradually wore United down.

Yet there were some highlights for Fergie. On 10 January 1998, his kids would knock out FA Cup holders Chelsea in the third round at Stamford Bridge. The Red Devils stormed to a 5-3 win – inflicting on Blues boss Ruud Gullit the most comprehensive defeat of his managerial career, one that would contribute to his sacking soon afterwards.

Disappointingly, after that tremendous win United would exit the FA Cup in the fifth round to Barnsley and would also lose out in the Champions League to Monaco in the quarter-finals. United exited on away-goals, drawing 1-1 at Old Trafford following a 0-0 scoreline in Monaco.

But for Fergie and his babes, the anguish would not last: United were just one year away from finally banishing the demons haunting them since 1968 due to their inability to reign again in Europe. After the darkness of that barren May in 1998, Alex Ferguson was on the brink of a dawn that would bring him his greatest-ever season in football – as he guided the Manchester United team to a magic Treble of the Premiership, the FA Cup and most importantly, the European Cup.

CHAPTER 6

MIRACLE IN THE CAMP NOU

The boss had dismissed out of hand those critics who warned that United were on a downward spiral after the disappointment of that barren 1997/98 season. 'We'll be back – and big time,' he had declared in his best Arnie Schwarzenegger voice. And how right he would be proved in that particular boast.

For just a year on from heartache, Sir Alex would lift the most amazing set of trophies ever in British football. By the end of the 1998/99 season, he would take home his greatest haul: medals for United's triumphs in the FA Cup, the Premier League and, of course, most important of all, the Champions League, as the club finally ended the hoodoo that had haunted Old Trafford for 31 years.

As usual, Fergie had headed down to the South of France for his annual month's vacation away from football. But, much to his wife Cathy's annoyance, he had not been idle – no, he was busy lining up two incoming deals that he believed would turn United into European champions.

When the boss rejoined the club for their pre-season tour to Scandinavia in July, he introduced the men who, along with Roy Keane, would establish a new, tougher spine to the United side. Arguably the world's best defender, Jaap Stam would also become one of United's greatest-ever defenders when he joined for what would prove a bargain £10.8 million from PSV Eindhoven.

Stam would add a granite-solid presence at the heart of the backline – he was already renowned as 'a one-man defence', back in his native Holland. Fergie also brought in the bubbly, likeable but deadly striker Dwight Yorke from Aston Villa for £12 million. Both would prove shrewd buys as Stam strengthened the backline, while Yorke grabbed goals galore. There was another indirect bonus with the arrival of Yorke – he would bring out the best in his new strike partner, Andy Cole.

Cole was a surprisingly introverted and introspective man but he somehow gelled with Yorkie, who was the exact opposite with his chirpy, happy-go-lucky demeanour. True, Cole had struck up a good partnership with Teddy Sheringham, but the pair had never got on off the pitch – in fact, they never spoke to each other. But Yorke would, I am told at the private behest of Fergie, take time to cajole Cole and take the heat off him – and, yes, it worked: we would eventually even see Coley smile!

Jesper Blomqvist was also brought in from Italian outfit Parma to add another option on the wing. He was fast and tricky, and would have a part to play in the final game of the season, the Champions League final in the Camp Nou, Barcelona.

Fergie told his players that he wanted them to begin the new campaign with a bang after the failed one just behind them. He warned that they needed to hit form quickly because they would be in the unfortunate position of having to qualify for the Champions League proper. But they hardly heeded the boss's words as they tumbled to an embarrassing 3-0 defeat to Arsenal in the Charity Shield. It did not bode well for the European qualifier, due three days later on 12 August.

Yet United, typically, defied the form book and beat Lodz 2-0 in the home leg, with goals from Giggs and Cole. A fortnight later, they would manage to hold their rivals to a 0-0 draw in Poland, thus booking their place in the group stage of the competition.

After the home win over Lodz, Fergie was fired up, telling the team that they needed to build on the result in their first League game that season. First up were Leicester and, amazingly, United looked tired, even though it was still opening week. They managed a 2-2 draw but had to come back from 2-0 down, with just 11 minutes remaining.

A week later the Reds travelled to West Ham and drew 0-0. All of a sudden the fans were scratching their heads and wondering if this was to be a re-run of the disappointing previous season. Fergie told them to be patient, that his new signings needed time to settle in – and that Keano had to get back into the pace of it all after his spell on the sidelines. But they needn't have worried for the team would now go on a run that would see them unbeaten in 19 out of 20 matches. The results in the League and Europe were commendable. In the Champions League group stages, they drew 3-3 twice with the might of Barcelona, drew 2-2 at Bayern Munich and thrashed Brondby 6-2 away. Meanwhile, in the League they beat Liverpool 2-0 at home and Everton 4-1 away, the double mugging of their Mersey rivals proving particularly sweet to United fans.

A 1-1 draw with Bayern in the final match of Champions

League Group D meant United successfully qualified for the next stage as runners-up to the Germans.

By Christmas Aston Villa were the unexpected League leaders, but they would come down with the lights on the tree as the festive season turned into the New Year. It then became a three-horse race for the title between United, Arsenal and Chelsea.

On 3 January, the Reds walloped Middlesbrough 3-1 in the third round of the FA Cup. Remarkably, that win over Boro was the first of 31 matches in the Cup, the League and the Champions League that United would play, from January 1999 to the end of the season in May 1999, in which they would stay unbeaten.

'It was a terrific achievement,' Fergie later observed, 'Just part of an overall magnificent season.'

It was all the more remarkable given the stress that the boss and his boys were under as they tried to stay in contention for the Treble by achieving at times back-to-back results in all three competitions. Arsenal were breathing down their necks in the League and the competition was exacting as they roared into the final stages of the Champions League, not forgetting the FA Cup. At the end of it all, it would come down to three season-defining games in 10 days.

The first was the home clash in the League against Spurs on 16 May, the second, on 22 May, was the FA Cup final against Newcastle and the denouement saw United head for Spain for a nerve-tingling encounter with old enemies Bayern Munich. That was to take place on 26 May, which would have been Sir Matt Busby's 90th birthday.

Fergie knew they had to beat Spurs to win the League; even a draw could see Arsenal overtake them. In a tense encounter they kept their nerve, eventually coming through 2-1 after falling behind to a Les Ferdinand goal on 24 minutes. Goals from

Beckham and Cole broke Spurs' surprisingly stubborn resistance (given their biggest rivals Arsenal could lift the title if they drew or won). The result meant United had won the League by a single point from the Gunners, with Chelsea third on 75.

Afterwards the boss was delighted and gave his players the nod when they asked if they could maybe take a victory drink or two. As pros, they knew they could not go over-the-top and he trusted them to stick to a couple and a celebratory meal.

It had been an emotional Sunday for Fergie, United and their fans. The great Peter Schmeichel took his final bow at Old Trafford in a United shirt as the club clinched their fifth title in seven years. Big Pete spoke to the fans, telling them, 'You will always be in my heart.'

Then Fergie took the mic, but typically, he was seeing the bigger picture. He said: 'Winning the title does take pressure off us in a sense for the two games we have got left. We know that we are going into next season's European Cup as champions. But if the players think that the FA Cup is the lesser of the two targets ahead of us, if a lot of them start thinking about Barcelona, they will soon wake up when I pick my team for Wembley next Friday.

'This club is not about egos: it is about maintaining success, about building on the bedrock that was laid down by Sir Matt. That is why I will make sure no one gets carried away.'

But then the boss went on to praise his team for what they had achieved already: winning the English Premier League was not to be sniffed at. In terms of toughness and constant pressure, it is probably harder than the Champions League, which is, after all, a knockout Cup after the mini league at the start. Fergie said: 'Titles are won over a year. We deserved our success – we are the best team in the country. They never give in; they were hanging on for a whole season of hard work.

'They suffered last year when they lost the title to Arsenal. They did not deserve that, but they got their act together and they rediscovered their work ethic. I know some people think of them as gods, but there is a sense of realism about them, too.'

Next up was the FA Cup Final against the Toon at Wembley. The Reds owed a major debt to Giggsy for getting them there – with that wonder goal against Arsenal in the semi-replay at Villa Park.

The magical moment – the one Ryan would describe as '...my best goal ever, and the one I'd like to be remembered by' – put United in the final with a 2-1 win. Fergie himself commented that it would always be remembered as one of the greatest of all time.

I can still remember that extra-time goal as if it were yesterday. A stray pass from Patrick Vieira was intercepted by Giggs and he ran all of 60 yards, dribbling past Vieira, Lee Dixon, Martin Keown and Tony Adams before unleashing an unstoppable shot that soared over David Seaman into the roof of the net. Even when he had seen off all those Arsenal defenders he still had to get the ball home from an acute angle.

David Beckham had put United ahead after 17 minutes at Villa Park that wondrous night, but Dennis Bergkamp equalised after 51 minutes before Nicolas Anelka had a goal disallowed and Keane was sent off. Schmeichel saved a 90th-minute penalty from Bergkamp, but, in the 19th minute of extra-time Giggs wriggled in to grab his goal of the season.

Fergie paid tribute to Giggs for what was arguably the greatest individual goal of the boss's tenure at United. 'It was a cracker, brilliant,' he said, adding: 'I think we deserved the win. We had no complaints about the sending-off of Roy Keane, the players have played in agony to get the victory.'

It would turn out to be a much more comfortable afternoon's

work at Wembley on 22 May. Newcastle simply did not turn up in their biggest match for three decades (when they had won the Inter-Cities Fairs Cup). They finished 13th in the league – it showed – and had hoped a bit of manager Ruud Gullit's magic would rub off on them. It didn't.

The night before the final I talked to the former AC Milan and Holland legend at the Kensington hotel where the Toon were based for the final – and he told me he was confident his team could end the long wait for major trophy glory. He was in a bubbly mood, as was key man Alan Shearer – the player Fergie feared most at Wembley.
Gullit gave me two VIP tickets for the final – as a sportswriter on the *Sun*, I was to escort a deserving Newcastle fan, who had won a competition set up by the club in tandem with the paper as his prize.

I must say the antics of the guests we were sitting among in the Newcastle VIP section were far more entertaining than the match itself. TV presenters Ant and Dec enjoyed several crafty fags – much to the annoyance of pop star Sting, who was nearby. Meanwhile, another rock legend – Bryan Ferry of Roxy Music fame – tried to look cool in the heat in a suit and tie. Everyone else was in short sleeves but still daft old Bryan insisted on striking a pose, even though the cool customer act was ruined as he consistently drew a hanky out of his pocket to mop his brow.

The hometown team were frankly a major disappointment, a real let-down to the loyal army of fans who had followed them to Wembley. Instead, it was United in red shirts who set the pace and sauntered to a 2-0 win with goals from Scholes and Sheringham.

Afterwards, Fergie purred with pride as his team paraded the FA Cup around the old stadium. He said: 'That's fantastic –

three doubles in five years. The boys were marvellous. This has been a tremendous season and once again the players produced when it mattered.'

He added that the three key men had been Sheringham, Beckham and Giggs – particularly after United suffered the massive blow of losing influential skipper Keane after just eight minutes with an ankle injury. Fergie continued: 'We tried to reorganise the team after Keane went off, but Teddy Sheringham was marvellous – great movement and a terrific finish. We had a big decision to make about whether to risk some players, but you have to trust them to tell you if they are OK. Now we can start thinking about Europe.'

The squad now moved on from Wembley to Bisham Abbey for a day's preparation for the big one. They watched videos of Bayern Munich and worked on tactics.

Before we analyse the biggest night in Alex Ferguson's footballing life, let's fill in the gaps of United's European campaign from the New Year of 1999. After successfully negotiating the group stages, the Reds were paired with Inter Milan in the last eight.

On 3 March 1999, they beat the Italians 2-0 at Old Trafford, thanks to a brace from Dwight Yorke, and drew the return 1-1 a fortnight later. That set up a tough showdown in the semis – with another trip to Italy against Juventus. United drew the first leg 1-1 at Old Trafford. The Italians took the lead on 25 minutes when Edgar Davids set up Antonio Conte – with the midfielder hammering the ball past a hapless Schmeichel. Juve held onto their lead until the last minute of normal time, when Giggs fired home from five yards after Juve failed to clear their lines.

A fortnight later, the return would see one of the greatest performances in the long and wonderful history of Manchester

United – certainly their best away from home in the European Cup as so much rested on the outcome.

Juve went 2-0 up within 11 minutes, thanks to a double from Filippo Inzaghi. United heads started to drop but cometh the hour, cometh the power, as Keane – urged on by 6,000 United fans in the Stade Delle Alpi – turned in a true captain's performance. By the end of the night those 6,000 loyalists would be celebrating, silencing the fireworks and taunts of the Old Lady's Ultra fanatics.

From a Beckham corner on 25 minutes, Keane rose superbly to head home, the precision and power of his effort giving keeper Peruzzi no chance. Eight minutes later, calamity struck when Keane received a yellow card for catching Zidane with a tackle. It would rule him out of the final, should United get there. But this was no Paul 'Gazza' Gascoigne; no, Roy Keane was made of much sterner stuff.

Ironically enough, it had been at the same stadium that Gazza suffered an emotional breakdown when booked nine years earlier. Playing for England against West Germany in the World Cup semi-final, he had burst into tears when it dawned on him that the indiscretion would rule him out of the final, should England make it.

Keane was more annoyed with himself for getting in a similar position. He would only wallow in his own loss after the match ended and rebuke himself for losing out on what should have been the greatest night of his footballing life because of a silly tackle. Two minutes after Keane's booking, United showed that they could never be written off, as Yorke put them level on the night, but ahead on the away-goals rule.

Six minutes on, the miracle comeback was complete when Andy Cole fired the ball home to take the Red Devils into the final.

Fergie was overjoyed at the result and hugged all his men. A few days later he said they had a great chance in the final, but Bayern would be tough and that they had an excellent manager in Ottmar Hitzfeld.

The German had masterminded Borussia Dortmund's victory over United in the Champions League semi in 1997 and Fergie said of him: 'He's a fantastic manager and also a very, very good man, a real gentleman and I admire him greatly. He is very focused as a manager and a bit like myself in that he gets agitated at times. Yet off the field, he is very calm and controlled.'

United and Bayern had met in the group stages when they drew 2-2 in the Olympic Stadium before a 1-1 draw at Old Trafford. Fergie added: 'I thought in the game in Munich that we were the better team. The game at Old Trafford was very, very even, with Bayern showing more experience than us for a good part of the match. Hopefully, we have improved enough to make a difference.'

The boss pinpointed midfield maestros Lothar Matthaus and Steffan Effenberg as principle threats to United glory. He said: 'I think Bayern's players of influence are Matthaus and Effenberg, and I think they are who we need to concentrate on. There's a history of European Cup finals being 1-0 or settled on penalty kicks over the last decade and a half. I hope Manchester United and Bayern will elevate themselves above that to produce a good game of football.'

Well, the play itself was rather mundane for the best part of 90 minutes but then it certainly did become a good game of football for United!

They had flown to Barcelona by Concorde and set up HQ at their hotel in the nearby coastal resort of Sitges. Fergie had rested two of his big players at Wembley – Stam and Yorke – but confirmed they would both play in Barcelona.

Of course, Keane and Scholes were out with suspension (although Roy would also have missed the match through the injury he picked up at Wembley), which meant the roles and performances of two other Red heroes would be vital. Beckham would be required to pick up the pieces in central midfield in their absence, while Giggs would be asked to start on the left, with Blomqvist in his traditional left-wing role.

Even on paper it looked unbalanced and so it would prove on the field of play. United were not the side they had been all season: let's be honest, they were lucky to win, but what the hell, the result was all that counted – and the ending of 31 years of hurt. And what could we really expect without Keane and Scholes? Yes, United were outplayed in that vital central midfield area, but it was hardly surprising.

Mario Basler put Bayern ahead after just six minutes and the Germans spent much of the match sitting back on their lead and relying on breakaways. It was difficult for United to get a foothold in the game, let alone break them down, and Beckham was not the player in the centre that he was on right wing. Yet fortune would favour the Reds that hot, humid night in Barca as those two late wonder strikes from Sheringham and Solskjaer brought the trophy back to Old Trafford. Completing the Treble as it did, this was surely the most wonderful night in the club's history – and in Fergie's long and glorious career as a manager.

It also felt good to see gloating Bayern fall back down to earth with an almighty bump. Their arrogance was breathtaking as they celebrated prematurely when the match ran into the final five minutes. Chief culprit was skipper Matthaus, who captained West Germany to World Cup victory in 1990. He could be seen pumping his right fist in celebration at the Bayern fans, but was distraught when the double act killed off his team.

Afterwards he spoke with sour grapes, not giving any credit to United and their fortitude, resilience and determination. He said: 'To lose a final is always hard, especially this way. Tonight it was not the best team that won, but the luckiest. But we must not blame anyone, especially in normal time. It's bitter, sad and unbelievable. We're all disappointed. You can't blame the team – we had the match in control for 90 minutes. We had bad luck, hitting the post and the crossbar. What happened afterwards is simply inexplicable.'

Of course, Fergie disagreed, saying United had deservedly triumphed: 'This is the best moment of my life. I'm really proud of my players, proud of my heritage and my family for what they have given me. I simply don't know where to begin, but you can't deny people with this spirit we have and that's why we have won this trophy. Football is such a funny game – it's a fairytale, really.'

It was certainly that: United had followed up the Miracle of Turin in the semis with the Miracle of the Camp Nou in the final. They deserved the utmost credit for their achievement and Matthaus would surely acknowledge that when his head cleared after the inevitable deflation the defeat brought.

The win meant United had become only the fourth side in history to win both their domestic League and Cup competitions, and Europe's premier club tournament in the same season. Only Celtic in 1967, Ajax Amsterdam in 1972 and PSV Eindhoven in 1988 had previously managed the same feat.

Out of a total of 62 competitive games in the Treble season, United had won 36, drew 22 and lost just four – three matches in the League and one in the Carling Cup when Ferguson fielded the reserves. They had scored a total of 128 goals, conceded 60 and remained unbeaten in all 13 European matches, winning six and drawing seven.

And they had become the first side to win the Champions League after having to qualify for the competition. Peter Schmeichel, who had played his last game for the club, summed up the general feeling of euphoria when he said: 'This is a fantastic finish for me and everything feels really good right now. When I announced that I would leave United at the end of the season, I promised I would do all I could to finish with United being at the top – it's difficult to get any higher than this. It's been an amazing thing, being part of a team like Manchester United.'

The team returned to their luxury hotel base in nearby Sitges for a rowdy celebratory meal and party (at which even the normally reserved and gentle Giggs would end up punching a bloke – none other than the chairman's son!). The celebrations would go on all night and well into the next week as the players deservedly let their hair down. But Fergie abstained after the night of the win. He was not a man to go overboard – sure, the win meant he was the most successful manager ever but it was done with, already in the past. Besides, he needed to keep his head clear and be on tip-top form a few weeks later as a very important date with Royalty loomed.

On 12 June, the boy from the Govan tenements was knighted at Buckingham Palace, becoming only the eighth football manager or player to receive the accolade. Sir Alex was awarded the title in the Queen's Birthday Honours List for his services to football and attended the ceremony with his wife Cathy. The honour followed on from the OBE he had received in 1984 and the CBE in 1995.

He said: 'I am delighted and honoured. I see this as an honour not just for me, but for the people who have supported me through my life and made me what I am. If my parents were still alive, they would be very proud. They gave me a good start in life, the values that have driven me and the confidence to believe in myself. It is not just down to me, but to the players who have to deliver on the pitch and to the people at Old Trafford, past and present, who have made it the greatest club in the world.

'Above all, I want to thank my wife Cathy. She knows better than anyone the pressures of the job and the demands they place upon me. She is the rock of stability in my life and I share this honour with her.'

The fans delivered their verdict on the achievement. Lee Hodgkiss, of the Manchester United Independent Supporters Club, told the BBC: 'We are all very pleased. I think it's deserved and in my opinion he stands alone as a football manager – and that's including all the managers who have gone before him.

'It's not just for the work he has done in Manchester, but what he did in Scotland. The success of Manchester United is now purely down to him and the players. He is responsible for Manchester United not only being the greatest football team on the pitch, but the biggest football club in the world.'

Lifelong United fan Terry Graham agreed: 'It's only right that he has been awarded the top honour,' he said. 'After all, he's the top manager – and I don't just mean in Britain. He's the best manager in the world. What he has done at Man United is unbelievable, turning us around from a middling-to-nowhere team and set-up to the best and biggest in the world. He's taken us back to the glory days of Sir Matt, but done it bigger and better. He has rebuilt the club and I hope he stays until he is 70!'

Fergie was grateful for all the plaudits, but cast them from his mind as he headed off for his annual vacation in the South of France. No, now it was time to think about the future: to start plotting how United could stay at this level and move on. That was how he had always done things, the secret of his success. Not allowing success to blind him or the grass to grow under his feet.

Only by starting again, with a blank canvas in front of him, could he take United forward once more. And he knew it would be difficult: it had been somewhat easier to motivate the players after they suffered a barren season in 1998, but had success gone to some of their heads? Would some of his players have lost their appetite for success, preferring to rest on their laurels?

He was about to find out.

CHAPTER 7

BOSH AND BECKS

'MY PROBLEM IS I CAN NEVER REMEMBER THE
PLAYERS I'M NOT TALKING TO. I HAVE A GO AT SO
MANY PEOPLE DURING GAMES THAT I NEVER KNOW
WHO'S TALKING TO ME AND WHO'S NOT.'
Roy Keane

'WHEN YOU ARE TALKING ABOUT MANCHESTER
UNITED 30 OR 500 YEARS FROM NOW, ROY KEANE
WILL STILL BE REGARDED AS ONE OF THE GREATEST
PLAYERS EVER AT THIS CLUB.'
Sir Alex Ferguson

'I HAVE A CAMERA UP MY BACKSIDE ALMOST
24 HOURS A DAY.'
David Beckham

After lifting the Champions League trophy in that never-to-be-forgotten night at the Camp Nou, it was inevitable Fergie might question if his men still had the will to win, the same unquestionable spirit and hunger for success that had taken them to such soaring heights as the Treble in the first place. He knew his own desire for glory remained as strong as ever, but what of the men he sent out on the pitch, millionaires who hardly needed to get out of bed, such was their wealth?

His skipper Keane shared the same fears, even more so than the boss because he stubbornly refused to accept that he had won the Champions League as a player. The medal he received was simply thrown into a drawer: in his eyes, Keano hadn't won it because he hadn't played in the final in Barca, even though United wouldn't have been there in the first place but for his remarkable show in Turin in the semis. Hardman Keano knew he had the same hunger because he still had the desire to win a 'first' Champions League medal. He remained the toughest guy on the pitch, the man who could make the opposition shudder with his challenges.

Meanwhile, there were private whispers that maybe David Beckham would be one of those who had lost that hunger – after all, he had won everything at club level and, in the eyes of certain critics, seemed to spend as much time boosting his 'Brand Beckham' profile with pop star wife Victoria, whom he had wed the year before the triumph in Barca. But those critics were way off line: he may have seemed more laidback than Keano, but Becks was just as determined and burning with desire for more success as his skipper.

As we move from that wondrous Champions League-winning season up to the arrival of Ronaldo and Rooney at the club (2003 and 2004), let's now assess how important Keane and Becks (the duo dubbed 'Bosh and Becks' by some of my Fleet Street colleagues because Keane hit you first and asked questions later!) were in Fergie's tenure. Indeed, after Cantona and Giggs, they were certainly the most influential stars for a big part of the boss's reign.

In the summer of August 1993 Fergie signed Keane for the then British record fee of £3.75 million. The Irishman's spell at the City Ground under legendary manager Brian Clough had been a good bedding-in exercise, a learning period for Old Trafford. Now he would work for a new, similarly top-class mentor in Alex Ferguson.

Keane departed the City Ground with this wonderful tribute from Clough ringing in his ears: 'The Irishman has everything he needs to go all the way. He can tackle, he can pass, he can head the ball and he can score. And he can do it all with the impression he has plenty of time, which is always the indication of a top-class player. You didn't have to be a genius to see he had something going for him – even my wife could have spotted it! He is one of the best headers of the ball I have come across. Blow me, I've not seen anyone jump so well since Red Rum called it a day!'

Keane had certainly given Forest good service for the £47,000 they paid for him. In his three years there he had played in a total of 154 games and scored 33 goals. Fergie was keeping tabs on him for some time before he signed up. The boss once admitted he loved the fiery way in which Keane played, his win-at-all-costs mentality. Of one game between United and Forest involving Keane the warrior, Ferguson said: 'The game kicked off, the ball went back to Bryan Robson and Roy absolutely creamed him. I thought, bloody cheek of him – how dare he come to Old Trafford and tackle Robbo like that! I made a mental note there and then that we had to get this boy to Old Trafford.'

Brian Clough had also gone out of his way to make sure the young Irishman was given every chance to develop under his control. He knew this was a boy who needed both reassurance and a certain freedom. Out on the pitch Keane would be aggressive, but away from it, he was shy and unsure of himself. Clough gave him leeway and one week early on in their relationship, he affectionately admitted that getting his footballing message over to Keane was never a problem, but making sense of his accent was: 'In his early days at the City ground, we thought about bringing in an interpreter. His Irish brogue was so pronounced and rich that, for a second or two, I thought we'd landed someone from the Continent!'

Fergie had no such misconceptions when the young Irishman finally walked through the doors at Old Trafford in July 1993 as United's most expensive signing. Keane would later tell how he felt a little choked up at finally making it to the Theatre of Dreams – United was the club he had wanted to sign for when he was a 16-year-old, back in Cork, but it had also been the only English club that he had not applied to for a trial simply because he had thought himself not good enough.

Fergie had snatched Keane from the clutches of Celtic legend Kenny Dalglish, then boss at Blackburn. Fergie and Dalglish were regularly at odds when Dalglish managed Liverpool from 1985 until 1991. Their most famous verbal spat was in 1988, when Fergie walked down the tunnel at Anfield complaining to the referee about a penalty decision. Nearby, Dalglish was cradling his baby daughter in his arms. With a wicked smile, he told newsmen: 'You'd get more sense out of my baby!'

Dalglish believed he had the Keane deal sewn up, that the Irishman was a shoo-in to follow Alan Shearer to Ewood Park. But he had reckoned without the determination and shrewd negotiating ability of Fergie. At the eleventh hour, the United boss sneaked in to talk to Keane and secured his signature, leaving Dalglish to bring in a player from Leeds as the rock on which his Blackburn ship would now prosper or flounder. He may have cost just £1 million less, but David Batty was lower league compared to the great Roy Keane.

The United Keane joined had just won the League title for the first time in 26 years and his team-mates included the likes of Bryan Robson, Paul Ince, Mark Hughes and Ryan Giggs. Keane would begin his United adventure at right-back, but Fergie knew Robson was on the last lap of a fine career so he had already earmarked Keane for his marauding midfield role. This was one element of the boss's genius: he could see when a long-serving star needed to be replaced and was quick to line up a player that he believed could take over.

And Keane's initial comments on why he joined the Reds rather than Rovers were pure music to Fergie's ears: 'I signed for Manchester United because they have got the best stadium, the best team and the greatest supporters in the country. Blackburn Rovers made me a fabulous offer, but as soon as United declared an interest there was only one outcome. This is a career move – to come to a club of this size is good for my future.'

His United debut came on 7 August 1993 in the Charity Shield win over Arsenal at Wembley. The match ended all square at 1-1, but Keane won his first piece of silverware with the club after United triumphed on penalties. Keane made his League debut at Norwich on 15 August 1993, setting up Ryan Giggs for the opener in the 2-0 win.

Roy grabbed a brace of goals in his next match, a memorable home debut on 18 August 1993 as the Red Devils crushed Sheffield United 3-0 in the Premiership. It was the start of a love-in that would last for 12 years between Keane and the United fans. In his first season he helped the club to the coveted League and FA Cup double – their second successive

Premiership win – and the icing on the cake was the 4-0 FA Cup final walkover against Chelsea.

The following season was a disappointment. After Bryan Robson left to become player-manager at Middlesbrough, Keane finally cemented his place in the heart of the United midfield at least, but the Red Devils ended the campaign trophyless. It was now time for 'Fergie's fledglings' – and Roy, along with Cantona, was just what they needed to drive them on to the next level, of more later.

When 'the King' departed in 1997, Keane would take the skipper's armband and hold it, unopposed, for the next eight years. Fergie would admit that Roy was 'his eyes and ears on the pitch' and together the pair would take United to an unprecedented list of honours over the decade.

In his boss's eyes, his greatest moment came in Turin in 1999, in that remarkable comeback at Juventus after United were 2-0 down – and looking for a miracle. Much to Fergie's eternal gratitude, it would come in the shape of Keane. As we have noted, he led United to victory, despite knowing that he would not play any part in the final after he was booked. But Keane did not let it get to him – instead he selflessly drove his troops on, covering every blade of grass as he dragged them over the line.

The battling skipper visibly slumped as the final whistle went. Now it truly sunk in: he would play no part in the final, but typical of this lionheart of a man, he blamed only himself when he eventually faced the waiting pressmen. He said he would never forgive himself for picking up a booking for dissent in the previous round at home to Inter Milan and that it was not his booking in Turin that was to blame for his predicament: 'I don't mind so much getting booked for making a tackle but to get one for dissent or arguing is a bit of a nightmare. I am annoyed

Sir Alex in his playing days. He began his career as an amateur at Queen's Park and also played for St Johnstone, Dunfermline Athletic, Rangers and Falkirk before ending up at Ayr United.

Above: Sir Alex collecting his OBE at Holyrood Palace with wife Cathy and sons Mark, Darren and Jason. Fergie received the honour in 1983.

Below: Capping his stint as manager of Aberdeen with a fourth Scottish Cup Final victory in 1986.

Above: Fergie with Walter Smith. Sir Alex took charge of Scotland for the 1986 World Cup following the sudden death of Jock Stein in November 1985.

Below: Sir Alex leads his Manchester United side out for the 1990 FA Cup final against Crystal Palace.

Above left and right: Fergie gets his first taste of English silverware as United beat Crystal Palace 1-0 in the 1990 FA Cup final replay (having drawn the first match 3-3).

Below: The trophy that ended United's 26-year wait for a League Championship – Sir Alex celebrates with assistant manager Brian Kidd after United clinch the 1993 Premier League crown.

Above left: Sir Alex with the 1993 Manager of the Year trophy.

Above right: Fergie celebrates again as United retain their Premier League title in 1994.

Below: Capping a remarkable season with victory in the 1994 FA Cup final – Sir Alex's first English League and Cup Double.

Sir Alex's United achieved yet another Double in 1996, clinching the Premier League title on the last day of the season before sealing victory in the FA Cup final thanks to an Eric Cantona goal against old enemies Liverpool.

The 1996 Double celebrations continue as the United managerial team pose with the
trophy and goalscorer Cantona, and then parade the trophies through Manchester
on an open-top bus.

Yet more success for Ferguson and Kidd in 1997, with their fourth Premier League title in five years and victory in the Charity Shield. 1996-97 also saw the signing of Norwegian unknown Ole Gunnar Solskjaer, who ended the season as top scorer.

because what really cost me was the booking I got against Inter in the quarter-final.'

Tributes for his performance in Turin poured in, but none meant so much to him as the words from his manager, Ferguson, who would later say: 'The minute he was booked and out of the final, he seemed to redouble his efforts to get the team there. It was the most emphatic display of selflessness I have ever seen on a football field.'

And that doyen of sportswriters, the *Sunday Times*' Hugh McIlvanney, had this to say after the 3-2 triumph over adversity: 'Keane is the most important player in the recent history of Manchester United.'

The last time Roy spoke of his 1999 Camp Nou disappointment he still maintained winning a medal meant nothing to him. He said: 'Football is a very selfish game. No matter how many people tell me I deserve that Champions League medal, I know I don't.'

Keane was to miss out on another couple of honours that he should have netted, too. Despite having led United to the treble, he did not win the Professional Footballers' Association (PFA) and the Football Writers' Association (FWA) Player of the Year awards in May 1999. Inexplicably, both bodies would honour the dilettante talents of Tottenham winger David Ginola – although Roy was to lift both the following season.

But the long soul search for Manchester United FC and Alex Ferguson was over with the Champions League win in Barcelona. Soon after he would be made a Knight of the Realm and the next season United would go on to play some fabulous attacking football, lifting yet another Premiership title in 2000, with the Scot also winning his fifth Manager of the Year award in eight years.

The first post-Treble season had turned out to be a bit of an anti-climax for Fergie and Co. – well, they could hardly win the Treble again as they opted out of the FA Cup to take part in the FIFA World Club Championship, but the players had shown the boss that they still meant business – and could do the business – by winning their sixth Premiership title in eight years in May 2000.

The Reds would also surrender their European crown that season, but the squad of players, which was essentially the same as the one that won the Treble apart from goalkeeping changes (Mark Bosnich coming in for Schmeichel), proved that they were still hungry and ambitious for more silverware by winning the League title. And they would do it in real style – lifting the crown with a record haul of 91 points, a massive twelve more than the previous season. At the same time, United would score 97 goals, as opposed to 80 the previous season and would lose only three games, the same number as 1998/99.

But while they finished 1998/99 on 79 points, just one ahead of Arsenal, now they would finish 18 points clear of the Gunners, who were again runners-up. Clearly, these were not statistics suggesting a team which had gone off the boil nor one taking it easy or living off its reputation. No, Fergie could see Keano and his team-mates were still as ambitious and greedy for success as they had ever been.

The following season the Red Devils secured their seventh Premiership title – and their third top-flight championship in a row, which put them in the illustrious company of the record breakers from Arsenal, Huddersfield and Liverpool. The 2001 triumph also meant Fergie became the first manager to achieve such a feat in English football and elevated him above the great Bob Paisley of Liverpool as the most successful manager ever in the English game – his 14 major trophies finally overtaking the 13 of Paisley.

Yet at the same time United crashed out of the Champions League in the quarter-finals, losing 3-1 on aggregate to Bayern Munich. While some observers saw the result as karmic retribution for United's last-gasp win in Barcelona against the same team, it was a devastating blow for the boss, who had been confident of lifting the trophy again. Instead Bayern would go on to win it, beating Spanish outfit Valencia in the final in Milan.

The disappointment suffered in United's early exit played a part in his decision to announce his retirement – just five days before that final in Milan. He told a stunned footballing world on 18 May 2001 that he would 'sever all ties with Manchester United the following season' – a decision he was to go back on in February 2002, when he signed a new three-year deal.

Shareholders United, the 22,000-strong umbrella group of small shareholders, had claimed that the club had forced the boss to quit. They said they would do all they could to persuade him not to leave the club – and that the United board had acted out of fear, believing if Fergie stayed he would cast a shadow over the club as Busby once had when he became general manager.

'We feared this would happen and the board should hang their heads in shame,' Shareholders United spokesman Oliver Houston told the BBC. 'The supposed Busby Syndrome is a smokescreen as any successor was going to have to have had the strength of character to work with him far more than be in the shadow of Ferguson.

'Instead we believe the plc feared giving Sir Alex a role with any real status or power because of his view that football should be more about supporters and local communities than just marketing and merchandising. He is highly regarded in the city and much loved on the terraces.'

But by the following February there would be no need for any protests as the boss changed his mind. He put pen to paper on a new three-year contract but made it clear that when that was up, in 2005, he would be off for good (which, of course, he wasn't!). 'I'm pleased to be staying but once this contract is up, that will be it,' Ferguson told the *Mail on Sunday*. 'I have no intention of staying on at the club in any capacity whatsoever.'

He added on BBC Radio Five Live: 'I just felt that I wasn't ready to retire and maybe I should not have announced it in the first place – it was too soon. Having thought it over with my family, we felt the right thing to do was to carry on and retire when I'm tired.'

The boss then explained to the *Scotsman* newspaper: 'It was really Cathy's idea. If she hadn't come up with it and the boys hadn't given full support, I wouldn't have considered a change of mind. But I do have to confess that maybe it was an idea I was hoping deep down she would come up with.'

He said he would not put his health in jeopardy, that he would not take on as much of a workload and would ease the pressure he was under: 'I'll tailor it a little differently – reduce the workload a bit.'

I am told that he also did not like the idea of Sven Göran Eriksson swanning into United and taking over; also that he had dreaded images of Bill Shankly and the way he had been treated after he retired prematurely at Liverpool. Images of the great Shanks not being welcomed at Liverpool's training ground and sitting aimlessly on the promenade at Blackpool, staring forlornly out over the Irish Sea, may have played vividly on Fergie's fevered imagination. Plus, Cathy had told him she could not stand the idea of him hanging around all day with nothing to motivate him. No, Fergie was like his mentor, the great Jock Stein – he had lived his life in the addictive world of football and would probably die in it, too.

That season was a write-off for United. Both the players and Fergie were too distracted by his on-off decisions and it was Arsène Wenger's Arsenal who stole the glory, lifting their own double of League title and FA Cup, as they had done in 1998.

The campaign got off to a bad start when defensive giant Jaap Stam was sold to Lazio for £16 million – and replaced by ageing tortoise Laurent Blanc. The 36-year-old wasn't a patch on Stam and United would suffer for it. By 8 December 2001, after one win and six defeats in their last seven League games, United were ninth in the Premier League – 11 points behind leaders Liverpool, who had a game in hand. Eventually, they would finish third in the League.

And in the April of 2002 Keane's – and Fergie's – obsession with winning the European Cup would again rear its head: this time both men were devastated as United crashed out in the semi-finals to the distinctly unremarkable German outfit, Bayer Leverkusen.

The first leg at Old Trafford ended 2-2 and United could only manage a 1-1 draw in Germany a fortnight later, going out of the competition on the away-goals ruling. Fergie's dream of recapturing the cup in his native Glasgow was dead and Keane's long sulk over his failure to play in a European Cup final would continue. For both men, this was a devastating blow.

The Irishman described the loss as 'a disaster' and criticised his team-mates. Already he had spoken sarcastically about some of them being only interested in their Rolex watches and big cars, now he would say of their performance in Germany: 'It is very hard to win the European Cup if you give away goals like we did in the semi-finals. This club deserves to win European Cup finals and we blew it. It was probably not the standard we expected over the two games.'

The following month his rage would flare again when United lost 1-0 at home to Arsenal, the team who would depose them as Premier League champs. Again, he attacked the efforts of his team-mates, but as Fergie was the man responsible for buying and picking them, Keane was indirectly criticising the work of his manager. As the pressure soared, their previously rock-solid bond was beginning to fray around the edges.

Keane observed: 'There are a lot of cover-ups sometimes and players need to stand up and be counted. I am not sure that happens a lot at this club.'

Meanwhile, Fergie broke the British transfer record yet again in the close season of 2002/03 when he paid Leeds United £30 million for 24-year-old central defender Rio Ferdinand. It was a massive amount for a defender but would prove money well spent in the long and short term. That season, Ferdinand was to settle in quickly and help United regain their Premiership crown from the Gunners – and of course would go on to become United and England skipper later on in his career.

But Keane's personal holy grail would once more elude him in 2003 when United exited the Champions League at the quarter-final stage to a rampant Real Madrid: he was left feeling bitter, resentful and ultimately unfulfilled. In 2003/04, United won the FA Cup but Keane saw that as small change. At 32 years old, his body creaked from the injuries he had sustained: ruptured cruciate ligament, hamstring strains (recurring), hip problems (career-threatening), hernias (recurring), knee ligaments (career-threatening) and back injuries (recurring and also career-threatening). Although his home life was happy, with wife Theresa and their five children, as far as football was concerned he remained an isolated, restless and unhappy soul.

Keane had continued to criticise his team-mates and had even fallen out with some of the United fans who helped pay his wages by dubbing them 'the prawn sandwich brigade'. By 2003/04 he looked burnt-out, a casualty of his own inner drive for perfection and unfulfilled longing for that unattainable European Cup final win he so craved. A year later, his era at Old Trafford was to come to a sad end: on 18 November 2005, he would leave the club after a long spell on the sidelines due to injury. His final competitive game was in the 0-0 draw at Liverpool in September 2005, during which he suffered a broken foot after a challenge with Luis Garcia.

In total, he had led United to 13 major honours, making him the most successful captain in the club's history. Keane's trophy haul with United included seven Premiership titles (1994, 1996, 1997, 1999, 2000, 2001, 2003), four FA Cups (1994, 1996, 1999, 2004), a European Cup (1999) and an Intercontinental Cup (1999). In 2004, he was inducted into the English Football Hall of Fame and was picked for the FIFA 100, a list of the 100 greatest living footballers selected by the great Pelé. Of his exit – and fallout at the time with the boss – more later.

David Beckham, one of Keano's greatest allies during the glory years around the time of the Treble, would also eventually fall out with Fergie (two years before Keane, in 2003 – and the fallout is again covered in more detail later on). But during his golden years, he, Roy and the boss would conquer all before them.

'Becks', as he would become known at the club and in the press, arrived at United as a schoolboy in 1993 and was to fully earn his place in the pantheon of United greats and wearers of the coveted No. 7 shirt. Fergie would send him out on the right wing and implicitly trust the golden boy from East London to drive in pinpoint crosses for his strikers. And how Becks would repay his faith: at United, his medals' haul read six Premiership titles, two FA Cup winners' medals and one European Cup winners' medal.

Lampooned as a numbskull, a man ruled by his wife, a clothes-horse whose main interest was celebrity and money, David Beckham was, in reality, a fine footballer – and the best crosser of a ball in the world. He was also a decent, likeable man who coped admirably with the demands of 24-hour press coverage and the fact that he would become the most celebrated footballer on the planet and one of its most famous people, too.

Similarly to Cantona, the man from whom he would inherit the No. 7 shirt, he knew the benefits of hard graft: that the hours spent perfecting his skills on the training pitch would pay dividends on the actual field of play on the Saturday. Beckham, who was born in Leytonstone, East London, on 2 May 1975, had always been a United fan and Fergie was quick to keep tabs when he heard 'good noises about a lad in East London'.

It was a sign of the boss's new scouting set-up that his men on the ground were first on the scene in London as Becks broke through. United sent their London scout Malcolm Fidgeon to watch Becks playing for Waltham Forest Under-12s and he was invited for a trial at Old Trafford in 1985, at the age of 10.

For the next three years, Fergie would continue to watch him progress and voice his approval of the boy's development. He wanted Becks to be part of his set-up from an early age and was delighted to secure him on a two-year schoolboy deal on his 13th birthday. When he was 16, Becks was faced with a dilemma as Spurs also moved in for his signature. Fergie worked swiftly and effectively to persuade the boy that Manchester was his rightful home. Becks duly signed as a trainee at Old Trafford on 8 July 1991.

By then Fergie was five years into his stewardship: his wooing and looking after the lad had worked and now he would join the other Fergie Babes in the youth team before progressing to the reserves and the senior side.

There had been some doubts about his size, but again Fergie stepped in, encouraging his staff to build the boy up so that he had a physique to match his undoubted skills. Youth team coach Eric Harrison recalled: 'I told David when he was 16 that if he continued his progress, he would definitely play in our first team. I was a little worried because, physically, he was behind everybody else and didn't have the strength. Then he shot up 6 inches overnight, at 16 going on 17.'

Fergie decided to blood him in the senior team on 23 September 1992, when he came on as a sub for Andrei Kanchelskis in the League Cup at Brighton. Then, on 23 January 1993, he signed as a pro for United and made his first full appearance in September 1994 against Port Vale, again in the League Cup. This would be the first of his 311 games for United, in which he scored 74 goals. He scored his first goal for the club in December 1994 in the 4-0 Champions League win over Turkish outfit Galatasaray.

Fergie knew all about the lad's progress and that he was none too far away from a regular spot in the first team. David rewarded his faith by scoring his first Premier League goal in the first match of the 1995/96 season, the 3-1 loss at Villa Park that prompted Alan Hansen's infamous 'Kids don't win titles' jibe.

At the time the boss liked the way his Cockney boy lived his life (although that wouldn't last, of course). David was the leading light of the new breed of English footballer who didn't drink, didn't do drugs, was clean-living and lived for his football. This new outlook coincided superbly with the hard-working, no-surrender ethos of Fergie and would propel both Fergie and his new signing to years of glory in the English game.

David saw the boss as a second father and came to rely on him for advice and help. For example, it was Fergie who gently eased him back into football after the nightmare of the 1998 World Cup, when he was sent off against Argentina – and subsequently blamed for England's early exit. A barrage of abuse and hatred was directed at Becks at football grounds all over the country when he finally re-emerged in a United shirt.

The golden boy of English football was at his lowest ebb as the tabloids gleefully laid into him and an effigy of him was strung up on a lamppost outside a pub in his home patch of East London. It was Fergie who came to the rescue when all around he heard only vitriolic criticism and hatred. Like a loyal father to his prodigal son, he told him: 'Get yourself back here, where people love you and support you. You can have your say back to the rest of them after the season begins.'

Of course, with the boss's support he did just that, helping United to the Treble the season after his darkest moment. It is worth noting how in two matches in particular in that glory campaign Becks proved just how much he had matured. Yes, in the Champions League quarter-final two-legger against Inter Milan he came up against his nemesis: the Argentine hardman Diego Simeone, who had him sent off in the World Cup.

United went through 3-1 on aggregate and David kept out of trouble, even swapping shirts with Simeone after the second leg – and I am told soon after he had the shirt framed on a wall at his English home in Hertfordshire.

But by 2002 there were rumours circulating around Old Trafford that Fergie was tiring of Becks and his celebrity lifestyle. The boss had been angered and crushed by the Champions League semi defeat to Bayer Leverkusen that April. He believed the Germans should have been beaten out of sight, that they were an average team who had only one brilliant player in Michael

Ballack. A few weeks later Fergie sat, grim-faced, at Hampden Park as Real Madrid beat Bayer 2-1 in the final – of course, it had been his dream to see United win the Champions League again in his native Glasgow. It was a sickener to watch Madrid lift the trophy instead, for a ninth time.

The boss watched the World Cup of 2002 from his holiday bolt-hole in the exclusive French resort of Cap Ferrat and remained unhappy. It is said he believed that United were suffering at the expense of England, that Becks cared more for the white shirt of his national team than he did for the red of Manchester. Beckham spoke of the situation in this way: 'I had the feeling he wasn't too happy, generally about the extra responsibility – and the extra attention – that came with me captaining England.'

It appears he was right: within 12 months Becks was gone from Old Trafford. That final season of 2002/03 started badly and gradually got worse for the golden boy. Fergie had welcomed him back from the World Cup by stressing how important a 100 per cent effort from him was for a successful campaign. After the bitter taste of watching Madrid's win at Hampden, the boss at least had another gilt-edged carrot to aim for: the 2003 Champions League final would be held at none other than Old Trafford. But it was not to be, and I'm afraid Fergie must take a large portion of the blame.

He may be the greatest manager ever produced on these shores – and arguably worldwide – but even he gets things wrong. Sometimes with personnel, sometimes with tactics, sometimes with substitutions: the man is only human, after all.

After an injury early in the season, Becks was unable to regain his place in the United starting line-up, with the boss preferring to play Solskjaer on the right side of midfield. Ole was a class act, and you can see why Fergie might persevere with the Norwegian until David reached peak fitness again. But it was impossible to defend the boss's antics in April 2003, when he stubbornly left him out of the team to face Real Madrid in the Champions League second-leg at Old Trafford. United had lost the first leg 3-1 and so this was the decider: a key match against a crack outfit, with the winner taking a step closer to the final at Old Trafford that Fergie so desired.

It was a match to field your strongest eleven, with no passengers carried, no worries about any man breaking down from an injury he had been carrying. Yet, instead of starting with Becks, Fergie stubbornly – and foolishly – sent out Juan Sebastian Veron in his place. Veron had been out injured for the previous seven weeks and was still half-fit, so it was a ludicrous decision.

I remember writing at the time that it seemed to be another chapter in the manager's doomed campaign to prove the Argentine was worth the £28.1 million he had splashed out on him. The facts tell the full story of how the boss's decision backfired that St George's Day, 23 April 2003.

A hat-trick by the Brazilian Ronaldo meant United were also losing 3-2 on the night when Fergie finally relented and took off the ineffective Veron – and sent on Becks. Within 21 minutes, David had scored twice and United finished 4-3 winners, but lost the tie 6-5 on aggregate.

Afterwards Fergie would claim he had kept Becks on the sidelines for Solskjaer, not Veron, saying: 'I saw it as quite a straightforward decision. Solskjaer's form has been fantastic on the right-hand side. I don't regard him as a sub any more – he deserved his place.'

Two months later Becks would be on his way to join the team who had ended Fergie's dream of competing in front of his own fans for the Champions League final. In the end, AC Milan would claim the trophy in Manchester after beating their Italian rivals Juventus 3-2 on penalties after the match ended 0-0.

In an interview some time later in *Sports Illustrated* magazine, published in New York, Fergie went some way towards explaining why he had decided to sell Becks for £25 million to Real Madrid – and it was not because of any declining powers of talent. No, the United manager admitted for the first time in public that the reason for the friction between himself and Beckham had been over his transformation into 'a celebrity footballer'.

Ferguson said: 'He [Beckham] was blessed with great stamina, the best of all the players I've had here. After training he'd always be practising, practising, practising. But his life changed when he met his wife. She's in pop and David got another image. He's developed this "fashion thing". I saw his transition to a different person.'

By the time David left, it was said that he and the man who had made him were barely speaking. Writing in the *Daily Telegraph* on 16 June 2003, the distinguished journalist Mihir Bose highlighted the unwillingness of United to keep their star player – an unwillingness that would cost them dear.

Bose wrote: 'David Beckham was offered a new contract by Manchester United on May 14 – three days after the England captain celebrated winning his sixth Premiership title with the club he joined on his 14th birthday. That was when SFX's Tony Stephens, Beckham's adviser, met Peter Kenyon, United's chief executive, at Old Trafford. But Beckham did not see this contract until Sunday, having spent the last month either with England or in the United States.

'By then, it was irrelevant. This time there was no disguising the end of their surrogate father/adopted son relationship.

'Beckham had his own circle and had replaced all his old

advisers with those supplied by his wife, Victoria, apart from Stephens. His treatment by England also seemed to put Beckham on a pedestal far removed from the collectivist team philosophy Ferguson espouses.'

It was a sad end to a wonderful partnership that had seen both men hit the heights. When Becks left, United would enter a period of transition and relative decline as Fergie now set about planning a future without the former golden boy – and proving United could prosper without that wonderful right foot.

CHAPTER 8
SWEET FA

In May 2003 Fergie had just won the Premier League title for the eighth time, yet 12 months later it was to look as if he and United were finished as the ultimate force in British football. Arsenal had made up ground and the ever-blossoming Roman Abramovich cash tree would propel Chelsea beyond both the Reds and the Gunners.

Darkness would suddenly descend on Fergie and Old Trafford without warning as he plunged into a second crisis era at the club (the first being from 1987 to 1990). Yet at the start of the new campaign he sincerely believed United were on the brink of more massive success. In August 2003, the United boss proclaimed: 'The best thing that could have happened to the players last season was winning the League. It brought back exactly where they were as a football team. It reinvigorated them. They got excited about it. Their form from Christmas was phenomenal and it is true what they say about people's character always being on the pitch and you saw that last season. It was fantastic for them.'

Yet the 2003/04 season would prove a major disappointment,

with only winning the FA Cup to shout about – and that, as Roy Keane had previously stated, was no big deal or consolation prize any more. Unbeknown to Keane (and Ferguson) the FA Cup win would be the final honour that they would share at United.

The boss was certainly busy in the transfer market that season. He had sent Becks to the exit door and now needed to replace him with like for like, or he would lose the goals of Ruud van Nistelrooy who had become so reliant on Beckham's mercurial crosses. It is worth noting here that after Becks departed, the Dutchman would never be the same player, certainly never the same goalscorer.

Ferguson would replace him with a youngster from Portugal called Cristiano Ronaldo, who had undeniably brilliant potential, but was far from the finished product when he arrived at Old Trafford for £12.24 million in the summer of 2003. Ronaldo would eventually become a world-class winger and the best player in the world, but no way would he replicate the work ethic or the pinpoint crosses that had become Beckham's trademark. Indeed, the most common sight in Ronaldo's first two seasons at Old Trafford was that of Van Nistelrooy clasping his head in dismay as Ronaldo wasted yet another cross or ran into trouble after some intricate dribbling. At the time he was an irritating show pony who had no final ball and whose free-kicks, unlike Becks', were always likely to head high over the cross bar.

The 18-year-old – whose full name is Cristiano Ronaldo dos Santos Aveiro – was signed from Sporting Lisbon on a five-year contract and Ronaldo was convinced he was joining a team that would win trophies galore. He said: 'I am very happy to be signing for the best team in the world, and especially proud to be the first Portuguese player to join Manchester United. I look forward to helping the team achieve even more success in the years to come.'

Fergie was also convinced that the glory days were still part of the club's immediate scenario and he gushed about how Ronaldo could take the club to a higher level. He said: 'We have been negotiating for Cristiano for quite some time, but the interest in him from other clubs accelerated in the last few weeks so we had to move quickly to get him. It was only through our association with Sporting that they honoured our agreement of months ago.

'He is an extremely talented footballer, a two-footed attacker who can play anywhere up front, right, left or through the middle. After we played Sporting (in a pre-season friendly in Lisbon) last week, the lads in the dressing room talked about him constantly and on the plane back from the game they urged me to sign him – that's how highly they rated him. He is one of the most exciting young players I've ever seen.'

True as that may be, the boy could not be expected to turn it on straightaway. By August 2003, United had gone backwards from the team that secured the Premiership three months earlier. The remainder of Fergie's buys that summer bordered on the disastrous: in came the 'talents' of Cameroon midfielder Eric Djemba-Djemba, French striker David Bellion, US goalkeeper Tim Howard and Brazilian midfielder José Kleberson.

Eric 2DJ, as the fans initially called Djemba-Djemba with an affection that would cynically drift away over the months, and Kleberson had been drafted in to learn from Keane and eventually take over from him. At least that's how the plot went. Both men were mighty flops and both were eventually taken away undercover of the night to Aston Villa and Besiktas (in Turkey) respectively.

Eric 2DJ was almost a candidate for the men in white coats rather than the boys in claret and blue when, in his goodbye speech, he ridiculously claimed that but for Keane being in his way he would have had a bright future at Old Trafford – this from a man who was one of the most ineffectual players ever to 'grace' the famous red shirt of Manchester United.

As for Kleberson, who had helped Brazil to their fifth World Cup win in 2002, the big question was: just how did he get into the Brazil side? He too was a major disappointment – unfit to even lace Keane's boots, let alone replace him as King of Old Trafford.

To be fair to Fergie, he was not to know that the men he was bringing in were as poor as they turned out to be. Indeed, on DVDs and scouting reports they looked the business and the boss had voiced great hopes for them, saying: 'The 22–23 age group is important. Having experience in the squad is obviously vital. In the past we've had some great experience with players in their 30s like Laurent Blanc, Denis Irwin and Teddy Sheringham. If you look after yourself there is no telling what age you can play to. We don't have that many in their 30s now, only Roy Keane, Fabien Barthez, Ryan Giggs and Ole Gunnar Solskjaer. But there is a group below them as well with great experience.

'When you are thinking about the future it is easier to construct your model with younger players so we had to look at that 22–23 age group. Eric Djemba-Djemba can go in there and challenge now. That's what you want and I think the boy is like that. He's broken into the Cameroon team and played all their games and he is only 22. He has a long future in front of him, but he is very much the present also.

'Kleberson is young and we certainly think he is one of the most progressive young players in Brazil at the moment. He is athletic, creative and quick. Roy Keane is 32, and Butt and Scholes are 29 in the winter, so Eric and Kleberson give us support for the experienced players.'

In a season of ups and downs, those words would come back to haunt the United boss. OK, by the end of term United had won the FA Cup for a record eleventh time but their failings in both the League and the Champions League were worrying indeed. The Reds would trail home in third place in the Premiership behind the resurgent Chelsea and the champions of Arsenal. And in Europe, they failed to make the last eight.

In the League, it all started to go pear-shaped when Rio Ferdinand failed to attend a drugs test and was banned for eight months from January 2004. The episode would cost him a place at Euro 2004, but as far as United were concerned, the debit account was far heavier as their League campaign fell apart – along with their pursuit of the so-called 'Invincibles' of Arsenal. Without Rio, United would certainly struggle at the back.

The Ferdinand ban was a particular blow to Fergie's hopes of regaining the European Cup. In the autumn and early winter of 2003, the defender had played a big part in United's battle with Arsenal at the top of the Premiership. The grim news arrived on Friday, 19 December, when the FA found Ferdinand guilty of misconduct after he failed to take the test on 23 September and handed out the ban, which would come into force on 12 January, and a £50,000 fine. Speaking for the club and with Ferdinand at his side, United director Maurice Watkins commented: 'We are extremely disappointed by the result in this case. It is a particularly savage and unprecedented sentence.'

The judgment had come 86 days after Ferdinand was asked to take a test at United's Carrington training headquarters but left without undergoing the procedure. Ferdinand claimed he had then contacted the club to offer to take the test, but was told it was too late. The Independent Commission did not have much choice but to hand out an eight-month ban – any less and it would encourage those who had taken drugs to claim they had forgotten to take a test. As a yardstick for the severity of the punishment, former United keeper Mark Bosnich had received a nine-month suspension from the game after failing a drugs test for cocaine.

World Anti-Doping Agency president Dick Pound said: 'The sentence is a third of the theoretical maximum he could have got, so he's done pretty well from his perspective.'

That same season Fergie's own judgment and credibility were called into question when he took on a legal battle – against, of all people, two men who had a majority shareholding in Manchester United. There were concerns that the manager was taking his eye off the ball in taking on the so-called 'Coolmore Mafia' of John Magnier and J.P. McManus over the ownership rights to the racehorse, Rock of Gibraltar.

The boss part-owned the horse with Magnier's wife Susan and watched it win a record seven Group One races as a three-year-old. But the Scot's name was dropped from the list of owners when the colt went to stud. Fergie contested the decision and Magnier and McManus criticised the United manager's behaviour, particularly over transfer deals, in a letter to the club's board. It appeared Fergie's United days might be numbered as rumours began to circulate about Coolmore forcing him out of Old Trafford. In the end the boss settled out of court, but the affair certainly rocked the club.

Also that season it was revealed that an American investor by the name of Malcolm Glazer had acquired a 3 per cent stake in the club. United were certainly changing with the times, but not for the better. According to the Glazer family foundation's website, he was a 'true American success story'. He started his working life in his father's watch-parts business at the age of 8 and at 15, took over the business when his father died. In 1995, he bought the struggling Tampa Bay Buccaneers and the team won the Super Bowl in 2003 – but surely his dream to own the Buccaneers *and* United was a mere pipe dream?

As if Fergie didn't have enough to worry about, his old adversary Arsène Wenger would be triumphant come May after his Arsenal team won the League and stayed unbeaten in the competition (to earn that 'Invincibles' tag) all season. In the modern era, only two other teams have won their leagues in Europe and remained unbeaten in their league programme: AC Milan in 1991/92 and Ajax (1994/95).

United's consolation was that they would still trump the Gunners on three counts during their unbeaten season – in the Charity Shield, the FA Cup and in signing Ronaldo, who had become a much more consistent performer by the end of the campaign. I am told Wenger was peeved that Fergie beat him to Ronaldo's signature – he had had him watched many times and had been planning a bid.

The agony of losing the Premiership title to the Gunners was matched for Fergie by the disastrous loss in the Champions League clash with Porto as United crashed out of the competition 3-2 on aggregate in the last 16, with Keane red-carded in the first leg. Foolishly, the United skipper stamped on Porto keeper Baia with just three minutes remaining. Fergie backed Keane, saying: 'There was no malice in the incident – it is not Roy's style to do anything like that. The goalkeeper made more of it than he should have done. Certainly he stood on the lad, but I don't know whether he could have got out of the way. I can understand why the linesman flagged, but the keeper made a meal of it.'

The Porto manager was amazed that Fergie was backing a

man who had hurt his keeper – in his eyes, there was no defence for Keane's actions. This would be the first clash between Ferguson and the man who would go on to win the European Cup with Porto and Inter Milan, as well as the Premiership with Chelsea: José Mourinho.

As the teams left the pitch in Portugal, the United boss confronted Mourinho over Baia's part in the sending-off. But Mourinho said: 'I understand why he is a bit emotional. You would be sad if your team gets as clearly dominated by opponents who have been built on 10 per cent of the budget. Ferguson told me in the tunnel that he thought Vitor had made the most of it. I said I wanted to see it on television before I would make a comment, but if he was right I would apologise.

'However, if he has no reason to make the claim he can apologise to me. Vitor told me he was diving for the ball, Keane left his foot in and he felt a bit of pain with the contact. I understand why he is a bit emotional – he has some of the top players in the world and they should be doing a lot better than that.'

Two lots of consolation for Fergie would come with winning the FA Cup: the first was that by beating Arsenal 1-0 in the semis, he and United had thwarted Wenger and his men from winning the trophy for a third successive season and at the same time, crushed their dreams of winning another double.

The second was that United ended a five-year wait for an 11th FA Cup triumph with the 3-0 win over First Division Millwall at Cardiff on 22 May 2004 – in which Ronaldo starred, giving a definite glimpse of what he could offer further down the road. Ruud van Nistelrooy killed off the battling South Londoners with a brace after the dazzling skills of Ronaldo, climaxing in a headed goal on the brink of half-time for the Portuguese, had sent them dizzy.

Afterwards skipper Gary Neville paid tribute to United's emerging star, Ronaldo. He told BBC Sport: 'Ryan Giggs and Ruud van Nistelrooy produced some good moments for us, but Cristiano Ronaldo was particularly outstanding. I think Ronaldo can be one of the top footballers in the world. To come with the price tag on his head and at his age, he has been outstanding for us this season.'

Fergie was happy enough to secure another FA Cup win and afterwards celebrated with his team at the dinner and party held at the Vale of Glamorgan hotel, traditionally United's base when they played in Cardiff. But there was still a feeling that, OK, he and United had won the FA Cup, but was that real success in the modern era? After all, it had not been that long ago when the club had even opted out of the FA Cup to play in Brazil. The general belief within the game – and it would get stronger as the years rolled by – was that the FA Cup was no longer that much of a prize, that United should be thinking of the Premier League and the Champions League rather than being sidetracked by domestic knockout cup competitions.

Certainly it was a view shared by some fans. One, Steven Haywood, summed up the opinion of many when he said: 'Yes, it was great to see Fergie winning another trophy – and for Ronaldo to get something in his first season at the club – but it all felt a bit of a consolation prize. We all knew Fergie was desperate to win the Champions League again. That's what he wanted more than anything else. So, yes, it was hard to believe that he was *that* elated just to win the bloody FA Cup!

'Certainly – and I know this will sound like we are spoiled – the fans weren't that elated. OK, it was a trophy – but it was now becoming distinctly second-rate, its importance moving more towards that of the Carling Cup.'

It was a theme which many other United fans would pick up. Big Bird, of Salford, was one of them: 'A Mickey Mouse cup, our consolation prize for a sickening season. It was a professional performance, nothing else. We played a team frightened of its own shadow with no idea what to do when it got the ball, mostly just kick in up field or kick it out to give their ten-man defence a rest. But credit where credit is due – we still won, yet let's not get carried away here.

'On this performance there was nothing to suggest a resurgence or anything to worry the rest of the Premier League about. There weren't any signs that we'll set the Premier alight next season. If Arsenal or Chelsea had been playing Millwall, the score would have been in double figures. It was a good day out, lovely weather, cool beer – but just a stroll in the park for an ordinary United team.'

But Fergie was jubilant – after all, it was the 17th trophy of his reign. He said: 'Ronaldo was outstanding. We need to look after him in the right way because he is going to be an outstanding footballer. You have to respect your opponents at all times and never take them for granted. It took most of the first half to open them up.

'We have professional players and expect a professional performance. I'm proud of everyone attached to the club. You always set out at the start of the season at this club to try and win a trophy and we've done that. I'm very pleased for the players and for the fans.'

His skipper Keane had set a post-war record of six FA Cup final appearances. Roy observed: 'It is always nice to win – the last one is always the nicest. All credit to Millwall, I thought they were outstanding. The goal before half-time was very important as Millwall had grown in confidence. Millwall had nothing to lose and we were on a hiding to nothing. It was about being patient and hoping that quality would tell, which it did.'

Neither Keane nor Fergie knew this would be as good as it got for a United in transition. The next two seasons were to be even more challenging as United were again edged out from the top table by rivals from London and Fergie received unacceptable abuse when some of his own fans turned against him.

CHAPTER 9

BARREN NIGHTS

After the FA Cup win over Millwall the boss had been banging the drum for his team and new signings, but was he really whistling in the wind? Did he truly believe they could hope to knock Arsenal off their perch and, more importantly given the bulging pockets of Roman Abramovich, keep a surging Chelsea at bay? Was a win over League One Millwall really a stepping stone – or was it a false dawn?

The reality of the situation was brought into some sort of focus for Fergie in the Community Shield, the charity showcase opener against Arsenal a week before the start of the new 2004/05 season. Certainly, it appeared that the cracks in Fergie's new team's make-up in the post-Beckham days had merely been papered over by that FA Cup win.

United struggled against a powerful Gunners outfit at Cardiff's Millennium Stadium. The Londoners strolled to a 3-1 win, with goals from Gilberto Silva, José Reyes and an own goal by Mikael Silvestre, the Reds' reply coming from Alan Smith.

The United line-up offered some clues as to why Red Devils

fans were perhaps not so effusive or as optimistic as the boss about the new campaign. The names David Bellion and Eric Djemba-Djemba in the starting line-up and those of Liam Miller and José Kleberson on the sidelines were indicative of a United in transition – or more worrying, a United in decline.

The manager's buys for the vital central midfield area, which needed addressing as Keane headed towards the sunset, were of concern. Juan Sebastian Veron had flopped and the triumvirate of mediocrity – Miller, Kleberson and Djemba-Djemba – would go the same way: they were simply not good enough for Manchester United.

Behind the scenes, there were also problems that the players – and certainly the manager – would be hard pushed to completely eradicate from their thoughts. All they wanted was to get on with the matches, but sometimes it wasn't easy when the boss himself (as already mentioned) was embroiled in a bitter dispute with two of the club's biggest shareholders, John Magnier and his partner, J.P. McManus.

In theory, he could lose his job if they forced through a takeover but there was also another possible takeover looming – from Malcolm Glazer. Throughout 2004, he had been increasing his stake in the club and by October, this would rise to 27.63 per cent. It would take him within touching distance of Magnier and McManus, who owned 28.9 per cent.

The shenanigans and uncertainty behind the scenes allied with United's struggle to maintain their No. 1 status on the field led to a tough season for the team, the fans and the boss. United would end up trophyless, but at least they would have the consolation of appearing in another Cardiff final.

There was a plus side too, of course. Ronaldo had had a debut season to bed in at the club and now Fergie expected greater things from him. And the boss showed he does have a canny eye with transfers when it comes to strikers, with the signing of Wayne Rooney from Everton for £27 million. Now he had the two best young talents in the world at Old Trafford: Rooney and Ronaldo, two boys who would eventually go on to conquer the world for him.

A bullish, brutish genius of a striker, Rooney was simply the best English player since Paul Gascoigne. Fergie had always wanted to sign Gazza, but the Geordie legend proved he was indeed 'daft as a brush' by sidestepping the boss's pleas and instead signing for Spurs and the bright lights of London. No way was Fergie about to lose out again. Rooney was only 18 when he joined United, but he had already played for England and would turn out to be a marvellous buy.

Fergie had also brought in the madman of Argentine football, Gabriel Heinze: he had a sneer and a smile akin to that of Jack Nicholson, axe in hand, on the poster accompanying the movie *The Shining*. He was another great buy, but would arrive late for the season's start, along with Ronaldo. Both men were playing in the Olympics for their country: Ronaldo with Portugal and Heinze for the eventual winners.

The excellence of these men and the mediocrity of the likes of Bellion, Miller, Kleberson and Djemba-Djemba sit uneasily when you examine Fergie's overall transfer buys. You can't always hit gold – as suggested, who would have thought Kleberson would be such a lightweight flop at Manchester United after he played for Brazil in the World Cup final? Overall, you would have to say that the boss got it right at least 75 per cent of the time and the majority of his biggest buys – Ronaldo, Rooney and Ferdinand – were terrific, even if the odd one or two (I'm thinking Veron again!) didn't work out.

Some critics have argued that Fergie was better at buying forwards because he was once a centre forward himself, but that denies his excellence in bringing in defenders of the calibre of Ferdinand, Stam, Nemanja Vidic and Patrice Evra over the years.

The season was a watershed one: on the one hand, Rooney and Ronaldo would come together to give a glimpse of the future, but old-timers like Keane would pass them in the opposite direction as their influence waned. That Keane actually played in 17 more competitive matches than the previous campaign was down to the manager's continued belief in him and of course, the fact that the alternatives he had brought in were simply not in the same class. At the very start of the season Fergie outlined his plan to use the skipper more, saying: 'What we're going to do with Roy this season, now he's had a good rest this summer followed by a good pre-season, we're going to work on the basis of how he feels. Roy's 33, but there's some players that are playing at 36 and 37, and doing well. There is nobody more respected than Roy Keane in this place, and I mean by the players – because he will do a lot for them. If they have a case to fight, he will fight it for them. He is an unusual person, he is a different breed of person to your normal footballer of today.'

Fergie also helped him out a bit by continuing to opt for the much-maligned 4-5-1 system, which allowed Darren Fletcher to do Keane's running. The fans, who had been brought up on Busby's style of attacking football, did not like it but at this stage of his United career Fergie had to be more pragmatist than entertainer, given the central midfield resources at his disposal.

Keane was as delighted as Fergie that Rooney had moved to Old Trafford. Even before the prodigy arrived, Roy commented: 'There are only two English players from the last 15 years I would pay to watch. One of them is Paul Gascoigne, the other is Wayne Rooney.'

Rooney would make his debut for United in that unforgettable 6-2 thrashing of Fenerbahce in the European Champions League. Keane did not play but Rooney, like some modern-day Maradona, would inspire a team containing Kleberson, Eric 2DJ and Bellion to play above themselves for one night only, much as the Argentine legend had cajoled a mundane national team to World Cup glory and an even worse Napoli to the Italian Scudetto.

Rooney grabbed a brilliant hat-trick and left the pitch with the cheers of the United fans ringing in his ears – the man who would eventually become the 'new King' had arrived.

Fergie had already admitted that he wanted Keane and Paul Scholes to be the youngster's minders on the pitch. And Keane, along with Ryan Giggs, would also be ordered to look after Rooney's co-partner-in-crime, the bubbly Ronaldo – especially to make sure he also stayed clear of major problems on the pitch. As Fergie had already noted, his two wonderboys had world-class tempers to match their talents!

Meanwhile, Giggs pleaded for patience from those fans who expected Ronaldo to mirror Rooney and immediately become a world-beater. He said: 'I can see similarities in how the manager handled me to the way he is handling Cristiano. Every time he has a good game he wants to play again, the fans want him to play and deep down, the manager probably wants him to as well. But you have to look at the bigger picture. To get the best out of Cristiano, he needs rest and help at the right points. It's not just physical, it's mental as well – there were times the manager did it with me.'

For Giggs himself the season would conjure up a couple of personal highlights, much to his and his boss's delight. In September 2004, he became only the third man to play 600 games for United. The landmark was achieved in the 2-1 home victory over Liverpool, but in typical style, Ryan refused to get carried away by the honour, telling manutd.com: 'I'm proud to reach 600 appearances – but I'm still as hungry for success as ever.'

United had trailed League leaders Arsenal by 10 points before the match, so the result was even more special. Surely there was something about United players making their comebacks against their biggest rivals after controversial bans: Cantona had done so back in 1995 and now, nine years later, Rio Ferdinand also turned out against Liverpool after his eight-month ban for failing to attend a drugs test.

It would be Rio's central defensive colleague Mikael Silvestre who grabbed the glory – scoring both United's goals, both of which were set up by Giggsy, the first from a free-kick, the winner from a corner.

That season, Ryan's second personal landmark came when he was inducted into the English Football Hall of Fame in 2005. He was honoured by the inclusion, but even more pleased when the boss told him shortly afterwards that David Gill had agreed to break United's unwritten rule of not offering players over 30 more than a one-year deal. A delighted Giggsy said at the time: 'I wanted three years, but we quickly settled on two.'

Another game that gave hope for the future during that transitional season came when Arsenal arrived at Old Trafford the following month. Rooney and Ronaldo ruined the Gunners' bid to make it 50 matches unbeaten. The heavyweight showdown ended with United 2-0 winners, thanks to goals from Ruud van Nistelrooy and Rooney.

It was Arsenal's first defeat since losing 3-2 to Leeds United in May 2003. Yet they remained top of the league on 25 points. Fergie said: 'It was an important victory. It's a great boost, we've been drawing too many games and hopefully we can get on a run now because we need wins to get alongside Arsenal.'

But he was to be disappointed. While United kept their sights on the Gunners, new kid on the block José Mourinho emerged from the shadows to steal in with his powerful Chelsea team. The Blues, who had beaten United 1-0 in the first match of the season at Stamford Bridge, proved simply too strong, with a squad powered by Abramovich's millions.

I was told that Fergie's favourite match of the season was the game at Arsenal in February 2005 as the Reds put on a fine show to dismantle the Gunners. The boss was said to be particularly impressed with his skipper's performance on the pitch – and off it, as he stood up for his team. What fan will ever forget the iconic image of Keane's snarling verbal attack on his Gunners counterpart, Patrick Vieira?

Keane clashed with the Frenchman after Vieira had a go at United defender Gary Neville, who had rowed with the Arsenal captain before the match. Afterwards, Keane insisted: 'I'd had enough of Vieira's behaviour and I would do what I did again tomorrow, if I had to.' Referee Graham Poll had to keep Keane away from Vieira when, with eyes and veins in his neck bulging, he pointed at the big Frenchman and threatened to sort him out.

Later, Keane admitted that Neville might also have been at fault over the incident, which added further ill feeling to an already-tense atmosphere: 'It takes two to tango. Maybe Gary deserves to be chased up a tunnel every now and then – there would be a queue for him, probably. But you have to draw a line eventually.'

Keane revealed that the trouble between Vieira and Neville was more serious than mere name-calling. 'I'm usually first out in the tunnel, but I had a problem with my shorts and I was maybe fourth or fifth out and by the time I got down I saw Vieira getting right into Gary Neville again,' he said. 'I mean physically as well now – I don't mean verbally.'

Later, Vieira would claim Keane had wound him up in the tunnel by condemning him for playing for France when he was born in Senegal. Vieira would hit back by saying: 'For someone who leaves his team in the World Cup he should keep the remark to himself. He does not know my background and I do not want him to make a comment like that because he is not in a good position to say something like that.

'I will not say I intimidated Neville, I would say I tried to make a point. Keane reacted the way I would react if somebody came to talk to one of the Arsenal players – that's what I would expect. It did not surprise me at all: it was a captain's, a leader's reaction. I have big respect for him and all the Manchester United players, no doubt about it.'

It was great entertainment – a feisty appetiser for the main course as United, much to Fergie's delight, went about their business with gusto.

Vieira did have the consolation of scoring Arsenal's opener, but a brace from Cristiano Ronaldo would go some way towards killing off the Frenchman's aim of retaining the Premiership crown. After the match Keane could not resist rubbing it in, repeating his criticism of Vieira: 'It makes me laugh, players going on about how they are saving this country and saving that country, but when they have the opportunity to play –well, it's probably none of my business.'

The victory kept United on the tails of Chelsea at the top, but the gap in points and class was too much to fill for Fergie's men. United would finish third in the League, a massive 18 points behind champions Chelsea and runners-up Arsenal. The Blues of Stamford Bridge, under the wily Mourinho, were emerging as the new dominant force in British football while off the pitch, United's army of fans were in sombre mood as each month, the takeover by the Glazers moved closer. It was clear that a takeover by the Americans would land United with unprecedented debt yet by the end of the season United would be in the hands of the Glazers. How would that impact on Sir Alex's spending plans? And how might he realistically be expected to turn the club around if the Glazers used profits to finance their debts – rather than for the good of the club itself?

Worrying times at Old Trafford, but at least the boss had the FA Cup final to look forward to. Yet again he would be up against his oldest adversary – indeed, the man who was overall surely the biggest adversary of his career: Arsène Wenger.

On this occasion, Fergie would end up proud, but beaten. His transitional team did well – after dominating the game against Arsenal at the Millennium Stadium they should have won the FA Cup. The disappointment was that they could not break them down in the final third; this would prove United's undoing and Fergie would take scant consolation that he had been in charge of the better team on the day as United lost the FA Cup final to the Gunners on penalties.

After extra-time, it ended 0-0 but the Gunners would lift the Cup after winning 5-4 on penalties. The boss had left Giggs on the bench so he could give his central midfield some pace in the form of Darren Fletcher, who did Keane's legwork while the old maestro led his troops forward in his usual fiery manner.

Afterwards, Keane said: 'We played quite well and had plenty of chances but it's about putting the ball in the back of the net and we didn't quite manage it. It's small consolation to say that we had all the chances. We dominated, but I'm sure the Arsenal players won't be too bothered about that – they've got the winners' medals and the cup, and we haven't.'

Sir Alex viewed it similarly to his skipper, but also claimed United should have been facing nine men by the end of the match. They were already up against 10 when José Antonio

Reyes was sent off in the dying seconds for a foul on Ronaldo (he had also been booked earlier).

And Fergie believed Gunners' skipper Vieira should also have taken an early bath earlier in the game for a series of indiscretions. He observed: 'Patrick seems to have an immunity to these kind of things so I'm not surprised. These games are very difficult for referees. Where do they start or stop? There were a lot of fouls and I don't think there were any really bad ones, although Reyes was perhaps a bit lucky not to be sent off for his tackle on Silvestre. You don't want to see players sent off in the final but referees are only human beings.'

Despite the crushing loss, the boss was still relatively up-tempo and confident about the future. He added: 'We've always been the sort of team that is galvanised by defeat and adversity, we're that sort of team. We'll get ourselves off the ground – cup football can do that to you sometimes. We are a very good team and in that form we can play against anybody. It was a really good performance and we got our game together today.

'You could toss a coin for Man of the Match out of Wayne Rooney and Cristiano Ronaldo because they were great, the pair of them. There's a great future for those boys and Darren Fletcher as well. The season's over now and we can reflect on what might have been as long as we like, but we now have to look forward to next season.'

He had every right to feel confident that things were turning around after his team's display against the Gunners but the boss would be badly scarred during the next campaign – or at least up until Christmas – when he found himself on the wrong end of some terrible abuse from his own fans as United struggled for form. It was certainly not a pleasant sight to behold.

CHAPTER 10

ON THE BOOS

By the close of 2005 it really seemed as if the Ferguson era at Old Trafford might be over. From August up to the end of the year, Fergie suffered his worst spell at the club since those dark days of 1989. After a series of insipid displays by the team his own fans booed him and following their falling-out, Roy Keane left the club in the November.

And then, in what looked like the final straw, United would exit the Champions League at the initial stage for the first time in a decade. The writing was on the wall and yet, digging deeper than he had done since the bad old days of his early reign, the boss somehow managed to rewrite a script that had him inexorably hurtling towards the exit door.

September 2005 was a particularly bad month for Fergie as his team could win only one out of five games. He was regularly booed by a section of United fans at Old Trafford. Angry at the direction the team seemed to be taking, they felt United were too negative; that they didn't have the attacking edge or penetration of the teams they had been reared on over the years at Old Trafford.

United lost 2-1 at home to Blackburn in the Premier League on the 24th of the month. After the defeat, the fans made their feelings known: they booed the team and Fergie, and two nutters even tried to charge a barrier to get to the United boss when he was in the dugout.

Fergie was immediately allocated extra security guards, but was confronted by more fans shouting abuse as he walked off at full-time. The incidents followed on from a bust-up at an airport in Budapest a month earlier when fans told him that he had 'sold out' by working for the Glazers.

It was easy to see why the supporters were down at the Blackburn match. United's best player, Rooney, had been left on the bench as a cautious approach was adopted. Rooney eventually emerged and played a major role in United's leveller midway through the second half. Blackburn goalkeeper Brad Friedel was unable to hold the striker's 25-yard shot and Ruud van Nistelrooy hit home the rebound.

The warning bells had been ringing four days before the home loss to Blackburn. Writing in the *Sun* on Tuesday, 20 September, Neil Custis reported the players were growing impatient with the style and quality of play being offered up by United's management duo. Custis wrote: 'Alex Ferguson is facing a Manchester United player revolt over tactics. United have had only five shots on target in their last three games and failed to score in 225 minutes of football. Many players are growing sick of what they see as a negative style of play, with a supposed 4-3-3 formation often turning into 4-5-1 with Ruud van Nistelrooy alone up front.

'Wayne Rooney is also growing frustrated at having to play a deeper role – sometimes out on the wing. He wants to play in attack and Van Nistelrooy wants him as a strike partner. But the tactics appear to be decided by Ferguson's No. 2 Carlos

Queiroz. And he is determined not to budge from what he sees as the right way to win back the Premiership....'

The defeat left United 10 points behind Chelsea, but Rovers boss Mark Hughes claimed the crisis at Old Trafford was not so bad as it had been depicted. The former United striker said: 'There are huge expectations at this club and those expectations will always be there. They work with that on a day-to-day basis but this defeat will make them stronger. Once they are backed into a corner, they come back stronger and stronger. I am sure that is the reaction they will get with this defeat.

'It is still very early days as far as the title is concerned. United were hoping to win today but they have not managed to do it. What makes it more difficult is the fact Chelsea are playing so well. If they give them too much of a lead, it will be very difficult to peg them back, so they will have to start doing it very soon.'

A few days earlier it appeared that the pressure was getting to Fergie when he stormed out of a Sky TV interview after being asked about Rooney's temperament. He had even refused to talk to MUTV after one programme on the club's in-house channel criticised his tactics.

Three days after the defeat to Blackburn the boss had to come out of his shell: he urgently needed to pep up his squad for the visit of Benfica in the Champions League. In the background, there was talk of demos being staged against his leadership and radio chat shows were peppered with 'fans' suggesting it was time Fergie headed off into the sunset. Some were also unhappy with Portuguese assistant manager Carlos Queiroz, whom they blamed for the more defensive United they were now witnessing.

Before the clash with Benfica at Old Trafford (the final game of that tricky month), Queiroz spoke out against the protestors.

He branded them 'stupid' and said: 'Football is a game of opinions – we do not play with one up front, nor two but with three. People have been crying out for us to use a 4-4-2 formation and in the Blackburn game we played with a 4-4-2 system for the first time and lost!

'We tried out the system that the fans had been demanding and we lose. That is why football is a game in which imagination and on many occasions, stupidity, have no limits.'

Even Arsène Wenger leapt to the defence of Fergie, saying: 'You know that I am not his best friend but I found it really appalling that they booed him. Of course, we – like the players – are only as good as our last game but considering what this guy has done for the club, I find it horrendous, nearly unbelievable.'

Fergie believed the barracking was from a minority, that true United fans would get behind him and his team against the Portuguese visitors. He said: 'The support will be great. It is a European night and that is always a special occasion at Old Trafford. There seems to be an extra edge on a European night and it will be good.

'In football terms when you lose a game there is always that opportunity to recover from a defeat. We have tasted defeats in the past and it will happen again. We have faced these problems before and we will face them again sometime. We are no different from anyone else in that respect: it happens. The Benfica match is important to me and we are doing a good job in terms of getting the players back up from the defeat last Saturday.'

His plea for help was certainly answered – and how. The fans sang his name throughout and got behind the team, and it paid off as United ran out 2-1 winners with goals from Giggs and Van Nistelrooy. Simão had equalised after Giggsy's opener.

In the middle of that prickly month Roy Keane played what would turn out to be his final game for the club – at Liverpool. It ended 0-0, with Keane heading off two minutes from time in front of a baying Kop. He had suffered a broken metatarsal bone in his left foot – the same injury that had sidelined David Beckham and Gary Neville.

Keane's injury couldn't have come at a worse time for an under-pressure Fergie. It would rule him out of the boss's plans for two months at a time when Chelsea were already pulling away in the battle for the Premiership.

For Keane, it was a particular blow. He had just returned from a hamstring problem and the layoff – like all the injury setbacks in his career – would not sit easily with him. Away from the action, he would brood, sulk and easily flare up. His time at Old Trafford was drawing to a dramatic close – by November 2005 he would be gone.

Asked at the time if the 0-0 draw at Anfield – the first between the clubs at Anfield since 1991 – had killed off his championship hopes for another season, Fergie bristled: 'It's far too early to say that. I don't think that games like this will be easy for Chelsea. I still think we had enough of the ball to win it and we showed good professionalism and composure, we just lacked a cutting edge.'

By November, United were in turmoil after Keane's banned outburst against his fellow players on MUTV made headline news. Roy had rattled his team-mates and the boss with his actions – he was living on borrowed time as a Manchester United player.

On the 6th of the month, United faced a cracker of a match with Chelsea coming to town. Fergie was clearly rankled by Keane's outburst before kick-off, warning that he would not tolerate public criticism of his players from those inside the club. He said: 'Of course there is criticism – the criticism has come from all directions. What you have to do as manager of our club is to make sure the criticism remains inside your doors. I am unremitting in that respect, totally unequivocal. My stance is there and it doesn't change: you don't criticise any Manchester United player outside the doors – I have never done and I won't.'

It had always been the boss's philosophy and it would remain that way until the day he finally walked away from Old Trafford. Over the years, it had served him remarkably well – the players knew they would never be mocked or verbally abused in public by the man who mattered and it had the effect of encouraging loyalty as part of a two-way street.

That Fergie felt he had to reiterate his belief publicly was a sign of how fractured the relationship between Keane and himself had become: it showed that the bond between himself and his injured skipper was broken for good.

The United manager continued: 'Criticism is not a problem for me – you expect it at a club like this. What I have to look at is how the players have been affected by it. It is natural, particularly in young players, that you have a dip in confidence when you lose games. They are no different to anyone else in that respect.'

The omens for the Chelsea match were not good – they were on a 40-game unbeaten run and were 13 points clear of United. Yet the Reds had a chance – they always seemed to rally when their backs were against the wall. Well, didn't they… don't they? Indeed, isn't that one of the most admirable characteristics of the great teams that Fergie has built over the years at United?

Fergie knew his boys could win the match – he was confident as he always is, whoever the opposition. He said: 'Chelsea are a very powerful team and very committed to defending. It is certainly not going to be easy to beat them but maybe what we need just now is the opportunity to play against a very good team. The start of the game will be so important and we need the crowd behind us. The question is can we usurp Chelsea and make them think for a bit? I know we have the ability to do it – and I think everyone else does too.'

And his optimism was not misplaced – his team beat the Blues although the win would ultimately prove to be yet another false dawn for this team in transition. Darren Fletcher, allegedly one of the youngsters on the back end of Keane's MUTV blast, grabbed the only goal of the game.

Inevitably the TV cameras focused on the lonely, grim-faced figure of Keane sitting in the main stand as United celebrated their precious goal. Unshaven, dark, determined, defensive – this was the great man's last stand at the ground where he was worshipped.

Twelve days later he would be gone.

By the end of December, there was talk that the boss was also on his way out after United fell further behind in the League and exited the Champions League by disgracefully finishing bottom of an easy group.

In his defence, it must be said that Fergie was hit by injuries. The hard-tackling Gabriel Heinze was ruled out for most of the season after damaging cruciate ligaments in his left knee during the Champions League group stage game against Villarreal – a cruel blow as he had only just returned from another injury layoff. And England full-back Gary Neville suffered a groin injury in United's Champions League qualifying second leg against Debrecen. When he resumed training, he seemed to be making a full recovery, only for him to break down again at Carrington. He needed surgery and was sidelined for another six weeks.

Ryan Giggs was also sidelined after a particularly nasty incident in the 0-0 home draw with Lille in the Champions League. The goalless draw on 18 October was indicative of the nightmares Fergie would experience in the competition that season when the French outfit cynically took Ryan out of the game. He had to undergo surgery after fracturing his cheekbone in three places in an aerial clash with Stathis Tavlaridis (ironically a former Arsenal man) and faced six weeks on the sidelines. The boss was infuriated by the incident and his anger worsened when the referee refused to allow Giggs to receive immediate treatment. It was only when he was replaced by Ji-Sung Park with seven minutes remaining that the full extent of the damage was uncovered.

Fergie said afterwards: 'The referee is supposed to stop the game when a player has a bad injury. When you see the incident, I am amazed the referee didn't allow the physio on. Our doctor is not happy about it and it is something we are looking at.

'Ryan has suffered three separate fractures and his cheek will have to be plated. If we had been able to get on the pitch we would have taken him off immediately because you can see the indentation in his cheek from the TV pictures. Ryan stayed on due to his own courage – the miracle is he didn't get any more knocks because something really serious could have happened. When he came off and we saw the damage, we realised Ryan had been very lucky.

'Lille are a very aggressive side who were committed to getting a result any way they could. I looked at the video and I have never seen as many elbows and aerial challenges in all my time in England. You have to give Lille credit in terms of how far they have come as a club since we last played them four years ago, but they certainly weren't prepared to gamble and try to win. They just wanted to make sure they didn't lose.'

Then came the injury at Anfield the following month that would bring down the curtain on the Keane era. Yet as well as the injury jinx, there was still the underlying problem that the strength of the squad in midfield was simply not good enough. The United boss appeared convinced striker Alan Smith was the answer to his prayers.

Smith, a £7 million summer signing from Leeds in the summer of 2004, was actually from Leeds – a Yorkshire lad born and bred, and, just as Rooney would be when he left Everton for the Reds, he was viciously condemned by his former fans. Never in their worst nightmares did they believe hometown hero Smith, a lifelong Leeds supporter, would end up joining the Whites' bitterest rivals.

Fergie admired the boy for his bravery, strength of character and determination, and believed those very elements would help him become another Roy Keane. When told in September 2005 that Smith had revealed to the press corps that Keane had taken an interest in him, offering advice and trying to encourage him, Ferguson purred: 'I am not surprised at that. Winning is as important to Roy as it is to me. He is one of the long-serving members of the club who wants us to do well all the time. He sees certain characteristics in Alan that he saw in himself as a young person. Those characteristics could help Alan develop into a very good player in that position.

'We are going through a spell of injuries at the moment but over the years we have handled this type of thing quite well. If that was to happen to Chelsea, and they lost people like John Terry and Frank Lampard, it could make a difference to them because up to now, they have not really had any injuries.'

But the truth of it was that Smith just wasn't a good enough central midfielder. Certainly, he was no Keane and he himself once admitted that he did not enjoy being thrust into the role.

At Leeds, in the 2001/02 season then Leeds boss David O'Leary deployed Smith there, so new signing Robbie Fowler could play upfront in place of him. But Smith was at pains to say he did not enjoy it – and when he signed for United he made it clear he had been signed as a forward.

It was hardly the glowing endorsement for a career in the centre of the park. His attitude and determination were beyond reproach, but his mistimed tackles and tendency to naturally wander upfield rather than maintain a holding position would pose problems for United.

The United fans seemed to agree that Smith and some of the other players now getting into the first team were simply not good enough. One fan, Ian Collins, said: 'Some of them would struggle to get into other teams – John O'Shea and Kieran Richardson spring to mind.'

And another, Rikki Mustill, added: 'Sure, players like Alan Smith and Darren Fletcher can do a reasonable job in their respective positions but that's not good enough when you play for a team like Manchester United – you must excel in your position week in, week out.'

As if 2005 hadn't already been bad enough for Manchester United – what with the boss being abused and Keano going – the club suffered another body blow on Friday, 25 November. Just a week after Keane's exit, Old Trafford was in mourning when George Best passed away. Arguably the greatest British footballer ever, he gave up the fight for life at the tender age of 59 at London's Cromwell Hospital.

George had been treated there since suffering flu-like symptoms two months earlier. He then contracted a kidney infection and towards the end, his condition deteriorated sharply with the development of a lung infection that led to internal bleeding. He had been particularly susceptible to infection because of the drugs he had had to take after his 2002 liver transplant. The final script in the drama that had been the Irish wonderboy's life had not been hard to work out: it was always going to end in tears, given his addiction to alcohol.

Inevitably, the news hit United – and Fergie – hard. The boss led the mourning and the tributes, saying: 'He was a fantastic player. Everybody at United regarded George as being one of the greatest of all time. It's very sad because he was a wonderful person, who was very likeable.'

But Fergie also had to focus his team on a crucial match 11 days later that could define his season and, some would claim, his future as United headed to Lisbon for their final Champions League group clash. Unfortunately, the Reds would lose to Benfica on 5 December 2005. The 2-1 defeat left them bottom of Group D without even the consolation of a UEFA Cup spot. It was, without any doubt, the lowest point of Sir Alex's reign for a good 15 years. Paul Scholes gave United an early lead, but Benfica came back to win, meaning it was the Portuguese champions who claimed a place in the knockout stage of the competition with Villarreal.

The tabloids, naturally, were full of speculation about the boss's future – but it wasn't just the red tops. Writing in the *Guardian*, the respected Kevin McCarra also joined in the doom-laden predictions, saying: 'There will be a reckoning that takes place in private and it is likely to see Sir Alex Ferguson's tenure at Manchester United terminated at the close of the season. The murmuring of rich men over the current balance sheet and the future prospects can be deadly, but no ruthlessness by the Glazer family will cause such heartache as failure on a football field does.

'This night at the home of Benfica will be the image of Ferguson's end. United hurled themselves on in a quest for an equaliser that never came. With Villarreal winning, a draw would have sufficed, but a side that had led could not grasp it. For the first time in 10 seasons, United will not feature in the Champions League knockout phase.'

And the *Independent* newspaper pointed out that the calls for Fergie to go were not just from those so-called fans who went to Old Trafford once or twice a season, but from diehards: 'Even United's official website, in its Fanzone section, reflected the dissent – much of it directed against the man whose 19 years at Old Trafford have been strewn with silverware. "It's time Fergie retired," one writer said. "I know we're in transition but the last consistent run we had was at the end of 2002/03." Another weighed in: "Big changes have to be made because we're not good enough." A third argued: "It's the lowest point in 10 years – they couldn't even get through a group with three very average teams."'

Fergie was typically defiant after the loss: he never even contemplated the end of his tenure being nigh despite the growing clamour for his head on phone-ins and other nationwide debates among United fans. Asked if he was worried about his future, he snarled and said: 'I am not going to answer that. I've got a job to do, it's a great job and I've confidence in my players. This club has always risen from difficult situations, and we will again.'

He added: 'I think we depended always on our home form. Even if we'd won the game I'd still be talking about our home form. That's where we've let ourselves down a little. We gave away possession far too easily, so we only have ourselves to blame in that sense. We were desperate to win the match and with that came a sense of anxiety. I give my team ten out of ten for determination and effort, but in the end it was not to be. You couldn't argue it was an unfair result, but I don't think it would have been unfair if we had got an equaliser, either.'

Skipper on the night Gary Neville was also defiant, arguing

that United could still turn their season around. He said: 'Qualifying for the knockout stages has been par for the course but we have not been good enough in this group. We know over the next few days people will criticise us and rightly so because our performances haven't been up to our standards. But we have to stick together and perform in the League because we have to close on Chelsea. The responsibilities of the senior players stay the same – we have to lift everybody.'

Fergie's record of achievement at the club quite rightly bought him time to turn things around. The players responded by turning in some determined shows and United now went unbeaten for 10 matches, only losing 3-1 at Manchester City in the League.

The team finished League runners-up to Chelsea (by eight points) that season and exited the FA Cup in a demoralising 1-0 defeat at arch rivals Liverpool on 18 February. The fifth round victory was Liverpool's first FA Cup win over United in 85 years – and was achieved thanks to a Peter Crouch header on 20 minutes.

Fergie was disappointed, but not despondent. He said: 'You need an element of luck in the Cup and we didn't have it. We lost Rio Ferdinand after training on Friday then Mikael Silvestre got a knock. It has been 85 years since Liverpool beat us in the FA Cup and I was hoping it would be another 85 years, then I wouldn't be around to see it. We found it hard to get our momentum going, but we stuck at it and I felt we dominated the second half.

'We started the game badly, but Liverpool can play for five minutes and win a game. They have got height up front, get balls into the box and make it an aerial battle. They are dangerous at set-pieces and maybe we just didn't have enough height in our team and their goal emphasised that.'

But that would be the last serious setback for another 15 months as Fergie now embarked on a resurrection from the dead worthy of Jesus Christ. Eight days after losing to the Scousers he would lead United to victory in the Carling Cup – and 15 months after that would bring the League title back to Old Trafford. It was a most remarkable turnaround, one that appeared impossible when the Reds lost to Benfica in that crushing Champions League clash.

On 26 February 2006, United thrashed Wigan 4-0 in Cardiff to lift the Carling Cup. Rooney grabbed a brace, with Saha and Ronaldo also getting onto the score sheet. In itself, this was small consolation but it was consolation for a tough, trying campaign for the boss. Fergie acknowledged as much after the win, which marked the first trophy of the Glazer era: 'I'm delighted for them [the Glazers] – they have put a lot of money in. I don't so much feel relief that we have won a trophy, more an assuredness in knowing we could win this cup. Any trophy you win is important and we're delighted. We've been criticised, but we've never devalued this cup.'

Yet there would be fallout from the only real high of that fractious season: Ruud van Nistelrooy was angry that he was a sub and not even brought on when the result was in the bag. He had already fallen out with Ronaldo during a training session in the January of that year over Ronaldo's closeness to assistant boss Queiroz. I am told Ruud scoffed at Ronaldo, saying, 'Off you go to see your father, then.'

His remark was hardly well timed – Ronaldo was still mourning the death of his real father. By May, the Dutch striker had joined Keane in exiting United. Fergie would explain the decision to offload Ruud was a result of a couple of incidents in training that concerned him in terms of the 'spirit of the club'.

It was also Rooney's first trophy at United, indeed his first pro medal ever, and he said: 'I am absolutely delighted. To win any trophy gives you a big buzz and this is the best feeling I have ever had. It is so long since I won anything, you can probably understand why I feel the way I do.'

Somehow, after the nightmare of Lisbon, Fergie had steadied the ship and won a trophy and there was little doubt his team were finally coming out of transition. By the end of the season, Keane was long gone, but after that Carling Cup win the new Reds were unbeaten in 11 of their 12 remaining League fixtures.

OK, that loss would come against the team who would once again beat them to the title but the 3-0 defeat at Chelsea apart, United were starting to look the business again and they notched up some pretty impressive results – including a 2-0 win at home over Arsenal and a 2-1 win at Spurs.

Both Rooney and Ronaldo were now outstanding on a regular basis and United finished a place higher in the Premiership than the previous campaign. They were runners-up to Chelsea, but had cut the points gap from 18 to eight. And the turnaround would be completed 12 months later when Fergie led United to a title triumph few would have dreamed possible that black night in Lisbon in December 2005. A triumph that merely confirmed he was the best manager in Britain and probably the world – and exactly why that was.

CHAPTER 11

BACK IN BUSINESS

'HE [SIR ALEX] IS A MAN WITH A MISSION,
MANCHESTER UNITED THROUGH AND THROUGH.
I'D SAY HIS DRIVE WAS MORE IMPORTANT TO OUR
SUCCESS THAN ANYTHING ELSE.'
David Beckham

The 2006/07 season was to be one of the most memorable of all Fergie's years as United boss for two specific reasons: the first was that in November 2006 he would celebrate 20 years in charge at Old Trafford. And the second was that he would do so with the team on course for a remarkable regaining of the Premiership crown.

The title win would certainly rank as one of the most brilliant of the boss's achievements at the club given, as already pointed out, the financial power and undoubted quality of the Chelsea players under José Mourinho and Roman Abramovich. It was achieved thanks to a wonderful coming together of several potent forces at Old Trafford.

Just as Fergie had promised, Rooney and Ronaldo both lived up to their wonderful potential with some magnificent performances. At the same time, veterans like Giggs and Scholes suddenly found a new lease of life and the defence started to look the most solid it had been since the glory days of Steve Bruce and Gary Pallister. It was well marshalled and rock-solid as Nemanja Vidic formed a fine partnership with Rio Ferdinand. Vidic, from Serbia, had arrived with Patrice Evra at Old Trafford just a month after the Lisbon débâcle. Evra got better and better as he settled in, and is surely now the best left-back in the world (forget the pleas of Ashley Cole's backers).

Behind them, Edwin van der Sar in goal may have been getting on, but for the first time since the great Schmeichel, United had a keeper they knew would generally be a reliable last line of defence. Plus, there was the beefing-up of the midfield that had been allowed to suffer and struggle since 2004. The days of the Klebersons and Djemba-Djembas were over. Fergie finally appeared to realise that there was no point in trying to find a direct like-for-like replacement for Keane – there was none. Keano was the master, with only Patrick Vieira in his prime possibly fit to lace his boots.

So, instead of trying to find another enforcer and power player, Fergie opted for the artistry and more refined industry of Michael Carrick. The manager splashed out what seemed an overblown £14 million – which would rise to £18.6 million – on 31 July 2006. The Tyne & Wear-born midfielder would eventually look a bargain as he drove United back to the top, providing a razor-sharp supply line of crosses and passes for Ronaldo, Giggs and co.

Although Fergie knew Carrick could not replace Keane as a warrior, he still handed him Roy's legendary No. 16 shirt, after Carrick asked for it. Fergie explained just why on MUTV: 'Michael has settled down fine. I spoke to him today – I said to him: "I'm giving you the No. 16 jersey," and he was delighted at that. I think that showed great courage because sometimes players are a bit superstitious about things like that, but he was keen and said he would gladly take No. 16.'

Carrick brought a calmness and reliability to what had been a wobbly inconsequential midfield and made some of us critics eat humble pie: at £18.6 million I myself argued he was at least £10 million overvalued. Even the fans were unsure. Mark Longden of the Independent Manchester United Supporters' Association, told BBC Sport: 'I cannot understand what is going on. I have not spoken to anybody who, when £18.6 million became available, would have spent that on Michael Carrick. But people have questioned Sir Alex Ferguson's judgment in the past and finished up with egg on their face, and I hope it happens again.'

And it did, Mark – it did. Carrick would have questionable moments, mostly when, jaws open wide, he would lose concentration and possession. (Some United wags in the crowd at Old Trafford even dubbed him 'Behind You' as he was often caught napping by rivals). And he could appear tortoise-slow at times. But he also had an ability to spray the ball around like no one at Old Trafford since Beckham at his peak and he would play a key role in the Premier League wins and the Champions League triumph of 2008.

In short, he was a class act. And Darren Fletcher, the lad often mocked in earlier years as 'Fergie's son' by the fans – because the boss continually picked him, even though he continually failed to deliver, finally started to come good. In itself, Fletcher's tale is one of forging triumph from adversity. In that dark year at Old Trafford in 2005, this was the lad that some sick United fans once tried to flog on the Internet for 1p. And he would prove them wrong: as this book went to press,

Fletcher was arguably Fergie's second most important player after Rooney – and he would certainly fetch more than 1p for his talents. Try closer to £15–20 million!

All United's new stars and rejuvenated existing ones would play their part in the club's first title for four seasons and certainly what was one of their least expected ever. But Fergie was the mastermind and credit where it is due. This was the man who had been written off and re-emerged with a new team that featured the fantastic attacking skills of two of the best three players in the world: Rooney and Ronaldo (the other being Barca's Lionel Messi).

United would win the League in 2006/07, finishing on 89 points; six ahead of runners-up Chelsea and a massive 21 ahead of third-placed Liverpool.

Fergie's haul of trophies at the club now read like this: one European Cup, one European Cup Winners' Cup, nine Premiership titles, four FA Cups, one League Cup and one Intercontinental Cup. In United's 2006/07 campaign the only letdowns for the boss had of course been the Champions League semi-final defeat in Milan and the FA Cup final loss to Chelsea. In both matches, United seemed fatigued and at the new Wembley Mourinho's suffocating tactics proved a bridge too far for tired legs, of more later.

Despite those two failings Fergie declared himself more than happy with the results of the campaign and revealed a little more about Alex Ferguson, the man away from the game. It emerged that he had a life away from work, too as he told of his passion for cooking Chinese meals, studying American history and listening to Scottish music on his iPod. Always an impressive name-dropper, the United manager also let it be known that he was a good friend of the then prime minister-in-waiting, Gordon Brown.

Fergie, a Labour supporter himself, said Brown shared his interest in the history of the United States, particularly the assassination of John F. Kennedy. He revealed: 'Gordon sent me 35 CDs on it, which was brilliant of him. I've got about seven books by the side of my bed and I have JFK's autopsy report. I also have a brand new copy of the Warren Report signed by Gerald Ford [the former US president], which is the only one he signed, so it's one of a kind.'

The United manager had opened up in an interview with Manchester radio station, Key 103 at Fairfields, the house in Wilmslow, Cheshire, named after the dockyard where Alex senior used to work. Movingly, he admitted that he wished his father, who died in 1979, had been around to share his success. 'He'd be very proud of me,' said Fergie. 'One of the sad things of my life is that he never saw me win anything. I went to Aberdeen and he didn't see any of it, which is unfortunate because he was football-mad.'

Despite the success the manager had delivered against the odds in 2007, there remained grumbles among the fans – primarily about his backing of the Glazers. Fergie had declared in public that he was happy with the new regime under the Americans; he contended they were easy-going, did not interfere, preferring to stay in the background, and it was easier to get transfer funds without the rigmarole of going through the previous red-tape procedures of the PLC.

This was not a view that sat easily with the majority of United's vast army of fans, who felt the American family was bleeding the club dry with the debt they had placed on it to buy it. Fair dues to Sir Alex, though, for standing up for what he believed in, even if it meant being on the opposite side of the fence to the fans he loved.

An indication of United's form that season could be found in the PFA Team of the Year chosen at the end of the season. Inevitably, it contained several United stars and read: Goalkeeper: Edwin van der Sar (Manchester United). Defence: Gary Neville, Patrice Evra, Rio Ferdinand, Nemanja Vidic (all United). Midfield: Steven Gerrard (Liverpool), Paul Scholes, Ryan Giggs, Cristiano Ronaldo (all United). Attack: Didier Drogba (Chelsea), Dimitar Berbatov (Tottenham Hotspur).

The excellence of the team's work was also reflected at the end of the campaign when Ronaldo won the Football Writers' Association Footballer of the Year award for 2007. And Ryan Giggs (third) and Paul Scholes (fourth) trailed in close behind Chelsea's Didier Drogba, who was runner-up.

As for the boss... well, Sir Alex won the Manager of the Year award. It was only right after he had somehow magically transformed his team from no-hopers to winners against all odds and in the space of 18 months, from December 2005 to May 2007. He declared himself delighted with the honour.

Earlier in the season he had also won a world version from the International Sports Press Association (AIPS). Fergie was presented with the 2007 World Manager of the Year award at United's Carrington training ground. He said: 'It is always great to receive awards and a big thank you to everyone who voted for me.'

The award certainly counted for something: it had been decided from votes cast from among the 9,100-strong membership of AIPS from over 150 countries across the world. AIPS president Gianni Merlo said: 'These awards are unique in football as they take into account the views of professional football media across the globe and not just one country.'

Of course, Fergie also celebrated his 20th anniversary in charge of United, on 6 November 2006. Some critics suggested it might be a good cue for him to retire, but in typical defiant style, he laced into them, saying he had no intention of doing so. The boss – who would be 65, the following 31 December – rapped: 'It is scandalous some people think I should retire – it is none of their business. Some people in this country don't want to work, so I don't think you should decry anyone who wants to! It disgusts me that people think that way.'

He added: 'I am proud of what we have achieved here. It has been an incredible spell and hopefully we will win more things at this club, but I also feel the way we have done it has been good. It has been the right way, the Manchester United way. We have not changed in that respect. Sometimes we get carried away with our attacking instincts, but you may as well die in a glorious way than not.'

Ryan Giggs, stand-in skipper at the time in Gary Neville's absence due to injury, said: 'The Manager is making sure the foundations are in place so that players like Rooney and Ronaldo can be the best in the world, a few years down the line. That's the way he works and that's why I think he will be around for a few more years yet.'

And Rio Ferdinand, the man who would eventually succeed Neville and Giggsy as United captain, said: 'The boss defends his players to the hilt and that's why he gets great respect from the players. They know they can trust him 100 per cent. It is something on which the whole foundations of this club are built.' While Roy Keane paid this tribute: 'For him to keep going is remarkable. He stands out with his will to win, he knows football, he knows his players and he knows his own club inside-out.'

Finally, Arsène Wenger set aside the differences he and Fergie had had over the years to say: 'When you think that the average life of a manager is one year and seven days, and somebody has done 20, it is a remarkable achievement. I feel we had some heated times, but time will settle things and there is a respect there now.'

Typically, Fergie said his players had been just as important in helping him survive in the hot-seat for two decades: 'Supporters who have followed this club for 50 years are very lucky people because we always seem to produce someone who can light up the stage. We have had players who put themselves on the canvas of artistry long before I came. Manchester United must have had more top players than any other club in the country and in that respect, I have been very lucky to work with some of them.'

Tributes poured in from his players, both past and present. United legend Sir Bobby Charlton led the way for former stars. He said: 'Alex Ferguson has revolutionised Manchester United. We had been in the doldrums for years under various different managers. Everyone knew Manchester United was the biggest club – they always had the biggest gates, but didn't get the results to show. It was a club that had really good players, but didn't play to its best potential.

'You have to have a boss. Matt Busby was the boss, Bill Shankly was the boss, Brian Clough was the boss and I thought Alex Ferguson was a boss. We knew we had the right man and we knew he would eventually come right. He always said being second was not good enough, you had to be first. What he meant was winning the FA Cup was not as important as winning the title, that was the main thing.

'He brought in players and has produced players over a period of 20 years. He has given Manchester United the most fantastic ride. For supporters of Manchester United, it has never been boring. We have had fantastic players who have come and gone, and he has made Manchester United what we always thought it was – number one.'

The *Independent* summed up just what Sir Alex had overcome to achieve the landmark when they wrote: 'In Ferguson's time at Old Trafford Chelsea have had nine managers, and Manchester City 11. When he succeeded Ron Atkinson in November 1986 the Berlin Wall was still standing, Nelson Mandela was languishing in jail and the Soviet Union was coming to terms with the Chernobyl nuclear accident in Ukraine.'

Yes, the boss had truly been one of football's (and life's) survivors.

The *Independent* also carried an interview with Fergie, in which he explained how much he felt he owed to his parents for the discipline and self-belief that had helped him become arguably the greatest football manager ever. He told them: 'My personal beliefs come from my family. I believe that I formulated all my disciplines from my family. My father was assiduous about timekeeping, I'm the same. I always have to get there early. It's a great discipline to make sure you're always early. It's ironic because my dad was a sheet-metal worker and in his latter years he became a timekeeper.

'My mother was Catholic and my father was Protestant, and even though he wasn't really a church man he'd make me go twice on Sunday. To morning service and Bible class. I was in the Boys Brigade too, from nine to 16. That all creates a certain foundation that's worthwhile. Because the Boys Brigade had a lot of discipline about it, too. You'd go for your badges, Bible class, your semaphore or Morse code, playing the chanter before you could play the bagpipes. It takes a lot of discipline. All that comes from your parenting.'

But the party was spoilt the day after his 20th anniversary celebration when United lost 1-0 to Southend in the fourth round of the Carling Cup. However, Fergie boosted spirits on 1

December when he announced that he had signed 35-year-old Henrik Larsson, a player he had coveted for many years. Then, on 23 December 2006, Cristiano Ronaldo scored the club's 2,000th goal under the helm of Sir Alex, in the 3-0 League win at Aston Villa.

As 2007 dawned, Fergie was confident his team would bring the title back to Old Trafford. His team were riding high, but suffered a setback when they went down 2-1 at rivals Arsenal on 21 January. Rooney had put the Reds ahead only for Van Persie and Henry to win the points for the Gunners.

They then proved the boss's optimism was not misplaced by winning their next four games, including 4-0 back-to-back wins against Watford and Spurs. The victory at White Hart Lane was a particularly stunning result and sounded out a real warning to United's rivals.

Nemanja Vidic headed home the opener from Michael Carrick's corner as the Red Devils made light work of their hosts. Goals from Ronaldo, Paul Scholes and Giggs completed the rout, leaving Fergie purring with delight. He said: 'The scoreline is very good. To come to Tottenham and win 4-0 is exceptional. It looked as if once we got in front we started to get a bit careless and casual. You can't do that: zeros against your name is all important when you are going for the title.'

The win at Spurs meant United were now six points clear of Chelsea at the top of the League and on their way to regaining their crown after two barren Premier League campaigns. It seemed to inspire Fergie and his boys: they now believed they were destined for greatness after a couple of years of struggling to stay afloat in Chelsea's slipstream.

The Reds embarked on a 10-match unbeaten run – a sequence that included some terrific results, including a 1-0 win at Liverpool in the League and a victory by a similar scoreline in the

Champions League over French side Lille at Old Trafford. The win over Lille, with Henrik Larsson heading home, meant United progressed to the next stage of the competition, the quarter-finals: 2-0 on aggregate.

The two-legger with Lille had not been without controversy, however. With seven minutes remaining, Giggs had grabbed the winner in France but the goal caused uproar among the Lille players. They claimed they were not ready with their wall when he cleverly scored from a free-kick after 83 minutes. Angrily, they walked off the pitch but eventually returned. Afterwards Fergie commented: 'I have never seen that before in all my years in football. That is a disgrace and UEFA have to do something about that because it was pure intimidation of the referee. The Lille staff encouraged their players to come off and that made it a hostile atmosphere inside the ground. Ryan asked the ref if he could take it quickly – and the ref agreed.'

Before the return leg in Manchester, Lille goalkeeper Tony Sylva then tried to stain the Welsh winger's impeccable reputation, much to Fergie's annoyance. Sylva said: 'Giggs is very intelligent, but I am not happy with the way he scored his goal at all. Football is a sport and it is necessary to play a clean game, to play without tricks. Giggs didn't do this. If you analyse the rules, I believe that the goal should have been cancelled and that Giggs should have received a yellow card. We are still furious with the referee that night and with the players of Manchester United.

'The English claim they are the kings of fair play, but that night they demonstrated they are experts in anti-sporting behaviour.'

Meanwhile, Fergie refused to be distracted as he and his team professionally finished off the job.

It was all systems go on three fronts – the Premiership,

Europe and the FA Cup – but Fergie was quick to point out that he would need a bit of luck and a lack of injuries if they were to succeed. Already he had admitted that a big part of United's success that season was down to the brilliant, rock-solid central defensive combination of Ferdinand and Vidic, so when both suffered injury problems at the business end of the campaign, the boss winced. He feared United would suffer without them and he would be proved right.

Disaster struck on the last day of March. The Reds were hosting Blackburn in what looked on paper to be an easy afternoon's stroll in the park. And so it proved as they ran out comfortable 4-1 winners – a victory that meant they needed just five more wins to wrap up the title. But the afternoon proved a nightmare for Vidic. His day would end 28 minutes into the match when he was forced off with a broken collarbone after he fell awkwardly while challenging for a header from a corner.

Fergie knew the loss of the big Serbian could be a major setback to his Champions League ambitions. He admitted: 'It's a real blow to lose Nemanja at this time of the season. The great thing we showed was the composure to not lose our heads, keep our nerve and keep on playing, and by doing that we kept on making chances.'

And he was right: it would seriously impact on United's quest for glory, effectively ending their European campaign. Vidic would be rushed back for the semi-final match against AC Milan when he was clearly unfit and United were to exit the competition.

When the injury struck, it was believed that Vidic would be absent for up to two months, with some pundits suggesting he might not even be fit until the following season. On the club's official fans' forum one United fan summed up the panic in the ranks when he posted: 'United have no chance in Europe now Vidic is out for a couple of months!'

In the event, Vidic would be sidelined for just five weeks, but he was not ready for top-class action.

Immediately after Vida suffered the injury Sir Alex was faced with the nightmare of shuffling of his pack for the Champions League quarter-final away tie at AS Roma. Mikael Silvestre was also missing with a dislocated shoulder and captain Gary Neville was out with ankle ligament damage suffered in the 4-1 home win over Bolton, a fortnight previously. It meant United had to field a makeshift central defensive pairing, with John O'Shea partnering Rio Ferdinand.

Given the last-minute disruption, it was little wonder the Reds lost 2-1 in the first leg of the tie. But they swamped the Italians in the return at Old Trafford, running out 7-1 winners to progress to the semi-finals.

Two weeks to the day after United suffered the blow of Vidic's injury at Blackburn, they would be dealt another setback when Ferdinand was also struck down by the injury jinx which had afflicted the backline. Playing in the FA Cup semi-final against Watford on 14 April, Rio limped off with a groin injury. United went on to win 4-1, with two goals from Rooney, one from Ronaldo and the other from Kieran Richardson, but the victory had been bought at a heavy cost. The last thing they needed was the loss of their other defensive lynchpin as the season reached the business end.

Even without Rio and Nemanja, United won two out of their next three League matches but Fergie also hankered after another one, or preferably two, Champions League wins before he headed off into the sunset. Yet the injuries to his key defenders – first, Nemanja, then Rio – would undermine and ultimately thwart his major ambition for at least one more season.

United would win the first leg of their Champions League semi 3-2 against AC Milan, with a battling performance and goals from Rooney (2) and Ronaldo. They had managed to achieve the win without Rio and Nemanja, but both men would be declared fit for the semi-final second-leg clash at Milan on 2 May 2007. Yet in reality, neither was fit in terms of match sharpness.

Vidic had not played since 31 March and Rio since 14 April. Both had struggled to overcome their injuries and Vidic suffered most with his collarbone agony. Fergie decided both would travel to Milan and that he would assess their relative strengths in training. Eventually, he plumped for Vidic. But the Serbian would have a stinker, definitely one of his worst showings in a United shirt, as he struggled for speed and sharpness in the tackle. United lost 3-0 in the San Siro, 5-3 on aggregate, after chasing shadows as a Kaka-inspired Milan left them for dead.

The Reds were out of the European Cup for another season.

Afterwards Fergie admitted: 'It is very disappointing, given how well we have done to get here. But I'd have to say we never came out the blocks. Milan were better prepared physically than us but we never coped with our start to the match. We lost two goals cheaply and you cannot do that at this level. Milan were fresher, but you have to say they put in a fantastic performance.

'If there was a difference in us tonight it was because we have been using the same players for the last two weeks without any respite. Milan have been resting players at the appropriate times but that is not taking anything away from their performance. We had a gruelling test at Everton on Saturday, where we had to go the extra mile, but I still expected more from my team. We just have to take it on the chin and see where we go from here.'

The boss did not pin the blame for defeat on Vidic, but instead pointed the finger at his forwards, Rooney and Ronaldo. He said: 'Wayne did OK but it was a disappointing night for Cristiano and he knows it. They are young and, on nights like this, the professionalism and experience of Milan gives a good indication of where we've got to go. That doesn't just apply to Rooney and Ronaldo, it applies to all the players.'

Yet three days later, United would show the boss the resilience and character he knew they possessed in abundance as they triumphed 1-0 in the League at Manchester City, thanks to a penalty converted by Ronaldo. They were now within a whisker of lifting the Premier League title that had been Chelsea's for the previous two seasons – and would secure just a day later when Chelsea could manage only a 1-1 draw in their match against Arsenal at the Emirates.

It was a remarkable turnaround. But the season wasn't over yet. One act of the drama remained: the FA Cup final against Chelsea, on 19 May 2007, and Fergie was intent on emerging victorious.

Unfortunately, it wasn't to be. A Didier Drogba goal ended the boss's hopes of yet another double as Chelsea won the FA Cup final by a goal to nil. It was a letdown as a spectacle and the boss felt cheated, too.

He believed Ryan Giggs had been denied a blatant penalty and goal after Michael Essien fouled the Welshman in extra time when he was trying to convert a cross from Rooney. Ryan's effort went straight at Chelsea keeper Petr Cech, who then seemed to lift the ball over his goal line as Giggs fell into him.

Giggs observed: 'It was clearly over the line – that's what I was asking for. I could see it was over the line and the referee didn't give a free-kick, so it was a goal. I felt I was getting to the ball quite comfortably and felt someone touch my leg.

'We're disappointed, obviously. The big decisions didn't go for us and if you don't get the big decisions, it is going to be hard for you. The referees are picked on merit and how they perform throughout the season.

'The FA Cup is a big occasion and you want the referees to get the big decisions right. They are only human and sometimes they get them wrong, but in the Cup final you hope they get them right and today they didn't.'

Fergie backed up his captain, saying: 'It's a penalty kick. Then the goalkeeper's spilled the ball behind the line. I think it would have been a difficult one for the linesman to call, but the referee should be in a better position. We couldn't see where we were, but when I see it now, it's a penalty.'

Fergie departed Wembley that night, thinking about what might have been. But amid the disappointment he knew he had much to celebrate – and much to look forward to. He had won back the Premier League crown and had only been denied glory in Europe because of bad luck with injuries to key men at a key time.

But Fergie and his boys were back in business – the best in England and hopefully soon the best in Europe, too... once again.

CHAPTER 12

FERGIE'S NEW DREAM TEAM

After miraculously leading Manchester United back to the promised land of the League title – and breaking the hold of Abramovich's Chelsea – Fergie heralded in a new era of optimism at Old Trafford. Now the lean years were over, normal service was resumed. The boss had seen off all those who claimed he was past his sell-by-date and re-emerged triumphant.

But there was still the little matter of the Champions League to put to bed before he finally hung up his tracksuit for good. Sure, the win in Barcelona almost a decade earlier had put him on a level playing field with Busby, but that wasn't enough: Sir Alex wanted to win the competition again – at least once before he packed it in.

And after the previous season's glory when he brought the Premier League title back to Old Trafford, he was seriously thinking he might never have as good a chance to do it again. In his mind, he had the players and the time was right to cash in on some more European glory.

In the close season he would throw down the gauntlet to his

rivals by strengthening his squad further. First, he snapped up England's midfielder enforcer Owen Hargreaves for £17 million and then paid similar fees for the dynamite potential of Brazilian Anderson and Portugal's Nani.

It was astute business: Hargreaves would add further weight to central midfield, while Nani and Anderson would one day hopefully be readymade replacements for Giggs and Scholes respectively.

The campaign began as it would again: against arch rivals Chelsea. Sir Alex's team met the Blues in the traditional charity curtain-raiser, the FA Community Shield at Wembley on 5 August 2007. It was an opportunity for revenge after the FA Cup final defeat the previous May – and this time it would be the Reds who emerged triumphant, winning 3-0 on penalties after the match ended 1-1. Ryan Giggs put them ahead on 35 minutes, only for Florent Malouda to level 10 minutes later. But in 30°C, the teams once again struggled to put on a show, just as they had in the FA Cup final.

There had been lethargy in United's play and it would still be apparent a week later when they opened their Premier League campaign with a 0-0 home draw with Reading. The loss of Wayne Rooney in the first half with what turned out to be a fractured foot did not help the boss's mood after the game: his team had not managed a breakthrough, even when the visitors were reduced to 10 men after substitute Dave Kitson was sent off for a disgraceful tackle on Evra.

In public at least the boss blamed the poor result on the loss of Rooney to injury, saying: 'If he'd been on the pitch, I think we'd have won the match. In the second half, chances started to come. We had some good chances and we just didn't take them.'

Three days later United were at Portsmouth and Fergie warned: 'Fratton Park is not an easy place to go to. It means

Portsmouth have a big advantage overall in terms of their likely home record.

'Harry [Redknapp] has made a few interesting additions, too, especially David Nugent, John Utaka and Sulley Muntari, who we have watched quite a bit, and I would expect improvement from them this season.'

He was spot-on: United had to settle for another point, coming away with a 1-1, after Paul Scholes put them ahead with a blistering drive on 15 minutes, only for Benjani to equalise just after the interval.

Carlos Tevez had marked his Manchester United debut by setting up Scholes for the goal, but the Reds stumbled after Ronaldo was sent off for violent conduct. He followed Portsmouth's Muntari in being red-carded five minutes from time for what looked like an attempted headbutt on Richard Hughes. Muntari had traipsed down the tunnel for an early bath two minutes before him for a second booking.

Fergie felt his Portuguese star had been harshly treated. He told Sky Sports: 'I've looked at the replays and there's nothing conclusive. My take was that he was provoked. He's fallen into the trap and he's paid the penalty – it's his own fault, really.

'It was a disappointing result, but not a disappointing performance. There was a great contribution from Carlos Tevez, even though he had to endure a lot of tackles from behind, a lot of abuse [for being Argentinean] and he came through that.'

But United's slow start to the campaign would continue into the next match – and in the eyes of the fans, the first defeat could hardly have come against worse opposition. OK, maybe a defeat to Liverpool would have gone down worse, but the 1-0 loss to neighbours Manchester City at Eastlands was hard to stomach, especially as the Blues had won courtesy of a deflected goal off Vidic.

While Tevez had made his League debut at Pompey, Hargreaves followed suit at City, lining up alongside Carrick and Scholes in midfield. It would take time for the new faces to settle in comfortably – and without the injured Rooney and the suspended Ronaldo, United lacked a little in terms of their usual flair and invention.

Fergie told the fans to keep calm and that his team would come good. He was right: just a week later the Reds finally got their 2007/08 title bid on the road with a 1-0 win over Spurs at Old Trafford, with Nani scoring his first goal for the club.

United had begun the match second bottom in the League, but rarely looked in any danger once they had settled down. Afterwards Sir Alex made the valid point that his team was finding it hard to fire on all cylinders because anxiety had crept in: an anxiety borne out of expectations after they had reclaimed their League title in the previous campaign. He admitted: 'That was narrow, touch and go, nothing to choose between the two sides. They dug in and got forward a bit and there was really nothing in it in the second half. I thought we lacked a little bit of confidence. Players are anxious, there is a lot of expectation here, and what was required was to dig in, show great commitment – and we did that.'

Certainly there was a feeling among the fans that this could be a very big year for United. Lifelong United fan Dave Moore explained to me: 'Right from the start of that season there was a tinge of excitement and anticipation in the air. We had finally brushed away the cobwebs of the transition years by winning back the title from Chelsea – and had proved we were No. 1 again, despite Abramovich's millions.

'We expected to retain the title but also felt we could go on and win the European Cup for the third time. There was all that stuff about the final coming on the 50th anniversary of the

Munich Air Disaster. It seemed as if we were predestined – that's why there was a little unrest and anxiety among the fans at the start of the season when we got off to such a stinker. It hadn't been expected: we had thought we would open up with all guns blazing, but we should have known better really, shouldn't we?

'United had always been renowned as poor starters and so why should it have been any different that year? The team started like a car that was stuttering but gradually picked up speed and ended the season like a Rolls-Royce. But it was still a blow to our pride to lose at Man City back in August!'

I asked Dave if he felt Fergie could still go on for a few years to come. 'Oh, definitely,' he replied. 'Many of us had written him off a few seasons back, but he proved once again last season that you do so at your peril, by winning the League again.

'That was a magnificent achievement – I must admit I never thought he would be able to outfox Abramovich and his millions. It just goes to show you: the boss knows what he is doing, he sees a bigger picture than the rest of us, so why shouldn't he go on and on at this club?

'I am sure he will know when it is time to go, but I honestly can't see that being for a good few years now. Why would he want to leave this exciting new team he has built for someone else to pick up and take the credit?'

United followed up the 1-0 win over Spurs with another 1-0 win, this time over Sunderland, again at Old Trafford. Their football was far from pretty but they were grinding out results and Sir Alex was pleased with that: in his eyes, it was part of the DNA that makes up champions.

On 15 September they attained a third consecutive 1-0 Premier League win – getting the better of Everton at Goodison

Park. Vidic was the hero of the hour, his headed goal seven minutes from time helping United continue their steady, if dour progress up the Premiership table.

Just four days later the Reds would chalk up yet another 1-0 triumph, overcoming old European foes Sporting in Lisbon. After the Champions League Group F win, it was back to the bread and butter of the Premiership and the first acid test of the new season for United. Yes, Chelsea were in town, determined to prove they could claw back the League crown United had taken from them.

But United were too strong for them, with goals from Tevez and Saha securing a 2-0 victory. Chelsea's cause was not helped by the dismissal of Jon Obi Mikel on the half-hour for a clumsy challenge on Evra. It was a bad start for new Chelsea boss Avram Grant, installed by owner Abramovich after the sacking of José Mourinho.

Now United were second in the League table and Fergie voiced the opinion that his team were about to hit their stride. Certainly, they kept on winning 1-0, with a fifth consecutive instalment of that scoreline coming at Birmingham on 29 September, and a sixth a few days later when they beat Roma in a Champions League group F clash at Old Trafford.

Then they crushed Wigan 4-0 at Old Trafford, but lost both Vidic and O'Shea to injury, much to the disappointment of Sir Alex, who said: 'Considering all the things that happened, I think we've done fantastically well. I was very pleased with the football in the second half. We had 10 players missing, but great credit to the players who played today. We speeded the game up in the second half, the flow of the game was much better. It's coming together.'

Indeed it was: the wins now became more emphatic and much to Fergie's delight United started to surge ahead. Stalwart defender Vidic said he believed they could do better than the previous season: 'We have a big squad this season. Last season we got a lot of injuries towards the end and did not have the power to go that one step further. Now we are much stronger and with the competition for places, everyone is pushing that much harder.'

They beat Sporting Lisbon 2-1 at home in December to secure their place in the last 16 of the Champions League and would now embark on a seven-match unbeaten run up to Christmas, which included two particularly impressive results: a Mersey double over Liverpool and Everton. The 1-0 triumph at Anfield on 16 December, with a goal from Carlos Tevez, left Fergie on cloud nine. Still, after all these years he liked nothing better than getting one over on the old enemy!

The win left Liverpool nine points behind United and was the beginning of the end of their title challenge, having a demoralising effect on them. It meant that Fergie could enjoy a happy Christmas with his family. He had beaten Liverpool and qualified from Group F with four wins – and that suggested to him that a real tilt at the Champions League was no pipe dream. Yes, he suspected it was well within his grasp to go one better than the semi-final exit of the previous season.

But he and the Reds would receive a setback just after Christmas 2007 when their unbeaten run came to a shuddering halt with a 2-1 loss at West Ham on 29 December. It was a setback, but hardly unexpected – over the years, United had often come unstuck at Upton Park and the Hammers had become a real bogey team. Ronaldo put United ahead, but goals from Rio's brother Anton and Matthew Upson killed them off.

Yet United would then go on another unbeaten run – this time seven matches – that would only end when they once again lost to neighbours Manchester City, who wrapped up an unlikely double at Old Trafford with a 2-1 win on 10 February 2008. Again, this would prove to be only a stutter and would be followed by a run of 16 matches unbeaten out of 17, with that single loss coming at home against Portsmouth in the FA Cup.

Two results in particular stand out in the run: against Liverpool and Roma. On 23 March 2008, United disposed of Liverpool 3-0 at Old Trafford in the League. The result left United six points clear of second-placed Chelsea, who had won 2-1 against Arsenal.

Full of praise for his team, Fergie said: 'It was a really good performance, a performance of maturity. The team has matured over the last six months and today they hit their peak.'

On 1 April, United triumphed 2-0 at the Olympic Stadium against Roma in the quarter-final of the Champions League. The win was all the more remarkable given that Vidic twisted his left knee and was replaced by Wes Brown after 35 minutes. Goals from Ronaldo and Rooney saw the Reds home, but Fergie expressed his hope that Vidic would return soon. No doubt the boss was mindful of how his team had suffered in the Champions League the previous season when the big Serb and his partner-in-crime Rio were injured.

Sir Alex said: 'I pray it is not serious because he is such an integral part of our team. We think it might be a nerve injury, but we can't be sure at this moment.'

Ronaldo was more upbeat, insisting: 'I think we have a great chance to win it. The team really played fantastically well in this game and has matured. Everybody knows what a tough game this was going to be for us and what a hard place Rome is to come to.'

Vidic would miss the return leg against Roma, but a 1-0 win, courtesy of a Tevez goal, was enough to ease United through,

3-0 on aggregate. Also, it set up a potentially mouthwatering, if nerve-racking semi-final clash against the attacking aristocrats of Barcelona.

To their credit, a patched-up United backline (without Vidic) held out 0-0 in the Nou Camp and went through, thanks to Paul Scholes' winner at Old Trafford.

The ties had threatened to be carnivals of entertaining football, but had not delivered. Not that Fergie was much bothered by that: no, all that mattered was that his beloved United were back in the final again.

Scholes' wonder strike helped erase his own personal nightmare and offered him the chance of redemption in Moscow – he had missed the final of the Champions League in 1999 because of suspension, but Ferguson promised he would be involved this time, fitness permitting.

A defeat at Chelsea, sandwiched in between the two ties against Barca, was a bad blow for Fergie as it meant the Blues were right back in the frame for the title – they were now joint top with United. But at least the Reds had the better goal difference.

Despite Rooney's equaliser, two goals from the powerful Michael Ballack – one a penalty – had won the points. But Fergie's new side was much like his other great United teams down the ages: tough, durable and battlers. On 3 May 2008, they returned to winning ways by beating West Ham 4-1 in the Premier League, thanks to a brace from Ronaldo and one apiece for Tevez and Michael Carrick.

And the win was achieved comfortably, even with 10 men – Nani was shown a red card on 37 minutes for headbutting Lucas Neill. Fergie now confidently expected his boys to retain the title they had won back off Chelsea, 12 months previously. To do so, they needed to win at Wigan the following week.

He said: 'The way Chelsea have been talking is that it'll be easy up there, but we know that's not the case. We have not won anything yet, but we hope we can win the League next week. There was a bit of nervousness in our play at times, but we killed the game in the second half to continue what has been a fantastic season so far.'

The boss also praised Cristiano Ronaldo for grabbing his 39th and 40th goals of the season and at the same time rapped Nani for his indiscipline. He said: 'How many players could score that many? He is improving all the time. Plus, he has spent 90 per cent of the season on the wing. It's been a great day for us and we've got a big chance.

'Our players have been absolutely fantastic this season. We were down to 10 men and I said to try to run the clock down, keep possession and be patient in the second half, and I'm very pleased because there was a bit of tiredness.

'There is no excuse [for Nani]. He showed a measure of immaturity and we will deal with it.'

In buoyant mood, United headed for Wigan on 11 May and strolled to a comfortable 2-0 win, securing their 17th League title in some style. Ronaldo put United ahead just after the half-hour and with 10 minutes remaining, Giggs scored the goal that secured his 10th title winner's medal (the same number as his boss had now achieved at the club).

It poured down, but that didn't stop the boss dancing in the rain with his players as they celebrated. Fergie admitted he was also delighted that Giggsy had equalled Sir Bobby Charlton's club record of 758 appearances for United: 'It was a tough old match. For most of the game we played well, but there were some nervous moments. I was pleased with that second goal. It makes it 10 today for Ryan Giggs, which is fantastic.'

The boss said he was confident that he and his team could

now go on to overwhelm Liverpool's record of 18 League titles: 'I think it will come – this side is young, there is plenty left in them. I said before the game that I am not bothered about records. This is what it is about, championships and trophies. I am at a great club, which makes it easier for me than the rest.'

But even as he was celebrating, the man who had built the modern legend of Manchester United was thinking about the Champions League final in Moscow that was now looming; it was the very nature of him. He would say: 'We are bouncing into that final now. If we'd lost the title, it would have been different. If this team goes on now and wins the European Cup, it will be my best ever.'

To achieve it, he would have to outfox his biggest rivals on the domestic stage: Chelsea. It was a match the whole world was anticipating with relish.

CHAPTER 13
CRÈME DE LA KREMLIN

There was no need to remind Sir Alex Ferguson of the significance of Manchester United's date with destiny in Moscow, in May 2008. He knew better than most that victory in the Champions League final against Chelsea would mean he had succeeded 40 years on from United's first European conquest and 50 years after the Munich air disaster.

That wonderful night was made all the sweeter when he led United to a third European Cup win. There he was, doing what he loved, making and rewriting history at his beloved United. It seemed unbelievable that just three years or so earlier, during some of his darkest hours at Old Trafford, many had written him off – over the hill, finished, unable to cope with the new kid on the block, José Mourinho. Yet there he was, back at the very top in a remarkable turnaround that proved his critics wrong.

Those same critics would have to eat humble pie in 2008, but rarely had it tasted so good for those among them who had been brought up as United fans (and that accounted for a considerable proportion of the press box).

In the build-up to the big game, Fergie had been ultra-confident. Even after United secured their 17th top-flight domestic crown by beating Wigan on 11 May, he predicted they would have enough in the tank to see off Chelsea in Moscow. After winning at the JJB he said: 'If we'd lost it today it would have been difficult for us in Moscow. When we lost the title in 1995 we went into the FA Cup final and were dead. But we are not dead this time – we're alive and kicking and can't wait to take on Chelsea.'

Sir Alex led a 24-man squad as his team flew out of Manchester airport on a private charter at lunchtime on Monday, 19 May, two days before the crunch match. Only three players had been part of the match-day squad that touched down in Barcelona a decade earlier for the 1999 final against Bayern Munich in the Camp Nou. Ryan Giggs and Gary Neville had been in the starting line-up that day, while Wes Brown was on the bench.

Chelsea arrived in town the same day – with an entourage of 44. It was their first European Cup final and they too were brimming with confidence. But when asked about United's own significance on that 50th anniversary of the Munich air disaster, Fergie insisted: 'We won't let the memory of the Busby Babes down.'

With Munich survivors including Sir Bobby Charlton in attendance, he was spot-on in that respect. 'It was only fitting,' Fergie would tell the press ranks after the match. 'It was such an emotional occasion. I said the day before the game that we would not let the memory of the Busby Babes down – we had a cause and people with causes are difficult to play against. I think fate was playing its hand today.'

Sir Alex also added to the growing impetus of the build-up by claiming the final was now the biggest event in world football: 'I think it is better than the World Cup now and has been for some time. The Champions League gets better each year, whereas World Cups are not what they used to be. You have to go back to 1986 in Mexico to get a real sense of what World Cups used to be like, or the one before that: in Spain. France and Brazil were both knocked out by the semi-finals that year – that shows how high the standard was. They were two of the best teams ever.'

Fergie was confident that he now had a strong enough squad to lift the trophy again after that 1999 success but added that the winning team would also need a bit of luck. He continued: 'You need a little bit in terms of who you've got on the Saturday before your Tuesday night game, or in domestic terms who you play on the Saturday after a Wednesday. The Premier League is so competitive you can't ease up for a minute and it can be difficult picking your teams if you are going for the League as well as Europe. You need a strong squad and we didn't have that last year, or at least not when we needed it.'

He said he was proud that the final would be between two English clubs – that it was a brilliant advert for the strength of the Premier League: 'There has been an English team in the last three finals. We are getting some consistency from English clubs in Europe now. The recent record suggests English clubs will get to the later stages and once you do that, there is always the chance of reaching the final or even winning it.

'Two European Cups over the history of the Premiership is not a lot, but there are reasons for that and the balance has been between Milan and Madrid, anyway. But the Premier League has improved, the quality of players in England has improved and although English clubs have no divine right to succeed, we have a better chance of consistency in Europe now.'

The Moscow showdown would be the third Champions League final between clubs from the same country in less than a decade. Spain's Real Madrid defeated Valencia in 2000, while AC Milan beat Juventus in an all-Italian final in 2003.

With the eyes of the world on the two clubs, it was a defining moment for English football and Fergie's United would not disappoint. The build-up was colourful and noisy as 25,000 fans from each club converged on the city the day before the big game, massing in Red Square, where special tents and entertainment had been lined up to keep them occupied. They mixed amicably for what one newspaper dubbed 'the biggest invasion since Napoleon'.

Of course, there were problems getting into the country and finding somewhere to stay. Queues at Immigration were long, tiring and testing, and all hotels in Moscow were booked up, but every Reds fan would agree afterwards that the aggro was well worth it.

The queues and delays would have been much greater for United's contingent of fans and staff, had the club's chief executive David Gill had his way. He believed they could have quadrupled their support for the match, saying: 'We have actually allocated the tickets broadly in accordance with UEFA instructions prior to knowing whether we would be there. Our allocation is just over 21,000 tickets and with season-ticket holders, box holders and other internal usage, it is a difficult process. We could sell well over 100,000 tickets for this final, so there will be a lot of disappointed people.'

Professor Simon Chadwick of the Centre of International Business of Sport summed up the sheer scale of the financial spin-off that the Old Trafford giants could expect when he told the *Sun*: 'The 2008 Champions League final will be the biggest prize yet in economic terms. The cumulative impact of this match could amount to upwards of £210 million – with more than half of that going to the two finalists.'

Which meant the final even eclipsed America's famed Super Bowl in terms of financial import – a remarkable feat on its own. In the match itself, United's creative, free-flowing football and more positive approach earned them a rightful victory. Chelsea were a far more pragmatic, physical outfit built from granite: rock-steady and rock-hard; big men who would not be pushed about, who could hold their own. John Terry, Michael Ballack and Didier Drogba formed a tough spine to an intimidating frame, but they were neither as positive nor creative as United.

To their credit, the Reds stood firm and refused to be bullied as Chelsea's hard men confronted them. At the end of the match it would be two of those men, Drogba and Terry, who would take it on the chin for their side's defeat. After extra time, the game finished 1-1, but Drogba would be sent off four minutes from the end for an assault on Vidic and England skipper Terry was to miss the penalty that would have won it for the Blues.

Drogba's petulance was extremely costly for his team-mates as he would certainly have been one of the key penalty takers in the shoot-out. In being sent off, the Ivory Coast striker also achieved the notorious distinction of becoming only the second player to see red in a Champions League final (Jens Lehmann being the first when he was dismissed for Arsenal against Barcelona, back in 2006).

Drogba was outraged and refused to go initially. When he eventually departed the field, many commentators believed it would be his last action in a Chelsea shirt although he was to prove them wrong.

At kick-off it had been clear that Fergie was well aware of Chelsea's midfield strength. He sent out a midfield of Scholes, Hargreaves and Carrick to counter Chelsea's own 'Big Three' in the centre of the park: Claude Makelele, Ballack and Frank Lampard.

The teams and formations read:

Manchester United (4-3-3): Van der Sar, Brown, Ferdinand, Vidic, Evra, Hargreaves, Scholes, Carrick, Ronaldo, Tevez and Rooney.

Chelsea (4-3-2-1): Cech, Essien, Carvalho, Terry, A. Cole, Makelele, Ballack, Lampard, J. Cole, Malouda and Drogba.

The Red Devils drew first blood, thanks to a 26th-minute goal from Ronaldo, who nodded home a cross from Wes Brown, the Portuguese's 42nd goal of the campaign. But the Blues equalised on the stroke of half-time as Lampard ghosted in to hammer home a ball floated in by Michael Essien.

At the half-time break Fergie worked his magic – convincing his men that they would still win if they kept things steady and did nothing stupid (like getting sent off, as would prove the case with Drogba).

Before the final, Vidic had warned about Drogba and now his words proved ominously spot-on. He had told the *Daily Telegraph*: 'Sometimes he [Drogba] goes in very strong and sometimes he pretends he is weak. He plays with your mind and tries to make the defender think about the next tackle.

'He can pretend he fell down to win a penalty, but referees know that. The Champions League final is a big game and I'm sure the ref will know his job. He's a great player and he's a top scorer – it's a hard job to stop him.'

United rode their luck in the penalty shoot-out to bring the trophy back to Old Trafford for the third time in the club's glorious history. For both players and fans alike, the shoot-out was a nerve-racking ordeal.

Tevez scored to make it 1-0 to United, Ballack made it 1-1, Carrick made it 2-1 to United, Belletti made it 2-2, Ronaldo missed, Lampard put Chelsea 3-2 up; Hargreaves kept United in it at 3-3, Ashley Cole put the Blues 4-3 up. Then Nani had to score or United were dead and buried: he did, but Chelsea still had the upper hand as the tension became unbearable. Luckily for United, Terry slipped and hit the post. Then Anderson put United ahead 5-4, only for Kalou to equalise. Ryan Giggs made it 6-5 to United. Finally, Nicolas Anelka had his kick palmed away by Van der Sar and the European Cup was on its way back to Manchester for the first time since 1999.

It did not escape anyone's notice, least of all Fergie's, that Ryan Giggs had broken Bobby Charlton's club appearances record. Already the club's most decorated player, with 10 Premier League titles and five FA Cups at the time, Giggs admitted his one regret was that he had only won the one European Cup winner's medal in 1999. In saying that, he was very much singing from the same hymn book as his boss.

Three minutes from the end of normal time, Giggsy came on for Scholes to overwhelm Sir Bobby's 46-year record of 758 appearances. Earlier it had been claimed the record was 759 until, just weeks before the final, it was revealed that Bobby had not, after all, played in a 1962 FA Cup tie against Bolton.

Giggs said: 'What appearing in tonight's game proved is that I was right to remain at United throughout my career. When I first came through, Serie A was the place to be and the best players went there. Now all the great players are playing in England.'

Naturally delighted and proud, Sir Alex said: 'It is a fantastic achievement – that is the first shoot-out I've won in a big game. When Cristiano Ronaldo missed his penalty we thought we were in trouble, but we deserved the win; we had the better chances. In the second half they had more control, but in extra time we were better.

'I thought we were fantastic in the first half and should have been three or four up, and they got a lucky break right on half-time. It gave them an impetus because I thought they were the better team in the second half – they had more power than us. Actually, I was quite glad to get extra time to change the formation a little and I thought in extra time we were the better team.'

The boss admitted that he had always thought victory would be United's destiny, with the result coming on that 50th anniversary of the Munich air disaster: 'We started the British sojourn into Europe in 1955 and we deserved to get the trophy tonight. I am delighted for the fans and the players.'

Typically, he was already looking ahead to the next campaign, making it clear both Giggs and Scholes would still have a role to play at the club. He explained: 'We have the issue of Scholes and Giggs getting to the twilight of their careers. They will contribute in a big way next season, as they normally do but not as many games. They will be eventually phased out, as you have to do in life.

'Ryan will be 35 in November – I think he'll play until he's 37, with maybe 25 to 30 games a season. I think Paul Scholes is 34 in November – 25 to 30 games next season because we have the back-up now.'

The triumph was Fergie's second Champions League crown, to go with the 10th Premier League title his side had already sewn up earlier in the month. But there was still work to be done and more trophies to win. As he enjoyed a celebratory drink in Moscow, he was already planning for the next season. Always one step ahead of the pack, even after winning the top club trophy in world football... it was the mark of a truly remarkable man.

CHAPTER 14

KOP THAT...
18 TITLES ALL

After the glory and celebrations of Moscow and that wonderful Champions League win, the horrid hangover... almost inevitably, I suppose. As the 2008/09 season got underway, United would win just two of their first seven games (including the FA Community Shield and the European Super Cup) – and it would be 23 September before they kicked on with a vengeance.

Obviously, the boss was annoyed about the slow start, but he didn't exaggerate the situation. He knew his boys would come good, that United were traditionally slow starters.

The campaign began at Wembley with a gentle run out in the FA Community Shield against Portsmouth – the FA Cup winners who had triumphed over Cardiff the previous May up against the Premier League champions. It ended all square at 0-0 and United eventually triumphed 3-1 in what was now becoming the traditional penalty shoot-out. ITN Sport conjured up a rather optimistic scenario after the Reds' huff-and-puff display, trumpeting, 'Manchester United will be the team to beat after this effective display.'

But Sir Alex was far keener to play down high hopes at this stage, preferring to gee up his troops rather than flatter them. He said: 'We dominated possession and had some good chances but it is this issue with scoring at the moment.'

Golden Boot winner of the previous campaign Ronaldo, with those incredible 42 goals, was out injured (for a month), while Rooney was suffering from a virus when Newcastle arrived at Old Trafford for the Premier League season opener a week later. Rooney had missed the Community Shield and still seemed to be suffering the after-effects of the virus as he teamed up with Frazier Campbell against the Toon. Because of a family bereavement Carlos Tevez missed the match, in which United struggled to a 1-1 draw.

Naturally, the result was a downer and Fergie was also faced with the loss of Michael Carrick and Ryan Giggs. The boss said: 'We played well in the first half and their goalkeeper made several good saves to keep them in the match. Our attacking play in the first half was good but as soon as we lost Giggs to a hamstring injury and Carrick with an ankle, which is swollen up badly – he'll be out for two to three weeks – we lost a bit of our experience in midfield.

'We had possession of the ball but didn't make it count at times but in light of the people we had missing, it was a creditable result for us.'

A week later United won 1-0 at Pompey in the League, with Darren Fletcher following up his equaliser against Newcastle with the winner. Fergie was pleased with the win and the way Vidic and Ferdinand had policed the Pompey Little-and-Large pairing of Crouch and Defoe, saying: 'They are so solid and reliable. Very little gets past them. We played some excellent football tonight. This is a difficult place to come, so it is a bonus to come here and win. We tried to play a system where the players would be comfortable. We wanted to have Anderson playing centrally, close to Carlos Tevez. We let Paul Scholes control the game and used Darren Fletcher's energy.'

But consistency would evade United for a month. The following Friday in Monaco, they blew their chances of winning the European Super Cup. United, as European Cup winners, lost 2-1 to UEFA Cup winners Zenit St Petersburg. It was the Reds' second Super Cup loss in a decade, the previous one coming in 1999.

On that occasion in the same Monaco stadium, the Reds crashed 1-0 to Italian outfit Lazio. Juan Sebastian Veron was the man of the match, performing so well that two years later Fergie would produce a cheque for £28.1 million in return for his signature.

United had made their debut in the Super Cup in 1991 with a happier outcome. As winners of the European Cup Winners' Cup after beating Barcelona, they overcame the challenge of Red Star Belgrade (who had lifted the European Cup) to take the trophy, thanks to Brian McClair's goal in a 1-0 victory. That match was due to be a two-legged affair (the permanent site of Monaco only came into being in 1998), but political unrest in Belgrade at the time meant only the Old Trafford leg was played.

Ironically, a 10-year-old Nemanja Vidic was cheering on Red Star that night in 1991, watching the match on TV with his father Dragoljub, back home in Uzice. He cried when the side he had supported as a boy lost but would find consolation five years later when Red Star signed him up for their youth team. And of course, he would eventually become a major player for Manchester United.

Against Zenit, United struggled for form. Six minutes before the interval, Pavel Pogrebnyak put Zenit ahead and Danny clinched the victory with the second goal just before the hour mark. But Vidic would find some consolation for United by heading home a pass from Tevez on 73 minutes.

Yet more agony would follow when Scholes attempted to punch the ball into the goal from a Wes Brown cross just a minute from the end – and was sent off. The ref showed him a second yellow card and the dismissal proved costly: he would now miss United's first Champions League game in September, at home to Villarreal.

Fergie claimed he was more disappointed about the loss of Scholes against Villarreal than losing the match, although he had said beforehand that he wanted to win the trophy. However, the United boss conceded his men had still not reached anything like the form he wanted from them: 'I think we played our best football at 2-0, unfortunately. It was a warm night and so I think my players did OK under the circumstances. I thought Tevez was outstanding, probably the best player on the park, and I thought we had chances to do something in the game, but Zenit are a very good team and have exceptional movement – they'll be a force in the Champions League, playing like that.'

Fergie had been lamenting the lack of goals since the Community Shield and a few days after the Zenit match, he would splash out serious money to remedy the problem – or so he hoped. He signed the Bulgarian striker Dimitar Berbatov from Spurs for a fee purported to be £31 million.

Berbatov, 27, put pen to paper on the £100,000-a-week, four-year deal at Old Trafford and said: 'Joining United is a dream come true. I look forward to playing my part in helping this club win more honours.'

Meanwhile, the boss was convinced Berbatov would deliver the goods and that the investment was good business. He said:

'This is a key signing. Dimitar is one of the best and most exciting strikers in world football. His style and ability will give the team a different dimension and I'm sure he will be a popular player with the fans.'

But Berba was not as popular with the fans as Fergie would have hoped. While many agree that the striker is classy and talented, they do not believe he justifies his massive fee. The general complaint was that he didn't put enough commitment into the United cause – and that he simply hadn't scored enough goals. Of course, the boss would continue to defend his man, but as United fans told me, he did the same with Veron, also deemed an expensive flop by the Old Trafford faithful.

Berba would make his debut in the hothouse of Anfield on 13 September 2008. It was memorable but for all the wrong reasons if you happened to be a United fan. They crashed 2-1 to their biggest rivals and Vidic was sent off for two bookable offences.

Carlos Tevez had shot United ahead after just three minutes – and all credit to Berba for setting him up. But an own goal from Wes Brown and a late winner from Ryan Babel did for United. It went from bad to worse when Vidic was sent off in the final minute of normal time for fouling Xabi Alonso.

Sir Alex admitted the result was a setback, but again refused to press the panic button. It was as if he knew his men would come good, although he must have prayed it would be by the time they travelled to Chelsea, eight days later! Fergie observed: 'Liverpool were far the better team: they tackled us, got about us and harassed us, forcing us to make mistakes and we didn't cope with that well. The two goals were absolute shockers – the defending was very, very poor. People will think they are watching a Conference side when they see the highlights. It's going to be difficult at

Chelsea and if we don't address the physical part of the game, then we'll struggle there too.'

In the event, United drew 1-1 at Stamford Bridge against the Blues and their new boss, Luiz Felipe Scolari – the Brazilian otherwise known as 'Big Phil'.

Finally, the Reds' season was starting to turn. They had been the better side and deserved a win after Ji-Sung Park put them ahead on 18 minutes, only for Salomon Kalou to equalise 10 minutes from time. Fergie admitted that he was disappointed United had not taken all three points: 'I feel we have missed a good chance, obviously. If we had had a bit more energy, we would have been OK. We started to drop off the pace a bit in terms of the speed we were playing at. That was a bit of a disappointment because it allowed them to regroup at half-time. We started to give the ball away in the second half and that got them back into the game. They had a couple of chances, but that's about all they had.'

The boss may have felt a bit let down that United had not left London with all three points, but now his team would lift his spirits by roaring into top gear. They notched up six consecutive wins, beginning with a 3-1 stroll over Middlesbrough in the Carling Cup and culminating in a 3-0 win over Celtic in the Champions League group stage. But then United slumped to a 2-1 defeat at Arsenal on 8 November 2008, with Samir Nasri grabbing both goals and the only consolation being a last-minute goal from young Brazilian fullback Rafael.

Fergie was uncharacteristically downcast, admitting: 'It is a big blow to us – we needed to win the game. Our results against the other big clubs are a big concern: we have got to get above 85 points to have a chance of the title, so we must keep going for it. Having every game away after a European tie is not easy.'

(He was referring to the 1-1 draw in the return match with Celtic, just three days earlier.)

His assistant Mike Phelan tried to inject some sense of optimism into proceedings, by claiming United could have taken something from the Arsenal game. He said: 'We are disappointed. We made enough chances to score a couple of goals, but that wasn't to be. It was an open game and very end-to-end, but we came out the wrong side of it. It was too open and we suffered from that.

'We put a lot of pressure on their goal and created about 20 chances. We were chasing the game at 2-0 down and it is always difficult. We didn't get the luck that we needed. Cristiano Ronaldo created a great opening for himself when we were 2-0 down, but he put it wide of the post. If we had got back to 2-1 then we could have gone on to get something from the game.'

Despite Phelan's attempts to boost morale, United left the Emirates in low spirits. The boss knew they had blown a good opportunity to put breathing space between themselves and major rivals.

The win lifted the Gunners into third place in the table above United and set alarm bells ringing at Old Trafford. After all, they had now lost to title rivals Arsenal and Liverpool, and only managed to draw at Chelsea. Would they now hit another slump in form and lose the chance to notch up an historic third Premier League title win on the bounce?

It would be one of the quiet men of Old Trafford who would inject some much-needed optimism – and realism – into the situation as United licked their wounds. Keeper Edwin van der Sar said: 'If we had won or drawn, we would have kept them below us in the table. Now we've let them back in. But Chelsea, Liverpool and Arsenal all have to come to Old Trafford. We have to make sure we get maximum points from those games.

'Am I concerned? No. I think we have been unlucky in all three of the games against the big teams. The belief is still strong.'

The belief was also right: Fergie and his team would soon go on to become World Champions in Japan, more of this in the next chapter, and embark upon one of the most remarkable runs in footballing history. Fergie would watch with pride and delight as his team stayed unbeaten for 16 matches in the Premier League, until 14 March 2009, as they strode towards that record-breaking title.

The turnaround simply demonstrated the impact one man could have on a football club. Sir Alex had cajoled and inspired his men, telling them the defeat at Arsenal was a mere setback, that they could still win the League – and that they could do it in style. It just went to show the brilliance, fortitude and mental and emotional strength of the man at the helm of the world's greatest football club. But you wouldn't expect him to do anything else but turn the show around, given the way he had done so many times before at Old Trafford. As the boss would remark later in the season when United needed to win in the Champions League at Porto: 'We at United are good at making firsts.'

That 16-match unbeaten run would take in some fine results, too. Straight after the loss at the Emirates, they would pummel an ever-improving, tough-to-beat Stoke City 5-0 at Old Trafford and then win 1-0 away at Manchester City. A fortnight after the win at the City of Manchester Stadium, United beat Sunderland 1-0 at Old Trafford. They then went on to crush Chelsea 3-0 at home in January and won 5-0 at West Brom, at the end of the same month. The demolition of Chelsea signalled the beginning of the end for Scolari's short, troubled reign at Stamford Bridge. Chelsea's defeat in Manchester meant they had taken just 10 points from their last eight games and set alarm bells ringing for Abramovich, who was now concerned they might even miss out on a Champions League spot.

A month later, the likeable Brazilian – a World Cup winner with Brazil – was gone from Stamford Bridge.

The win meant United moved up to third in the Premier League and now the pressure was right on Liverpool, who still led the pack. Liverpool boss Rafa Benítez crowed that United might be 'a little bit scared' at the sight of the Kop kings at the top of the pile. In the event, it would be his own players – and himself – who would suffer the heebie-jeebies, while Fergie would privately laugh off his rival's feeble attempts at mind games.

By the end of January, United leapfrogged Liverpool at the top courtesy of a free-flowing display of football at the Hawthorns that left hosts West Brom demoralised and at the wrong end of a 5-0 drubbing.

Fergie had seen his team amass a maximum 21 points from their last seven games, compared to 13 for Liverpool. The last time United dropped points was in the 0-0 draw at Tottenham on 13 December. The last time they had conceded a goal in the Premier League was the previous year: in the 2-1 defeat at Arsenal on 8 November 2008. And the 5-0 win also meant United kept a clean sheet for an 11th successive Premier League match – a new record. It also led to another record for Edwin van der Sar had not conceded a goal for 1,032 minutes, beating Chelsea keeper Petr Cech's previous best of 1,025 minutes.

Fergie heaped fulsome praise on his defence for those 11 consecutive clean sheets record: 'I am proud of them – they have been fantastic in this run. Edwin van der Sar has had a fantastic career, but he was really pleased to get this record. You look at him and what happened has really thrilled him.

'The scoreline was important. We showed a ruthless streak about us, possibly for the first time this season. It has been a long time coming and we needed it because I think goal difference could play a part. It is a satisfying result in that respect.'

Van der Sar broke the record, having kept West Brom at bay for 84 minutes. After collecting the match ball, he said: 'The most important thing is the win, but of course it is great for the team to get the record. I just needed to keep the concentration levels high and fire up the defenders and midfielders. We are delighted with the record because we haven't even had a settled defence, with players injured and others coming in and out.'

Four days after they thrashed Albion, United chalked up a 12th league shutout in the 1-0 win over Everton at Old Trafford. Van der Sar then went on to claim the British record for clean sheets when the Reds won 1-0 at West Ham on 8 February 2009.

The big Dutchman overwhelmed the achievement of Bobby Clark, a former Scotland international, who went 1,155 minutes without conceding between the Aberdeen posts in the 1970/71 Scottish First Division season. Ironically, Clark would also play a part in the Dons side managed by Sir Alex that would win the Scottish First Division in 1980. Van der Sar had beaten his record after walking away from East London with his goal not breached for 1,212 minutes.

Clark told *The Times* that Fergie's United side of 2008/09 were a masterclass defensively. He said: 'I love watching him [Van der Sar]. He does so many things very well, but he's got two very good centre-backs in front of him as well. It was the same back in 1971 – Martin Buchan was in the middle of the defence alongside a big lad, Tommy McMillan.'

Thirteen days later, United would finally concede in a Premier League match in the 2-1 win over Blackburn at Old Trafford, but Van der Sar could hardly be blamed. He missed the game through injury, with Tomasz Kuszczak deputising.

Two weeks later, United conceded another goal and now it was finally the end of a remarkable record for Van der Sar as Newcastle scored at St James' Park on 4 March. Edwin was at fault for the goal – fumbling a shot from Jonás Gutiérrez and setting up Peter Lovenkrands. The consolation was that United still went on to win 2-1, with Rooney and Berbatov finding the net, and the victory established a seven-point lead at the top of the table. The result also meant United had made it 11 victories out of 11.

But the boss was not interested in apportioning any blame for the soft goal – and who could blame him after his keeper had taken United to such an incredible run of results? Fergie conceded: 'It wasn't a great performance – we got off to a terrible start and Newcastle were pumped up for it. We expected that and we should have dealt with it better, but coming from 1-0 down was a good result for us. It required a lot of grit.

'Edwin says himself he made a mess of it and they had a couple of near things after that. It was going to happen some time and it is out of the road now.'

Plus, Fergie was already on a high after lifting his second trophy of the season, just three days before the goalless record ran out at St James' Park. Yes, he held aloft the League Cup – or as it is more commonly known nowadays, the Carling Cup – just a couple of months after bringing home the World Club Championship from Japan.

The Carling Cup triumph came on the first day of March 2009 as United finally ground down a gritty Spurs team at Wembley, although it would take penalties to do so. When the match fizzled out to a 0-0 draw after 120 minutes, the Reds won 4-1 on penalties.

Fergie traditionally used this distinctly second-tier competition to blood youngsters, but it was a more experienced team than many had expected that started at Wembley. The line-up read: Foster, O'Shea, Ferdinand, Evans, Evra, Nani, Gibson, Scholes, Ronaldo, Welbeck and Tevez. It would also later be augmented with Vidic, Giggs and Anderson. In the end, reserve keeper Ben Foster would take the plaudits – thwarting Aaron Lennon in a one-on-one contest in normal time and saving Jamie O'Hara's penalty kick in the shoot-out. When David Bentley also missed from the spot and Anderson scored for United, the match was won. Giggs, Tevez and Ronaldo also scored from the spot for the Red Devils, with only Vedran Corluka doing so for holders Spurs.

Defeated Spurs' boss Harry Redknapp said he could envisage United now going on to win a unique quintuple: 'They have got a big chance – they are the team to beat. They have a fantastic squad, it looks as if the League is going their way and you wouldn't bet against them in the Champions League and the FA Cup.'

Fergie was quick to play down such talk, however. He tried to keep his squad's feet on the ground by saying: 'I'm certainly not getting carried away with it, only the media will. We will keep our feet on the ground. We could go to Fulham in the FA Cup, the ball comes off someone's backside and we are out of that one.'

But he was wrong about Fulham – the Reds drubbed them 4-0 in the FA Cup 6th round, although they would eventually crash out in the semi-finals, losing on penalties to Everton. Fergie remained on course for a Champions League and Premier League double, though: his team beat Inter Milan 2-0 in the Champions League last 16, 2nd leg tie, making it through to the last eight by the same scoreline.

After the win over Inter, coached by Fergie's old adversary

José Mourinho, the United boss said: 'When Vidic scored the first goal, I thought we'd kill them off. I thought we could score a few goals but then we started doing flicks and back heels. We can play better than that, but I am happy to get through it.'

But then United suffered a temporary blip of form, crashing 4-1 at home to Liverpool in a disastrous match that also saw Nemanja Vidic sent off. Just days later, they lost again, 2-0 away at Fulham. The Fulham loss left Fergie angry and perplexed – at the referee! United had gone down to goals from Danny Murphy (from the penalty spot after Scholes stopped a Bobby Zamora shot with his hands) and Zoltan Gera. Scholes was red carded for his indiscretion and Rooney joined him three minutes from time when he earned a second yellow card for throwing the ball aggressively.

Afterwards Fergie rapped: 'Did Rooney throw the ball at the referee? The ball was thrown direct to where the free-kick was taken and did it hit the referee? No, the ball didn't hit the referee. Was it thrown in anger? Yes, because he wanted the game hurried up, he threw with pace to get the game going.'

But he cooled down sufficiently to say that he felt his boys still had enough in the tank to bring home the title for that third consecutive occasion, adding: 'I was disappointed with the first half – we didn't get started at all and that cost us the game. In the second half they responded to the half-time talk and we were unlucky not to get something out of it. If we'd have got the goal, we could even have won it. If you lose games in March and April then it can cost you, but fortunately we have a little slender lead at the moment.'

The boss would now direct operations and lead his team to the title as they went unbeaten in the remaining eight League games. Liverpool, to their credit, kept up the chase up until the penultimate fixture. But when United drew 0-0 with Arsenal at

Old Trafford on 16 May, the race was over. With a game to spare, Fergie and his men had made it.

The boss was delighted with his 11th Premier League crown – and that he had now equalled Liverpool's record of 18 top-flight title wins. But as usual, he was thinking ahead, planning ahead, dreaming ahead, even as he held the trophy aloft. He said: 'The great challenge now is to try to win it next year because that would be something special. A 19th league title would give us a special place in the club's history.'

First, he had another ambition to achieve, though. A week after lifting the title, United won 1-0 at Hull in the Premier League to wrap up their domestic campaign for 08/09. However, there was no time for relaxation and celebration: three days later, the boss would be heading for Rome and a showdown with Barcelona in the Champions League final.

It was time for him to tackle the holy grail of winning a third European Cup for his beloved United, but he would have to do it against the odds, against a team many critics dubbed the Finest of the Decade. United would play Barcelona – and the man those same critics had already labelled the Best Player in the World, Lionel Messi.

But before we examine Fergie's Roman mission, let's conclude our look at the 2008/09 season with United's trip to Japan – and remind ourselves just how they became World Champions.

CHAPTER 15

WORLD
BEATER

Many in English football had scoffed and poured disdain on FIFA's attempts to establish a 'World Cup for club football' in 2000 – they said it had no meaning, was a sideshow of an irrelevance and that winning meant absolutely nothing. Predictably, given his love of contrariness, Sir Alex Ferguson was not among those cynics.

For him, the World Club Cup was worthwhile and full of prestige and when United got the chance to compete in it after winning the 2008 European Champions League, he was determined not only would they do so, but they would win it, too. For Fergie, a win would make United champions of England, champions of Europe... and champions of the world.

There was another element, perhaps: as a player, the boss had never even won a cap for his native Scotland – indeed, his only sprinkling of stardust at international level came in the summer of 1986, when he had managed the Scottish national side at the World Cup after the tragic death of Jock Stein. And that had hardly been a qualified success as the Scots struggled to make an impact and exited the competition at the group stage. So there was probably some credence in the oft-mooted idea that Fergie took the World Club competitions so very seriously as a manager precisely because he himself had never tasted glory at international level, as a player or a manager. It was his chance to show that he could be a world beater – and he would do just that.

Such was his commitment to the tournament in 2008 that he even admitted he didn't mind if it meant his team stuttered a little in the Premier League after they had won it, as they tried to catch up with lost fixtures and play their way back into League action. He explained his feelings to the assembled press corps as United arrived in the Far East for the tournament in December 2008, saying: 'The nitty-gritty of this is that in 30 years, I hope people will look back in the record books and see "Manchester United: World Champions" – that is what this football club is about, and that is why it is important for us to win it. A trophy like that adds prestige to a club.

'Playing different opposition does not do us any harm, either, so that is exciting, but our biggest incentive for being here is that this is the World Championship. We cannot win the Premier League in December, but we can become World Champions so our aim is to do that first and the rest maybe later.

'Yes, there is a bit of a handicap coming here while the League is going on, but that is what happens when you are successful. We're here because we won the European Cup and as far as I am concerned, without any question the benefits of being here outweigh what is happening in the Premier League.'

That December, he would achieve his aim when United came home from Japan with the FIFA World Club Cup.

And when you look at his stance from a United history point of view, you can see that the boss was doing the right thing: his attitude was spot-on. After all, he was only following the blueprint set out by Matt Busby, many decades earlier.

Sir Matt was the pioneer who had insisted that England should not miss out when the idea was mooted of teams playing each other throughout the Continent. In 1956, he took United into the European Cup, much against the advice and wishes of most senior footballing figures within the British game. In September of that year, United's first competitive European encounter had taken them to Anderlecht – a first-round first-leg European Cup tie, which the English club won 2-0, a month before a certain Bobby Charlton made his first-team debut.

Even now Sir Bobby remains convinced Busby's insistence that United and English clubs should play in Europe is one of his greatest legacies for the club, as well as football in general. Charlton said: 'It was a great adventure back then, an exciting time. Having to go to places you had never been before, having to alter the food you took, the medical side, everything – nothing was available as it is now but that didn't matter.

'People forget, we played our first few "home" matches at Maine Road, and you ask anybody who was there, the floodlights weren't great. We had to play in silky shirts so that what little light there was would reflect off them. It was still a great, great time and if you are a big club, like we always assumed we were, the place you had to be was in Europe and beating those teams. We all thought the English game was good, but you can't measure yourself properly until you have played the very best.'

And that's just the way Sir Alex saw it when he contemplated United's involvement in the World Club Cup. Rather than being cynical and dismissive, much to his credit he was visionary and welcoming.

Of course, the competition was hardly a new idea although it certainly had much more backing and weight behind it than previous shadowy incarnations. Nine years earlier, Fergie had won it in its first incarnation – when it was a one-off match rather than a mini-tournament and was known as the Toyota Cup.

Previous to that, it was called the Intercontinental Cup – and once again, Busby had been a cheerleader for British clubs to take part. In 1968, after winning the European Cup for the first time, he and United were invited to take part in the Intercontinental Cup, which pitched the champions of Europe against the champions of South America.

George Best and United had battled gamely ('battle' being the operative word) to bring the trophy home. Like Fergie, Best had also been desperate to be crowned a World Champion, albeit at club level – but it was not to be. United came up against a cynical team called Estudiantes, from Argentina, and they were kicked off the park, taunted and the victims of dreadful tackling and provocation. United would lose the first leg 1-0 at Boca Juniors Stadium, going down to Marcos Conigliaro's 27th-minute header. Nobby Stiles was sent off for dissent, but it would be Best's dismissal in the return at Old Trafford that would hog the headlines.

United would draw 1-1, thus losing the match 2-1 on aggregate, after George was sent off when the provocation proved too much for him too handle. Indeed, both sides finished a man short as both George and José Hugo Medina were shown the red card for fighting. Estudiantes had scored first through Juan Ramon Veron and Willie Morgan's last-minute equaliser was not enough to save United. Ironically, Veron was the father of Juan Sebastian Veron, who would join United as their then most expensive signing at £28.1 million in July 2001.

The next time United would get the chance to play in the event was 31 years later, after that terrific night in Barcelona. Fergie, like Busby, was all for the Reds taking part – and he would get one over Matt, as already mentioned: by winning the

Toyota Cup, as it was now known. Roy Keane grabbed the winner as the Red Devils overcame Brazil's Palmeiras in Tokyo.

Victory meant United became the first British team to win the coveted trophy. Their team that day read:

1 Mark Bosnich, 2 Gary Neville, 6 Jaap Stam, 27 Mikael Silvestre, 3 Denis Irwin, 7 David Beckham, 16 Roy Keane, 18 Paul Scholes (10 Teddy Sheringham), 8 Nicky Butt, 20 Ole Gunnar Solskjaer (19 Dwight Yorke), 11 Ryan Giggs.

Some line-up – formidable, tough and yet full of talent and ability: apart from Mark Bosnich (in goal for the now-retired Peter Schmeichel), easily a stronger line-up than the one that had secured United's second European Cup triumph in Barcelona, six months earlier, with the return of Keane and Scholes.

The winning goal in Tokyo had come on 35 minutes after Giggs set off on one of his trademark runs, leaving Junior Baiano for dead and driving in a cross that Keane tapped in for the easiest of goals.

Giggs, who won a Toyota car after being voted Man of the Match, admitted he had been surprised to lift the trophy. He revealed that he had never expected his cross to beat keeper Marcos and find Keano for the winner. 'The balls have been flying about in training and they definitely seem to be a lot lighter,' he said. 'I didn't know if it would beat the goalkeeper when I first crossed it and I thought he would reach it, so I was surprised when it went over him and Keano got on the end of it.'

Even in 1999, Fergie was ecstatic that he and his team had made footballing history: 'We wanted really badly to win the World Championship. We wanted to win firstly, because no British team had won it and secondly, because it makes us World Champions -- and we are proud of that.' In typical

Fergie mode, he also said it was vital they build on the Toyota Cup triumph to win the Champions League again: 'I'm very pleased to win the World Championship and to become the first English team to win it. The World Championship is very special and I'm very proud of what my players have done, but you've got to win the European Cup firstly to get here and no matter how you place this, the European Cup is always going to be the golden goose for us. It got us here tonight by winning it and we've come here and won again, which makes us very proud.'

And the boss of the Brazilians would also pay a nice tribute to his counterpart. The man rapidly becoming known as 'Big Phil' – yes, Luiz Felipe Scolari, who would go on to manage Brazil, Portugal and Chelsea – was full of admiration for Ferguson and the team he had built. Big Phil, who had also lost the Toyota Cup with Gremio in 1995, declared: 'We gave our all, but we learnt once again that Manchester United are a great and a tough team, who can fight. I would like to congratulate Alex Ferguson and Manchester United – he is a great leader and a great coach. Maybe it will be my turn next time!'

Fergie and United would not have to wait long for their turn. By now the competition had morphed into the prototype of the current tournament and would be known as the Club World Championship. From its inception in 2000 until 2006, it would run under that banner when it finally took on the moniker, World Club Cup.

Of course, United would, controversially, miss out on the FA Cup in 2000 to concentrate their energies on the competition which took place in Brazil – and what a disaster it would prove. Having pulled out of the FA Cup, they performed poorly in Brazil and made fools of themselves with some abject PR. The tournament featured eight teams – United, Real Madrid,

Necaxa, Corinthians, Vasco de Gama, South Melbourne, Al-Nassr and Raja Casablanca, with a group stage, a final and a third- and fourth-place play-off. United finished third in their group, just above minnows South Melbourne but below Necaxa and group winners, Vasco.

As his team slouched home in disarray Fergie was typically defiant, saying: 'It's been fantastic here – what a chance for us to come out and get some sun! Back home, we would have been freezing our toes off.'

Privately, though, I am told he was fuming that his team had performed so poorly on such a world stage. It would be eight years before he had a chance to put things right, in what was now known as the World Club Cup, after United's win over Chelsea in the Champions League final in May 2008 set them up to take part.

The event was now permanently staged in Japan over a 10-day period and United had been told they would enter at the semi-final stage – along with South American champions, Liga de Quito. The two teams were the top seeds as the Ecuadorians had won the South American version of the Champions League, the Copa Libertadores.

On Sunday, 14 December, the day after the 0-0 Premier League draw at Spurs, United headed out to Japan. Fergie's squad indicated just how seriously the manager was taking the event:

Goalkeepers: Van der Sar, Kuszczak and Foster
Defenders: Neville, Evra, Ferdinand, Vidic, O'Shea, Evans and Rafael
Midfielders: Ronaldo, Anderson, Giggs, Park, Carrick, Nani, Scholes, Fletcher and Gibson
Strikers: Berbatov, Rooney, Tevez and Welbeck.

With all the top men making the journey out to the Far East, it was full-strength.

The boss was happy that United would enter the competition at the last four stage in Yokohama on Thursday, 18 December – and that their opponents would be Japanese outfit Gamba Osaka. The final, if they made it, would be three days later at the Yokahama Stadium, the venue that had staged the 2002 World Cup final between eventual winners Brazil and runners-up Germany.

At 4pm on the Monday, United touched down in Japan at Tokyo's Narita airport – and Sir Alex got straight down to business. Hours after the boys had booked into their hotel, he had them out training! But he also allowed the squad to do a tour of the sights and some shopping over the next couple of days, although he stressed that United were there essentially on business, not as idling tourists, and he would ensure the boys were involved in two more training sessions before the semi-final clash.

Gamba had won the Asian Champions League and had beaten Adelaide United in Sunday's quarter-final to earn the right to meet United. In a 5-3 defeat, they put on a spirited display to score three times.

Wayne Rooney was the big name missing from the starting line-up – he had suffered a knock in training – but the team Fergie put out was a strong one: Van der Sar, Neville, Ferdinand, Vidic, Evra, Nani, Anderson, Scholes, Giggs, Ronaldo and Tevez. Rooney was on the bench, along with Michael Carrick and Darren Fletcher, among others.

By the Friday morning United were preparing for the final, but also the Premier League match against Stoke that would follow it the following Friday. Fergie may have been keen to show he was committed to the World Club Cup, but he was also a pragmatist. He knew United would face a battering when they returned to the English cold and Stoke's dogs of war and so he implemented a brilliant plan that saw his players preparing for two matches at once. From 9am that Friday morning in Japan, players, management and staff started to switch back to UK time to be in sync for the return to England and the build-up to the Stoke match at the Britannia Stadium on Boxing Day.

Tokyo was eight hours ahead of Manchester, so although it was 9am there, it was 1am in United's world. For the next three days, the players would experience a slightly surreal lifestyle. They would have their breakfast at 4pm, Tokyo time (the equivalent of 8am), lunch at 9pm, Tokyo time (1pm in England) – and dinner at 3am in Tokyo (7pm back in England). Finally, they would retire to their rooms for a good night's sleep at 7am in Tokyo, the equivalent of 11pm in England.

This cycle was repeated on Saturday and Sunday, which meant that when they arrived back in England on the Monday, they were fresh and alert, their bodies in tune with local Manchester time. All this was possible because the club had their own chef travelling with them, as well as a nutritionist and a medical adviser.

The final kicked off at 6.30pm local time in Japan (10.30am, GMT), so Rooney and the boys would not have to play in the middle of the night in their own peculiar time zone. To stave off hunger pangs, United's nutritionists supplied them with energy bars and drinks.

And the gamble paid off. United beat Liga de Quito 1-0 in the final to lift the World Club Cup trophy, thanks to a late winner from the brilliant Rooney.

The only downside was the sending-off of Vidic four minutes after the break for elbowing striker Claudio Bieler. This would lead to him being banned from the first leg of United's next Champions League match, the tough last-16 clash with Inter Milan.

With a fine shot, low into the net after 75 minutes, Rooney won the game. United became the first English club to win the event in its revamped format: they were now champions of England, champions of Europe and champions of the world, just as Fergie had dreamed.

The boss said: 'The sending-off made it difficult for us – it's a soft sending-off, but he swung an elbow. When you do that in front of the referee you've got no chance; he gave the referee no option.

'Half an hour to go is a long road with 10 men, but Wayne scored a magnificent goal. After Vidic was sent off it was important that we didn't lose the ball. It was important to keep passing and hope Ronaldo or Rooney did something special. The collective spirit of the team won the day. With 10 men we played with great expression and tried to win. It is a measure of the players' ambition.

'In 30 years, you'll look back and see Manchester United's name on the trophy, although I won't be around to enjoy it.'

He allowed his team a celebratory glass or two of wine with their meal, but that was it. OK, another honour might be heading for the Old Trafford trophy cupboard, but there was still some serious business to deal with in the Premier League. Onwards and upwards, as Sir Alex liked to say, with the Premier League and Stoke's Britannia Stadium the next pit stop on an incredible journey of unrelenting glory. As already noted in the previous chapter, Fergie would now go on to bring home an unprecedented third Premier League crown on the trot – but what of the Champions League final against Barca at the end of the 2008/09 season?

Let's head to Rome to complete the picture and assess just what went right and what went wrong as Fergie attempted to bring home his third European Cup to Old Trafford.

1999: the most successful year of Sir Alex's career to date. Manchester United notched up an incredible Treble of Premier League, FA Cup and Champions League trophies before Fergie received a Knighthood for his services to football.

Above left: Sir Alex at his testimonial match in 1999.

Above right and below: Celebrating his and United's sixth Premier League title in 2000 – meaning United were Champions for the third year running.

Above: Signing autographs for young fans at Old Trafford.

Below: At Ascot in 2003 – Sir Alex is a big fan of horse racing and owns several racehorses.

Above left: The years following United's title hat-trick were tough, with Sir Alex scheduling his retirement for the end of the 2002 season, but to the delight of United fans everywhere he changed his mind and agreed to stay at Old Trafford.

Above right: Sir Alex salutes the crowd after United's 4-0 win over Millwall in the 2004 FA Cup final.

Below: United fans worldwide are in dreamland again as the team clinch the Champions League trophy after a nail-biting penalty shoot-out against Chelsea in 2008.

Sir Alex proudly shows off the Champions League trophy as the team returns from Moscow in 2008. It was Fergie's second Champions League victory and Manchester United's third, having also won the European Cup in 1968.

Above left: Sir Alex with Cristiano Ronaldo. Although the player would become a hate figure for many England fans following the 2006 World Cup, he was instrumental in securing United's 11th Premier League title in 2009.

Above right: Applauding his players after victory over Arsenal in the 2009 Champions League semi-final second leg.

Below: Fergie looks relaxed as United prepare for their second Champions League final in a row, against Barcelona in Rome.

Above: Sadly things didn't go to plan in Rome, as Barcelona won the 2009 Champions League final 2-0. Here, Sir Alex is pictured receiving his runner's-up medal from UEFA president Michel Platini.

Below: Joking on the training ground with star player Wayne Rooney.

After an incredible 26 years at United, Sir Alex finally announced his retirement on 8 May 2013. Just a few days later, the team paraded their 13th Premier League trophy – a 20th League title overall – in front of thousands of fans who lined the streets of Manchester.

CHAPTER 16

ROMAN RUINS

The aim was daunting, but typical of Fergie and United: just weeks after winning the Champions League final against Chelsea, the boss sat his men down for pre-season training and told them he now wanted them to notch what would be another remarkable first in the annals of the Old Trafford giants.

You've guessed it – he told them that he would love it for them to become the first team, and for him to become the first manager ever to retain the Champions League – and that he believed they could do it. True, AC Milan had won the old-style European Cup in the 1989/90 and 1990/91 seasons, but no team had cracked it since the Champions League format was introduced in 1992.

After collecting his 11th Premier League title crown at the start of May 2009, the boss might have been forgiven for thinking his team would make his European dream come true when the day of the final in Rome dawned on the 27th of the month.

The omens were good: his men were clearly in fine fettle (as their League title win showed) and victory for United meant they would have achieved a magnificent 'quadruple' – as they had already put the World Club Cup and the Carling Cup in the trophy cabinet, along with the Premier League.

Another omen the Reds hoped would be lucky was that they would be wearing their white away kit in the final – the same colour worn when they triumphed in the 1991 European Cup Winners' Cup final in Rotterdam. And on the day before the final, in what appeared yet another sign of good hope, it was announced that Sir Alex had scooped one more honour: his ninth Manager of the Year award. The boss was delighted with the accolade and dedicated it to his backroom staff and players who, he was quick to point out, were just as much responsible for United having won their third successive Premier League title. He insisted: 'It is a great honour and a great reflection on the work of everyone at the club.'

Meanwhile, he had more pressing matters to deal with, like ensuring he did everything he possibly could to retain the Champions League the following night in Rome. He knew it wouldn't be easy: Barcelona, along with United, were the best in Europe, but it was about time the Reds were bracketed with European greats of bygone eras – the likes of AC Milan and Real Madrid, who had won the trophy many times.

Before the match he said: 'This is an opportunity for us to be put alongside a lot of the great teams of Europe. If you look back, sides like Ajax, AC Milan and Bayern Munich regularly won it on consecutive seasons. There have been a lot of unlucky teams in world football, but when you look at the pantheon of great teams you need to have won the European Cup to have that tag. There is no question about that, it has always been that way. Teams like Manchester United and Barcelona have to win the trophy to be regarded in that respect.

'It is unusual that no one has done it since the Champions League started, but we are good at doing things first and this is our opportunity. Great teams used to do it, but not now. We have an opportunity and hopefully it is something we can tick off.

'There are times we should have done better in Europe. This particular team has that type of future and the experience to do well over the next few years – and hopefully, on Wednesday we can endorse that.'

Fergie's most experienced campaigner, the evergreen Giggsy, was just as keen to carve out the niche in history his boss was demanding – and he too felt they could do it. Giggsy said: 'I have played in some really good teams. In 1999 it was obviously the Treble side, while the 1994 team sometimes seemed unbeatable, but this season we have won the League for a third successive time and I think if we win the Champions League as well, you will not get very many people arguing against it being rated as the best-ever United side.

'Nobody has ever defended the Champions League. To accept that challenge and succeed would, on its own, be brilliant. But to have won a hat-trick of leagues as well, you have to talk in terms of this being the best team the club have had.

'It is hard work winning the Champions League. Mentally and physically, it is draining – it is about going again and having the desire and hunger to do it all again. This season there has been the same desire at the club because we recognised that nobody has defended it and the players look for those challenges. Everybody wants to beat the champions, whether it is the League or Champions League, that is why it is so difficult to retain.'

United had progressed to the final after beating Porto in the quarter-finals (3-2 on aggregate) and Arsenal in the semis (4-1 on aggregate). The Porto two-legger had seen United jittery in the first-leg, which ended 2-2, but commanding in the away leg – which they won, thanks to a Ronaldo wonder goal.

United, as holders, were the scalp every club wanted – none more so than Arsenal, who awaited them in the semis after they had finally put Porto to bed.

In the first leg at Old Trafford on 29 April United squeezed home with a 1-0 win, courtesy of John O'Shea's 18th-minute goal, a close-range strike. Ronaldo hit the bar with a brilliant shot after the interval and Gunners keeper Manuel Almunia was the Man of the Match.

Even though they had lost the first leg Arsenal were on something of a high. At 1-0, they felt that they had escaped lightly; that their turn to show their mettle in London would come. Sir Alex agreed they should have suffered a bigger beating, but warned United would score in the return: 'We played at a good high tempo and maybe we should have scored four goals, but before the game I wanted to win without losing a goal. We know we can go there and score, and that is the big problem Arsenal have.'

Indeed, it was – as Arsenal shipped another three goals and could only reply with a single effort.

Robin van Persie made the scoreline respectable for the Gunners when he hit the net on 75 minutes, but it was in controversial circumstances. He netted from the penalty spot after Darren Fletcher was wrongly sent off for bringing down Cesc Fabregas. TV replays showed the Scotland skipper had won the ball fairly. That he would now miss out on the Champions League final against Barcelona was a travesty.

Meanwhile, in the Arsenal camp there was equal disappointment that they had fluffed their big chance. Boss Arsène Wenger called it 'the most disappointing night of my career' and added: 'I felt the fans were really up for a big night and to disappoint people who stand behind the team so much hurts.'

The Frenchman went on to add: 'The most difficult thing is that we do not have a feeling that we played a semi-final of the Champions League.'

A telling comment and a prophetic one, if you applied it to United and their own destiny in the final of the competition, a month later. For just as Wenger had said the Gunners had not shown up for the semi against United, so the Red Devils did not show – apart from a rousing opening 10 minutes – against Barcelona in Rome.

So, what went wrong? My view, and one shared by some of the United players, was that the team froze after a cracking 10-minute opening. Like Ivan Drago in the movie *Rocky IV*, they were thinking they were unbeatable and immortal until they got cut. When Rocky caused Drago to bleed, the big Russian looked stunned and began to lose his nerve. Similarly, when Samuel Eto'o turned Nemanja Vidic to fire Barca ahead on 10 minutes United fell to pieces: they bought into the nonsense that Barca were unbeatable and almost looked on in awe for the remaining 80 minutes, allowing them to run wild and dictate the game.

Which was a mighty pity for as Chelsea would tell you, Barca are far from invincible, as the Blues showed by outscheming them over two legs in the semi-final. The Stamford Bridge boys should have progressed, no doubt about it: they outfought and outthought Barca and would have made the final but for weak finishing by Drogba and the dismal refereeing of Norwegian Tom Henning Ovrebo, who denied them two blatant penalties.

After the first goal United just didn't turn up and it was an incredibly disappointed Giggs who would lead them up for their losers' medals after Lionel Messi confirmed Barca's victory as he rose above Ferdinand to head home after 70 minutes.

On a humid night in the Eternal City it had been a collective loss of form and nerve. And with no solid midfield to battle against the wondrous Andreas Iniesta and Xavi, United's backline would always be in for a busy night at the office. Afterwards, a demoralised skipper-on-the-night Giggsy admitted that had been the case: 'At times Barcelona can make you look silly because they keep the ball so well. At times we maybe chased it and didn't keep our shape as well as we should have, but still, we created chances – and probably more chances than Barcelona.

'We said whoever turned up on the night would win and that proved to be the case. They turned up and played some great football – we didn't, really. I think if we had gone a goal ahead, we're capable of keeping the ball like they are – but credit to them, they deserved it.'

Sir Alex was just as gutted as his on-field general, but collected a loser's medal with dignity and encouraged his men to do the same. He also stood up and admitted United had been outplayed, saying: 'I think the first goal was a killer for us, it was their first attack and they scored. We had started brightly but we got a bit nervous after that, and of course with a goal lead, they could keep the ball all night.

'In fairness we were beaten by a better team. We weren't at our best – after the first goal it was very difficult for us. They defended quite well, actually – we thought we could get at their back four better than we did. Losing is the best part of the game because in adversity you always move forwards quicker.

'Of course we are disappointed, but we've done well: it's been a long season, we've had 66 games, and you've got to give the players credit for their courage and resilience. Next season we'll be better.'

He also paid tribute to Messi and the midfield partnership of Xavi and Iniesta, but pointed out that United had been without their own key midfielder, Darren Fletcher, because of suspension. 'He is a big-game player,' said the boss. 'It was a loss, but they had losses also, and it is difficult to measure how big a loss it was. The disappointment was the use of the ball when we got possession. You have to wait minutes to get it back off them. Could be it was an off night, could be it was a mountain too big to climb.'

His vice-captain Rio Ferdinand voiced similar sentiments: 'We have played better 99 per cent of the time this season, but saying that we created four or five good opportunities to score, but they scored two goals at crucial times and two bad goals on our part.

'We have no arguments: they were the better team on the day – you have got to do it on the day. If we played better or played to our strengths it would have been a different game but if you don't do it on the day, you don't deserve to win.'

Disappointed and down, United headed home to Manchester. It was a measure of how far Sir Alex had brought the club during his then 23-year tenure that heads were hung so low after a campaign that had brought three trophies to Old Trafford: the Premier League, the Carling Cup and the World Club Championship. The boss jetted off for his traditional holiday in the South of France determined he and his team would use the experience to return stronger the next season.

However, he knew something the fans and the majority of his employees did not: that he was about to lose his best player. On 11 June, just a fortnight after the defeat in Rome, United posted a brief, but devastating news item on their official website: www.manutd.com. It revealed the news many supporters had been dreading: 'Manchester United have received a world-record, unconditional offer of £80 million for Cristiano Ronaldo from Real Madrid. At the request of Cristiano – who has again expressed his desire to leave – and after discussion with t he player's representatives, United have agreed to give Real Madrid permission to talk to the player. Matters are expected to be concluded by 30 June. The club will not comment until further notice.'

It was a body blow: just how could United step up a gear if their best player was gone? Who was Fergie planning to buy with the world record £80 million fee that Real were prepared to pay for the Portuguese genius? Did the boss really believe he and his team could improve without the best player in the world?

Well, yes, it seemed he did because he already had at the club the young man who was now ready to step up to the plate and challenge Ronaldo for that accolade. Wayne Rooney was to become the main man at the Theatre of Dreams, but did he have enough quality to take United back to the European summit or would the Reds now go through another soul-destroying period of transition, similar to 2003/05? There were many questions, but only one man had the answers.

First, Fergie was determined to enjoy his summer vacation. He would then return with his batteries recharged, his ambitions and demands of his players as lofty as ever.

CHAPTER 17

RETIREMENT, EH? BLOODY HELL!

When Liverpool lost at home to Chelsea on 1 May 2010, many United fans blamed their old enemy Steven Gerrard for costing the Red Devils the title. Had the self-styled 'Stevie G' not set Carlo Ancelotti's men on the road to a 2-0 win with his terrible back pass (eagerly gobbled up and despatched by Didier Drogba for the first goal), they argued, the Kop boys could have clung on and held the Blues to the draw that would have put United in the title driving seat.

A draw would have meant United would have been top of the pile on 82 points to Chelsea's 81, going into the final match of the season. From that position, United would certainly have been expected to see off Stoke at home, a result that would have rendered a Chelsea win over Wigan irrelevant.

Yet laying the blame at Gerrard's door was all too simplistic, even if it did provide a more than acceptable bogeyman in the eyes of United fans. OK, Gerrard hates United – indeed, he once said: 'Growing up in Huyton, I was taught to loathe United, their fans, players, manager, kit-man, mascot... everyone associated with Old Trafford.'

And, yes, Fergie did make a big thing of the blunder, saying: 'I just saw it after the game. It was a great gift. There is nothing you can do about it – you just have to get on with it.'

But no, Gerrard was not the culprit – and no, he did not mess up deliberately to thwart United in their bid for that record 19th championship crown (one that would have put them clear of Liverpool in the all-time record stakes). The Liverpool skipper was visibly shocked that he had been caught out with a poor pass, but let's not forget his past. In Euro 2004, a similar back-pass from him gifted the match to France. And in the 2005/06 season his back-pass at Highbury resulted in an easy goal for Thierry Henry.

In fact, the real reasons for Fergie's title woe in May 2010 were twofold: his problems in attack and defence. The boss never effectively replaced Cristiano Ronaldo and subsequently suffered injuries to key defensive stalwarts at key times, with centre-halves Vidic and Ferdinand missing. United's success of the previous two seasons had been built around the goals of Ronaldo and the rock-steady partnership of Rio and Nemanja so you didn't need to be a rocket scientist to work out that without the three in tandem, United would not be so effective.

Yet there was one consolation for those United fans still determined to blame Gerrard for the title loss: it meant that Fergie would definitely stay on for another season.

My sources at Old Trafford told me that, yes, the manager was giving serious thought to quitting in May 2010 if he had won the record-breaking 19th crown. Sure, in public, he had declared he had no plans to leave and hoped to continue in the hot seat for years to come.

Towards the end of April 2010, stories had been emerging in the press claiming Fergie would leave his job the following May (2011), with José Mourinho lined up as his successor. The boss laughed it off, saying: 'It is rubbish! There is no truth in it – I have no intention of retiring and if I did, the people I would tell are [chief executive] David Gill and the Glazer family.'

My source told me: 'Well, he would say that, wouldn't he? Of course, there is truth in it – many people behind the scenes had been whispering that he would probably do one more season and then we would go for Fabio Capello or Louis Van Gaal to steady the ship. He wouldn't announce it a year in advance, would he? When he flirted with retiring in 2002, he announced it 12 months in advance and United struggled. It rocked the boat, causing uncertainty among the players and staff.

'But there were also strong indications that the boss might even have gone this year [2010] if he got that 19th title. Everyone thinks he is obsessed with the Champions League but that is not altogether the case – you've got to remember that his main ambition has always been to supplant Liverpool at the top of the tree and that 19th title has always been his No. 1 motivation.'

So, there you have it: the great man had even contemplated going in 2010, had United pipped Chelsea at the post, rather than the other way round. Maybe those United fans discontented with Gerrard should actually have been thanking him! While the Gerrard backpass proved costly, indirectly it also had a positive effect. Losing out to Chelsea for the title had perhaps persuaded Fergie that he definitely needed to stick around for at least another season, if only to try to clinch that 19th title.

Another surprise was that my insider at United talked of Capello and Bayern's Van Gaal as being the men 'to steady the ship'. What, no Mourinho? 'Of course, he's a winner,' I was told, 'but he's not everyone's cup of tea at United. His football is more functional than entertaining, and United have always liked to win with style. You've also got to remember that Sir Bobby once said in public he had reservations about José – and that Van Gaal was on the shortlist of two with Eriksson to take over, when Sir Alex said he was going to retire in 2002 before changing his mind.'

Sir Alex may have lost out to Chelsea at the last hurdle of the 2009/10 season, but was his 24th season in charge at the club a success otherwise? Well, he did achieve the basic goal he demands of himself and his staff – 'one trophy a season is a success' – by winning the Carling Cup again, but these days that trophy, as already noted, is only regarded as loose change by many inside Old Trafford (and at the other top four clubs). Within the much tougher terms and parameters he privately sets himself and his players, the season was a letdown for Fergie.

Second in the League, out of the Champions League at the quarter-final stage against a team they should have comfortably beaten and out of the FA Cup at the third round to League One Leeds, a side they should have crushed – it was a real letdown. The campaign began on a low note when United lost out to Chelsea in the Community Shield at Wembley on 8 August 2009. The match ended 2-2, with Nani and Rooney scoring for the Reds, but Chelsea triumphed 4-1 on penalties.

Nani was impressive for the Reds and he would build on that showing as the season progressed, becoming arguably the second star performer overall after jewel-in-the-crown Rooney. But he was to fall victim to the early-season injury jinx that was hitting United as he dislocated his shoulder in a clash with John Terry in the Wembley showcase. 'He's out for a while, the worry is that we couldn't put it back in place,' said a clearly anxious Fergie after the loss to Chelsea.

United were already without keeper Van der Sar for two months after he needed surgery on a broken finger and bone in his left hand. And Vidic was also out, with a calf injury. These were setbacks that Fergie could have done without as he tried to plot an early-season surge but he was to be thwarted again and again by injuries throughout the campaign.

Michael Owen had come on as a 74th-minute sub at Wembley, making his competitive debut after being signed up on a free during the close season. His arrival at the Theatre of Dreams was certainly a calculated gamble by the boss: Owen's injury record was woeful and many pundits believed he was past his sell-by (or buy-by) date. After his contract ran out at Newcastle, the striker joined the club at the start of July 2009.

The former Liverpool man showed enthusiasm for a new start by agreeing to a massive drop in wages, from the £115,000-a-week he earned at the Toon to a more modest £50,000-a-week at Old Trafford. Owen admitted he was keen to become a United player as the move would provide him with Champions League football and would hopefully allow him a stage to enhance his chances of making Fabio Capello's England squad for the 2010 World Cup finals.

United legend Bryan Robson was confident Owen could do a job at United. He told the *Daily Telegraph*: 'Michael is a natural goal-scorer and natural goal-scorers who can do the business at the highest level are few and far between. I definitely think that he is capable of being a Champions League striker because he's only 29 and he still has plenty of good years left in him yet.'

Sir Alex also believed Owen could plug one of the gaps left in his forward line with the departure of Ronaldo and

Carlos Tevez. He said: 'Michael is a world-class forward with a proven goalscoring record at the highest level and that has never been in question. Coming to Manchester United with the expectations that we have is something that Michael will relish.'

And Owen himself displayed a boyish enthusiasm when quizzed over how he viewed his transfer. He revealed: 'I had just begun to talk to other clubs when out of the blue, Sir Alex phoned me and invited me to have breakfast with him the next morning, during which he told me that he wanted to sign me. I agreed without a moment's thought.

'This is a fantastic opportunity for me and I intend to seize it with both hands. I am now looking forward to being a Manchester United player and I am fortunate that I already know so many of the players here. I missed pre-season last year and am pleased that I will be starting at Carrington from day one.

'I want to thank Sir Alex for the faith he has shown in me and I give him my assurance that I will repay him with my goals and performances.'

Owen signed a two-year deal on a free transfer.

He had certainly fallen from the heights when he walked into Old Trafford. Just eight years earlier, he had been European Footballer of the Year after inspiring Liverpool to a cup treble of the FA Cup, League Cup and UEFA Cup in the 2000/01 season. In August 2004, he moved to Real Madrid and that was the beginning of his star waning as a nightmare run with injuries began, with Owen eventually ending up at Newcastle a year later.

Was he the answer to United's dilemma after the departure of Tevez and Ronaldo? United's fans were certainly not convinced. Lifelong supporter Steven Haywood told me at the time: 'He's too much of a gamble – he's had too many injuries and he's lost at least a yard of pace. You watch: he'll end up injured and be out for months.' Back in July 2009, those were prophetic words for Owen's season would end the following March when he suffered a hamstring problem. Yet he would score nine goals during the season, including two vital ones – the memorable Premier League injury-time winner over Manchester City at the end of September and the first goal in the Carling Cup final win over Aston Villa at Wembley, the match that brought the hamstring injury that would KO his campaign.

The *Guardian*'s Kevin McCarra succinctly summed up the importance of the Owen goal against City – and the player's overall impact thus far – when he wrote: 'The decider was claimed by the substitute Michael Owen, with an expert finish across the goalkeeper Shay Given after a pass from the superb Ryan Giggs.

'There has been debate over the signing of Owen, since it is hard to tell how he can be a regular starter, but this impact as a lethal specialist more than vindicated his involvement.'

The importance of Owen's goal against Villa at Wembley was simple: it put United back in it, it spurred them to victory, to what would be their one trophy that campaign, after the Midlanders had taken the lead. United had fallen behind through a James Milner penalty after five minutes when Gabriel Agbonalahor was fouled by Vidic. Owen levelled seven minutes later, easing the ball past Brad Friedel and setting United up for Rooney's winner, 16 minutes from time.

So, Owen did OK in his first season: given his injury problems, he should have effectively have been United's No. 4 striker after Rooney, Berbatov and one other. The only problem was that Fergie did not sign the one other who could step in to fill the breach brought about by the departure of Ronaldo and

Tevez. Instead, United had to rely on the burgeoning talent of young Italian Federico Macheda and, from December, new-boy Mame Biram Diouf.

Rooney, Berbatov, Owen, Macheda/Diouf… it hardly adds up to Yorke, Cole, Sheringham and Solskjaer.

Ronaldo, inevitably, had headed off to the Madrid sunshine at the end of the 2008/09 campaign. He had wanted to join the Spanish giants a year earlier, but I am reliably informed by my man on the inside at United that he was persuaded to stay – with the proviso that he would definitely make his dream move to his boyhood idols 12 months on.

He quit after the demoralising Champions League final defeat to Barcelona in Rome. Just a fortnight after the letdown, he was gone.

United were adamant Fergie had made the decision to allow the Portuguese to leave and told the BBC: 'It was purely a football decision and had nothing to do with the financial structure of the club.' But the fans were not so convinced – many believed the money would be used to finance the crippling debts the Glazer family had dropped on the club to buy it.

Their fears appeared to have foundation when the only incoming transfers at Old Trafford in the summer of 2009 were Owen and Antonio Valencia – a promising, though not fully developed winger from Wigan, who would cost £17 million.

The £80 million world-record transfer fee was some consolation for the loss of the man who was arguably the best player in the world at the time, but the likes of Lionel Messi, Karim Benzema or Franck Ribery would not be Ronaldo's replacement, much to the chagrin of the United fans who eyed the Glazers with deep mistrust.

Of course, it wasn't just the brilliant Ronaldo who United

had been lost from their forward line that summer: the ever-busy, ever-dynamic, ever-praiseworthy Carlos Tevez also quit the club. Along with Cristiano, the loss of the Argentine was a hammer blow for United, although Fergie would play down claims that Tevez's exit was anything like that and argue that Tevez was simply not worth the £25 million demanded by his 'rights owner', Kia Joorabchian.

The boss outlined his view in July 2009 when he told the press: 'We made contact with Carlos, I sent him texts and spoke to him when he was in Argentina. David Gill [United chief executive] made an offer to Kia Joorabchian, so I spoke to Carlos before the Inter Milan game [in the spring] and said that we had spoken to Kia.

'But we never heard back. In my opinion I didn't think he was worth £25 million – that's just my judgment, maybe I'm wrong. The fans quite rightly have their heroes, and I respect the fans, so I was happy to go along with a deal as long as it was the right deal. Our success is down to the fans and their support – we need them when we are away from home to the likes of Fulham and Arsenal – but simply he was not worth £25 million.'

As the season progressed, many fans would disagree with Fergie: they would much rather have seen the back of Berbatov than Tevez. While the Argentine regularly busted a gut for the club, Berbatov's languid – some would say lazy – contributions drove the supporters mad. For them, Berba may have had style, but his final product was lacking. And it showed in their final goals' tally at the end of the season: Berbatov scored just 12 goals for United, while Tevez scored 29 for Manchester City.

Former England boss Terry Venables summed up the general feeling of the United fans towards Tevez's exit, saying United had made few mistakes during Fergie's reign, but letting Tevez walk away was one of them. Venables said: 'None of us really know why the Argentine striker left for City in the summer. Was it that Fergie didn't fancy him? Didn't he have the money to pay Tevez's owners the £25 million they allegedly wanted for his services? Or was Tevez determined to leave because he believed he was not loved at Old Trafford? As I say, nobody really knows why. All we know is it now seems United made a big mistake.'

Fergie's comments on Ronaldo made at the same press conference show the stark difference in his views on the relative merits of the two men. While he felt Tevez was not worth the transfer fee, it was tough to say goodbye to Ronaldo: 'I had a good chat with the boy about it. He had made up his mind about it. Last year he was begging me and this year, it was a sensible discussion.

'I felt it was right. I told him I'd let him go on one condition and that was that we got the biggest fee ever for a player. And he said: "Right, that will do me."'

My sources say there is another side: that Tevez did not make it easy for Fergie to keep him; that he was angling for a move because he did not feel he was valued enough at Old Trafford. And of course, there was also the fact that he could earn much more money at Eastlands – he would earn £150,000 a week, £50k more than he got at United. I am also told the transfer fee City paid was a full £22 million more than United would have had to fork out. Yes, a cool £47 million! It would have been surprising had the Argentine not taken a small percentage of that for joining City.

So, big-time mercenary or a guy who just felt he wasn't loved enough? Probably a bit of both, but his departure was certainly Fergie's – and United's – loss.

At the end of the season, United would just fall short – it was too much to accommodate the departure of two world-class talents such as Tevez and Ronaldo, and not replace them with like-for-like genius, although Fergie would still go close to pulling off the miracle in the League, ending up just a point behind Chelsea.

But the striker left behind when Tevez and Ronaldo exited would be the man who took Fergie so close to pulling off mission impossible. Yes, Wayne Rooney, with his 35 goals, his United Player of the Year award, his PFA Player of the Year award, his FWA Player of the Year award and his Premier League Fans' Player of the Season, was Fergie's inspiration. After Ronaldo left, he stepped up to the plate to prove that he was now *the* man at United.

Fergie owed him big-time. OK, United weren't a one-man team, but how they struggled when Rooney was absent from duty. Fergie paid tribute to his top man when Rooney collected the FWA award shortly after winning the PFA gong. He said: 'It was a foregone conclusion. I thought he would win both awards and deservedly so because he has elevated himself to a tremendous level now.

'He has brought maturity and authority to his game. It usually starts to show itself when young players move into their mid-20s and that is the case with Wayne now.'

It was Rooney who got United off to a flier in the League when they beat Birmingham 1-0 at Old Trafford on 16 August. He was also on the scoresheet with a well-earned brace as United trounced Wigan 5-0 away, after the ignominy of the 1-0 loss at Burnley, three days earlier. As August merged into September, Rooney was at it again as United chalked up mighty impressive wins against Arsenal (2-1 at home) and Spurs (3-1 away). Wayne opened the scoring against the Gunners from the penalty spot and helped himself to the final goal at White Hart Lane.

By the end of 2009 United were lying second in the table, two points behind Chelsea. They had suffered a wobbly December, losing 1-0 at home to Aston Villa and 3-0 away at Fulham. That wobble would reach its climax three days into 2010 when they crashed out of the FA Cup 1-0 at home to old rivals Leeds United. Jermaine Beckford grabbed the goal for the League One outfit – it was the first time United had been knocked out in the third round and by a lower-division team in Fergie's 23-year reign as manager.

OK, the boss had made several changes from the team that had hammered Wigan 5-0 three days earlier, but Rooney and Berbatov were in the line-up and the Reds should have been able to sleepwalk their way through. Sir Alex, inevitably, was none too pleased by the abject surrender and I am told he lashed out at his men in the dressing room afterwards. He may have mellowed over the years, but he could still turn purple with rage if he felt he – and more importantly the loyal army of United fans – were being short-changed. Fergie said: 'I didn't expect that performance, it was shocking. I've no complaints about the result: Leeds deserved to win. They got breaks at times, but deserved their luck – I'm disappointed.

'We were caught napping, really – it was a bad goal for us to lose. The whole performance in the first half was bad. We never got going and the quality of the passing, the whole performance was just bad.

'I don't think any of the players can say they had a good day. Maybe only Valencia, when he came on, can say that. Even then it took us about 10 minutes to get the ball to him. You expect us to get a goal at Old Trafford and the intensity of our game improved a little bit in the second half. We had a lot of chances in the box, but on the day we didn't take them.'

For him, the only consolation was that he and his team would not have to wait long to try and put things right. Three days later they would be up against local rivals City in the first leg of the Carling Cup semi at Eastlands. Fergie told MUTV: 'We have to get this result out of our system as quickly as possible. We have a semi-final on Wednesday and a lot of these players won't be playing. You have to view this performance in the right light. We'll make sure we're ready for Wednesday now – we had a team in mind, but there will maybe be a few changes for that.'

In the event, the match would not be played for another fortnight because of bad weather, but in the meantime Fergie led United to a 1-1 draw at Birmingham and a 3-0 win over Burnley in the League. But it would be Manchester City who would draw first blood in the semi first leg at Eastlands on 19 January, winning 2-1 with, ironically, two goals from Tevez condemning the Reds to defeat after Giggs put them ahead early on. The boss showed his growing regard for City's progress under new head coach Roberto Mancini by fielding his strongest side, albeit without key defenders Ferdinand and Vidic.

Fergie declared he would not agonise over the defeat; indeed he fully expected his men to overturn the deficit at Old Trafford when the second leg came around, eight days later. He also reiterated his belief that the sale of Tevez had been the correct decision despite the Argentine's winning brace, saying: 'We've had a few players who have left the club and scored against us. It is not an issue. For most of the game we were in control. The crowd will make a difference at United and if we perform like we did tonight, we will be OK.'

United warmed up for the return leg with a 4-0 crushing of Hull at Old Trafford. Tensions were high on the night of 27 January, when City finally arrived for the showdown. True, this was just the relatively unimportant Carling Cup (at least in the eyes of the Big Four, unless they were struggling to win silverware elsewhere!), but it had thrown up a gem in this semi-final. For United, this was the opportunity to put down a marker that said they were still top dogs despite the growing strength of City, who Fergie had dubbed 'noisy neighbours'.

For City, it was a chance to reach a Wembley final and to end an agonising 34-year wait for a trophy.

Inevitably, Fergie triumphed, denying City their moment of glory and emphasising that United remained No. 1 in Manchester, however many millions City's Abu Dhabi puppet masters might care to throw at 'the project'. In an emotionally charged match that saw goals from Scholes, Carrick and Rooney take the Reds to Wembley, United won 3-1 on the night, 4-3 on aggregate. Just as inevitably as Fergie's triumph, Tevez proved a thorn in his side once again, grabbing City's consolation goal. That strike would be enough to secure him the accolade of again being top goalscorer in the competition for the second year running, with six goals for City – the same number he netted in the Carling Cup at United, the previous campaign.

Yet it was Rooney's injury-time header that sent United through and the boss was unstinting in his praise of his mercurial frontman. Fergie said: 'His control, his leading of the line, his penetration was absolutely fantastic. It was a wonderful performance, truly world-class.

'You like to win your derbies. The atmosphere tonight and the fact it was a semi-final tie added a lot of spice to the match. We kept our patience – that was important. Once we got into the last third of the field we always looked a threat.'

The win would set Fergie up for a final at Wembley against Aston Villa at the end of February. He was to retain the trophy that United had won a year previously against Spurs. On this occasion, there would be no need for a penalty shoot-out; the Reds ran out 2-1 winners in normal time. A James

Milner penalty put Villa ahead, but that Owen equaliser we have already talked about and a header from sub Rooney meant the trophy would return to Old Trafford. The major talking point was ref Phil Dowd's decision not to send off Vidic after he fouled Gabriel Agbonlahor in the box to give away the penalty.

Fuming Villa boss Martin O'Neill claimed the decision had cost his team the final: 'I think it would be universally accepted they should be down to 10 men. It's not a good decision by an otherwise fine referee. It's poor. Obviously at Wembley we score the penalty – they are down to 10 men for virtually the whole game. It's a major point in the game.

'It does not matter if it is in the first, second or the 89th minute of the game, the decision is straightforward. It is so straightforward, it is incredible.'

Even Sir Alex agreed United had been lucky in that respect, saying: 'We got a lucky break, he could have been sent off.'

Fortune was less favourable to the boss when Owen was forced off with the hamstring that would end his season early. The boss said: 'He did really well for us and it was a good performance from him. It's maybe our fault, too. He's not had a lot of minutes recently and that soft pitch didn't help him. It's a bad blow for us.'

United would celebrate at their London hotel and then head back home to prepare for their next match, away at Molineux, six days later. The season was hotting up now: they were still battling with Chelsea at the top of the table and were also progressing in Europe. The Reds secured a vital win at Wolverhampton, courtesy of the only goal of the game from Scholes on 72 minutes. Directly after that win Fergie had to inspire his troops to finish off the job they had started against AC Milan in the last-16 second leg of the Champions League.

A fortnight earlier, United had won 3-2 in Milan and now demolished their ageing visitors 4-0. A seventh successive goal from Rooney set them on their way and ruined the return to Old Trafford of former Reds hero David Beckham. Rooney scored a second as United roared into the last eight of the competition and Fergie reflected on an Italian job extremely well done. The brace had taken Rooney on to 30 goals for the season – 12 short of Ronaldo's 42, which led United to Euro glory in 2007/08. And Fergie reckoned Wayne could overtake him, saying: 'It's a challenge. I am happy he's got to the 30 mark, but to be honest, he just keeps on improving.' In the event, injury would thwart Rooney's bid – but at the time his boss was purring with delight at the striker and the team's majestic form.

Fergie added: 'It was a marvellous performance. When we play at that tempo, we are very difficult to play against – it was a solid performance. With the kind of team I have got, it doesn't matter who we are playing in the next round.'

That might be true, but you can't build in the unexpected, something such as bad luck or even a sending-off...

Following the mighty demolition of Milan, the Reds chalked up two fine home League victories, beating Fulham 3-0 and Liverpool 2-1. A diving headed goal by Ji-Sung Park sent them back to the top of the League. As Fergie moved ever closer to the day when he would retire as United manager, the win was just as sweet as all the others he had achieved against the Mersey giants. In his programme notes he wryly remembered how his main aim when he took over in 1986 was to 'knock Liverpool off their fuckin' perch' – well, he had certainly achieved that. They were a pale imitation of the giants they had been back then and collapsed after Rooney equalised from the penalty spot and Park nicked in for the winner.

Over the years the invincibles from another era had truly been put in their place by Fergie. Their season would now peter out, with defeat in the Europa Cup semis, followed by a poor seventh-place finish in the League, with a 63-point tally, 22 behind United.

After the win, Fergie was bullish about his side's chances against Bayern Munich in the last eight of the Champions League, saying: 'We've lost Cristiano Ronaldo and that would hit any team but there's an impressive maturity about the team in Europe nowadays – that's where we have improved.

'And it's reflected in our away-form as we've not lost in 16 games in Europe. It is easy for them now – there isn't the panic there used to be when we had young players.'

But he would be proved wrong: that 16-game unbeaten record crashed as United went down 2-1 in the impressive Allianz Arena in Munich on 30 March. Rooney (inevitably) had put the Reds ahead on two minutes, but late goals by Franck Ribery and Ivica Olic led to their downfall. United seemed a little overconfident and on cruise control after the early lead – and paid a heavy price. The loss would be the first of three consecutive 'must-win' games that would end in misery and wreck their season – and United fans had the added agony of seeing Wayne Rooney limp off with an ankle injury that threatened to keep him out for up to three weeks.

Four days later, they crashed 2-1 at home to Chelsea – and four days after that, would go out of the Champions League.

The Chelsea defeat was seismic: to lose against your biggest rivals at that stage of the campaign. It was a sickener and took the wind out of the team. United looked old, slow and out-of-touch without the injured Rooney. Once again it showed the folly of not beefing up the attack earlier in the campaign: Berbatov looked what he was: a costly luxury. The modern-day

Juan Sebastian Veron, who, as we have noted earlier, had similarly struggled at Old Trafford after Fergie splashed out £28.1 million for his services in 2001. Just as Fergie once persevered with the Argentine (often at Beckham's expense), as if to prove he *was* worth the outlay, so he now did the same with the hapless Berbatov.

In the Chelsea game and subsequent matches until the end of the season, the man would miss chances that Rooney would doubtless have buried. It was an unedifying experience watching him struggle while Fergie stubbornly continued to maintain he was a genius who was worth the money.

Inside the corridors of Old Trafford there had been a general delight when United were drawn out of the hat with Bayern. The feeling was that they had been given the luck of the draw and that once Bayern were disposed of, it would be a relatively gentle ride into the final when they met Lyons in the semis. But I had a bad feeling, a feeling of gloom and doom when the Munich giants came out of the hat. OK, eight times out of ten United would beat them, but they had two of the best, fastest, wingers in the world in Ribery and the wonderful, if exasperatingly inconsistent Dutchman Arjen Robben.

Robben had missed the first leg, but Bayern still won. So, I felt unease when fellow critics started talking about the semis and a possible re-run with Barca in the final. Robben would be back for the match at Old Trafford and I seriously doubted whether the likes of the ageing Gary Neville, Scholes and Giggs could cope with Robben and Ribery.

To give him all due credit Fergie shook up the side – injecting youth and pace to throw Bayern onto the back foot. With the enthusiasm and daring raids of Nani, Darron Gibson and the wonderful Brazilian right-back Rafael, United had the Germans rocking. They went 3-0 up and it looked as if the boss's excellent ploy of cancelling out the threat of Ribery and Robben had worked: their menace was nullified because they simply could not get the ball. United were all over Munich, while the visitors were tied up in their own half, desperately trying to stem the onslaught.

United were now 4-2 ahead on aggregate, thanks to a brace from Nani and one from Gibson, and heading confidently for the semis. Then fate dealt them the cruellest hand.

Olic pulled one back for Bayern before the break and United's Rafael was dismissed. The young Brazilian had already been booked and was sent off in the 50th minute for an innocuous challenge on Ribery. But the Frenchman made a real song and dance about the challenge, demanding that the ref should red-card the boy who had been a thorn in Bayern's side with his attacking threat and speed and delivery of crosses. The dismissal was the pivotal moment of the tie and, it could be argued, United's season.

From being a constant menace, the Reds were now forced to adapt a 40-odd minute role as defiant defenders. Rooney, who had started as a calculated gamble by Fergie after making an early return from injury, was withdrawn five minutes after Rafael's sending-off and it would now take a miracle for United either to score again or not concede.

They say miracles only happen once in a lifetime: maybe Fergie had used all his up against Bayern that memorable night in Barcelona, 11 years earlier. This time it would be United who would be grieving and Bayern unexpectedly celebrating.

Resilient at the back, the Reds did so well to hold out, but would crack eventually. And it would be Robben who would kill theirs and Fergie's European dream dead for another year, hitting a fantastic volley into the net from Ribery's corner.

United would hold on to their 3-2 win but they were out, on

the away-goals rule. It was a cruel way to exit the competition and Sir Alex was understandably in some agony afterwards, laying the blame for the defeat at the visitors' door, branding them 'typical Germans' for what he perceived as deliberate attempts to injure Wayne Rooney and persuade the ref to send off Rafael.

'They got him sent off,' Sir Alex fumed. 'There's no doubt about that and they would have never won if we had 11 men. He [Rafael] is a young boy, inexperienced and there's a bit of immaturity about what happened, but they got him sent off. Typical Germans!

'That sending-off changed the game. I thought they were typical professionals in the way they saw the opportunity and forced the referee. It was only a slight tug at the boy – and Jesus, he was 35 yards from goal! He [Rafael] was having a marvellous game and it's a tragedy for him, but the ref wasn't going to do anything until they forced him to get a card out. But we've seen that before from teams like that.

'I don't think the best team got through. They got a deflected free-kick [in the first leg] and a goal in injury-time, so you have to say they carried their luck. We have had occasions when we have had luck and I think they have this time. It's hard to digest. In one way we could say we have thrown it away, in another we've been very unlucky.'

You could certainly understand the boss's discontent, if not his reasoning. Typical Germans? Well, Ribery is French and Robben is Dutch, as is the club's manager, Louis van Gaal!

One thing Fergie knew was you couldn't change the result. The European odyssey was over for another campaign: now he had to lift his demoralised troops to go on to win the League. But even that would be beyond him in what was ultimately a frustrating season of so-close, so-far scenarios. Yes, they should have beaten Bayern, and yes, they should have beaten Blackburn in a key match directly after that European loss.

With hindsight, the 0-0 draw at Ewood Park four days later was a disaster. Had United won, which they should have and comfortably, they would have gone on to win the League by two points if all the results had still panned out as they did. As it was, they suffered yet again for Berbatov's profligacy in front of goal and when the Premier League trophy was handed out a month later, it would be presented to John Terry rather than Rio Ferdinand, with United finishing that single point beyond champions Chelsea.

The dream of four-in-a-row titles was gone, as was the chance of notching up that record 19th crown, but at least the boss still had something to aim for, something to keep him at the helm at Old Trafford, if only for another season. No way would he walk away when there remained two major goals to achieve in the 2010/11 season: the chance to grab that 19th title and to win the Champions League one final time at the home of English football, Wembley Stadium.

CHAPTER 18

RECORD BREAKER

Back in 1986, when he first walked into the manager's office at Old Trafford, Fergie had famously declared he wanted 'to knock Liverpool right off their fuckin' perch'. It was some want: at that time the mighty Liverpool had 18 top-flight titles to their name, while United had seven. To close such a cavernous gap would take some doing – and it is a measure of the big man from Govan that he not only declared war on Liverpool, but won against such massive odds.

And so, in May 2011, Sir Alex proudly addressed the Old Trafford faithful after finally overhauling Liverpool's tally of 18 titles. United's 19th was secured with one game of the season to go. Along with loyal servant Ryan Giggs, Fergie had notched up the 12 titles he had needed to silence the Scousers. 1993, 1994, 1996, 1997, 1999, 2000, 2001, 2003, 2007, 2008, 2009 and 2011 – all years that brought Premier League trophies to Old Trafford.

And what made the record-breaking 19th all the more remarkable was that Fergie had achieved it with a squad that had been largely written off as unremarkable by the majority of pundits. A squad that supposedly did not compare to the class of 2008, who had won the Champions League and Premier League Double. A squad that, shorn of the services of Cristiano Ronaldo and Carlos Tevez, had apparently lost its two best players (a statement that ignores, of course, the merits of the brilliant Wayne Rooney). A squad with no star players; at best merely a functional unit that had no glitz, no flair and no genius.

Yet somehow this team would win the Premier League for that record 19th time and waltz through to the final of the Champions League, only to lose out 3-1 to arguably the best club side ever to grace world football – the mighty Barcelona of Messi, Xavi and Iniesta.

Let's straight away put to bed that silly argument that United had 'no stars' during that record-breaking 2010/11 season. What about the aforementioned Rooney, not to mention Giggs, Valencia, Ferdinand, Vidic...and the best new player in the Premier League, Javier 'Chicharito' Hernandez! Those six players have stardust sprinkled all over them – and that's without giving a nod of the head to the likes of Berbatov, who ended up joint top scorer in the Premier League, Nani and Park.

United may have been a more disciplined, compact unit in 2010/11 but they still had their share of creativity, magic and wonder. If anything, you could argue that their all-round excellence and ability to operate as a team only went to prove, once again, what a managerial genius Sir Alex is. He moulded his new team over the season and turned them into a force that was hard to beat and a side that never gave in. He created a team of true fighters with undoubted skill: a United for the modern era, if you like.

After narrowly losing out to Chelsea in the Premier League

title race the previous year – thereby missing out on the chance to overhaul Liverpool's 18 titles – the ultimate target for Sir Alex in 2010/11 was always to regain that lost crown. But the boss also had one eye on the Champions League, especially as the final would be at Wembley in May 2011. He believed that winning the league was a definite possibility and that the Champions League could also be won, although you needed much more good fortune along the way in Europe with the knockout competition after the opening group stage. With the Premier League, you could work out a tactical plan based on the full nine-month campaign.

Sir Alex's optimism looked well founded as United opened the season in the traditional Community Shield curtain-raiser at Wembley with a 3-1 win over Chelsea in August 2010. The goalscorers gave an indication of how the new United would thrive during the ensuing campaign, with Valencia, Hernandez and Berbatov laying down a marker. Fergie was particularly pleased that Berbatov had scored – a frustrating campaign the year before had seen him hit just 12 goals and become the butt of the fans' jibes. Fergie said, 'He has great talent. You can't dispute the man's ability – he's a genius at times. He had a mixed last season but maybe it's going to be his season now.'

The boss also had words of praise and encouragement for another striker who would play a key role in the triumphs of the season – new boy Hernandez. Fergie added, 'He's quick to get in the box – he's a really good finisher. He's got a bubbly character and speaks good English. He's settled in very well.'

The season proper got underway with a comprehensive 3-0 drubbing of Newcastle at Old Trafford on Sunday 8 August 2010. Remarkably, United would not lose in the league for a full six months after that, with their next defeat coming at

Wolverhampton on 6 February 2011. In fact, their only other defeat in any competition during that time would be the 4-0 drubbing a second-string selection suffered at West Ham in the Carling Cup on 30 November 2010.

It was an incredible sequence of results that left them firmly at the top of the table – and they were also safely into the next round of the Champions League after topping their group with convincing wins over Valencia, Glasgow Rangers and Bursaspor of Hungary. Also included in that heady run was a 3-2 win over Liverpool, a 2-0 triumph over Tottenham, a 1-0 win over Liverpool in the FA Cup, a 5-0 crushing of Birmingham and the incredible 7-1 licking of Blackburn.

And straight after the disappointment of losing that game at Molineux, Fergie's new-style team showed exactly what they were made of by beating bitter local rivals Manchester City 2-1 in the Premier League.

In fact, the only real problem the United boss encountered in the run-up to the Christmas 2010 arose when his star player, Wayne Rooney, tried to engineer a move away from the club. On Tuesday 19 October, Rooney issued a statement claiming that he wanted to leave United because the squad was simply not strong enough and the club did not share his vision of future success.

The striker still had 18 months of his current deal to run and sources within the club claimed the feeling at Old Trafford was that Rooney's 'vision' actually had more to do with the money he was set to take home. Basically, he wanted more wonga – or else.

Fergie spoke of his dismay and bewilderment at the development: 'We've done nothing but help him since he's been at this club. We cannot quite understand why he would want to leave. No one can deny this club is one of the most successful in British football.

'We have won 40 major trophies, countless cup finals, have a fantastic history, a great stadium, great training arrangements.

'We don't understand it. I can't answer any questions about why he is doing it. We can speculate. We can have opinions. It won't matter a dickie-bird, simply because the player is adamant he wants to leave.'

But he cleverly did not rule out the chance of a U-turn by the player, stressing that there had been no fall-out between him and Rooney – and that he still valued him. 'I feel that we still have to keep the door open for him, especially as he's such a good player', Sir Alex revealed.

This was Fergie at his brilliant best. He had no intention of allowing his best player to leave; sources within the club have hinted that Sir Alex felt the boy was being manipulated by his agent and that, if the club played things correctly, the whole thing would blow over and Rooney would stay.

The following day, Rooney issued a statement. It read: 'I was interested to hear what Sir Alex had to say and surprised by some of it. I have never had anything but complete respect for the club. How could I not have done given its fantastic history and especially the last six years in which I have been lucky to play a part?

'For me it's all about winning trophies – as the club has always done under Sir Alex. Because of that I think the questions I was asking were justified. Despite recent difficulties, I know I will always owe Sir Alex Ferguson a huge debt. He is a great manager and mentor who has helped and supported me from the day he signed me from Everton when I was only 18.'

And within two days, Rooney had performed the very U-turn Sir Alex had apparently anticipated, after he was offered a new deal (and more money) to stay. He would still be turning out with the same players – but hadn't he said that he felt the club hadn't shown enough ambition in signing new stars?

So why the change of mind when he was offered a new deal? Fergie had called his bluff.

On Friday 22 October, the boss and Rooney were all smiles as it was announced the player had signed a new five-year contract. Rooney said: 'I said on Wednesday the manager's a genius and it's his belief and support that convinced me to stay. I'm delighted to sign another deal at United. I've spoken to the manager and the owners and they've convinced me this is where I belong. I am signing a new deal in the absolute belief that the management, coaching staff, board and owners are totally committed to making sure United maintains its proud winning history – which is the reason I joined the club in the first place.

'I am sure the fans over the last week have felt let down by what they have read and seen. But my position was from concern over the future. The fans have been brilliant with me since I arrived and it's up to me through my performances to win them over again.'

So was it the bigger salary, or the fear that the fans might turn on him if he went to say, Manchester City, who could have offered him even more money? Whatever the reason, it was clear that Fergie's persuasive powers had been instrumental in encouraging Wayne to pen a new deal – the boy had admitted as much. 'The manager's a genius and it's his belief and support that convinced me to stay'. And it was Fergie's powers that had persuaded the club's owners to sanction such a deal.

Fergie was pleased with the outcome. He told the club's website: 'I'm delighted Wayne's agreed to stay. It's been a difficult week but the intensity of the coverage is what we expect at Manchester United. Sometimes, when you're in a club, it can be hard to realise just how big it is and it takes something like the events of the last few days to make you understand. I think Wayne now understands what a great club Manchester United is.

'I'm pleased he has accepted the challenge to guide the younger players and establish himself as one of United's great players. It shows character and belief in what we stand for. I'm sure everyone involved with the club will now get behind Wayne and show him the support he needs to produce the performances we know he is capable of.'

After a nightmare spell on the pitch, Rooney now started to buckle down and by the New Year was showing signs of the form that had made him one of the world's most wanted players in the first place. He certainly owed the manager and the fans after his display of petulance: once again Fergie had shown just who was boss at United, that no one was bigger than him or the club and how his own brand of man-management – often fiery and confrontational but just as likely consolatory and conciliatory with an arm around the shoulders – worked wonders.

Just hours after Rooney's new contract was announced, Rio Ferdinand tweeted: 'It was never in doubt in my mind tweeps, Wazza is Man Utd through and through there's no way I could have seen him playing for another club, defo not a Prem club anyway.'

But that does a disservice to the excellent job Fergie had done. 'Wazza' had already proved he was a man who would do what he felt was best for his career (and his pocket) by leaving his beloved Everton for United in 2004. If he could leave his hometown club, the club he had supported and loved as a boy and a player, why would he necessarily feel any more loyalty to United?

No, Fergie had delivered for United once again in cleverly ushering the boy into signing a new deal with the club.

By the end of March 2011, Rooney was returning the favour with much improved form as Fergie's boys stormed into the quarter-finals of the Champions League, seeing off French outfit Marseille 2-1 on aggregate, and also made it into the semi-finals of the FA Cup by dumping Arsenal 2-0 out with a clinical display at Old Trafford.

But Fergie and his team suffered two setbacks in the Premier League at the dawn of March 2011 – a 2-1 Premier League loss at Chelsea and a 3-1 defeat at Liverpool five days later. The Stamford Bridge defeat was down to considerable bad fortune. The Blues triumphed through an 81st-minute Frank Lampard penalty that was extremely hard on United. Yury Zhirkov made the most of a light touch from Chris Smalling, collapsing as if he had been shot to win the spot kick.

Earlier, Brazilian David Luiz should have been dismissed for a number of cynical fouls, so it was all the more grating for Fergie when it was Luiz who grabbed Chelsea's first goal on 54 minutes, equalising Rooney's opener on the half-hour.

It was only United's second league defeat of the season but it was a blow – and a setback made all the worse as Vidic received his marching orders for two yellow cards. It meant the skipper and commanding centre-back would miss the match at Liverpool five days later. Without Vidic and fellow lynchpin Ferdinand United struggled at the heart of their back four – with Wes Brown and John O'Shea deputising. A Dirk Kuyt hat-trick destroyed the Red Devils, with only a late consolation goal from Chicharito easing the misery on the return journey back down the East Lancs Road. Fergie's side remained top of the table but second-placed Arsenal were now only three points behind with a game in hand.

Fergie sat his men down after the double defeat and told them they were still in the driving seat for that record 19th title

– but that they would need to raise their game. They would need to get back on a winning run and show their mettle. They did just that – now going on a seven-match unbeaten run that included that FA Cup quarter-final win over Arsenal and a brilliant two-legged demolition of Chelsea in the last eight of the Champions League.

The 3-1 aggregate win over the Blues would set United up for a semi-final encounter with Schalke 04 of Germany, the surprise team of the tournament, and ultimately lead to the sacking of Carlo Ancelotti as Chelsea manager. Owner Roman Abramovich was unrepentant; even though the Italian had won the domestic double of FA Cup and league title the previous year, he had not delivered in the competition the Russian coveted more than any other. Yes, that very same Champions League.

United had won the first leg 1-0 at Stamford Bridge on April 6, with Rooney paying back the manager's faith in him with another vital goal. Fergie saluted his star man's efforts, saying, 'Wayne's now more regular with his goalscoring which, in the last part of the season, is going to be important to us. It was important tonight – we are pleased with that performance. Work-rate, desire, he was top quality. He took a lot of abuse and late tackles, but he was excellent.'

Chelsea felt aggrieved that they were refused a late penalty for Patrice Evra's rasping tackle on Ramires.

But Fergie laughed it off, saying United were due the rub of the green. He said, 'Yeah, someone said it could have been a penalty but it was the first penalty decision we've got here in seven years, so I think we're due one. I don't feel guilty about that at all. It was a 50-50 from where I was and I don't know what the contact situation was.'

But he did not smile when asked whether the tie could now be considered in the bag for the Red Devils. He shook his head and said, 'No, we have to be very careful and have to give a top performance in the second leg, but the atmosphere will help us.' He was right about that.

Before the crunch match, Fergie had predicted that United would finish the job – telling a UEFA press conference that his team now had the momentum, and that the form of Rooney could prove the difference between the teams. The boss said, 'Momentum is key: it's what keeps you from going off your stride. Every game from this point on is like a cup final – the players thrive on that. In that respect I see similarities to 1999, but the circumstances are completely different as we didn't have any injuries back then. We've coped very well this season, particularly with the injuries we've had in defensive positions. Having the likes of Anderson, Rio [Ferdinand], and [Antonio] Valencia back makes an incredible difference at this time of the season. They're fresh and they know how to play for the club, so it's not like signing new players as they don't need time to adapt.

'In the first leg, Wayne Rooney adapted very well to the role we asked him to play. He had to combine partly defensive duties but with an attacking thrust, so in that respect he did very well and of course he put in a good performance. He is capable of causing problems no one else can. Balance, power, speed and a great tactical brain – the boy's got everything.'

The United faithful also played their part in the triumph as he had anticipated, roaring their team home at Old Trafford six days after the first leg at Stamford Bridge. Goals from Chicharito and Ji-Sung Park saw United into the semis for the fourth time in five seasons with Didier Drogba grabbing Chelsea's consolation.

Ryan Giggs had played a key role in all three goals over the two legs and the boss now singled his veteran out for special praise, saying, 'He's incredible, a unique person and player. It's a great contribution and his experience and composure were vital. He's lucky with his physique, he's never carried weight and has got fantastic balance. He looks after himself. To play at 37 it must be a great sacrifice to do that.'

Even Ancelotti, who was hurting badly after the defeat, had praise for Fergie and his team and their terrific achievement in reaching yet another Champions League semi-final. He said, 'Sir Alex is one of the greatest managers in the world ever, if not the greatest. He keeps going and never gives in. Our performance was not so bad but I think of the two teams, United deserved to win.'

Fergie was in celebratory mood – he could afford to be as he knew that his team would now face Schalke in the semis. The Germans had surprised everyone by making it thus far, but Fergie knew they were the dream draw. It would have been much harder to progress to that Wembley final had the opponents been Barca or Real Madrid, who now proceeded to knock six bells out of each other, with Barca eventually emerging triumphant.

But before the clash with Schalke, Fergie had to negotiate a tough FA Cup semi against Manchester City – just four days after that Champions League win over Chelsea. It was a match too far for his tired heroes – they would lose 1-0 at Wembley, with Yaya Toure grabbing the winner. United struggled without Rooney, who had been banned for two domestic games by the FA for swearing into a TV camera after scoring a hat-trick in the 4-2 Premier League win at West Ham a fortnight earlier.

The Reds now had nine games remaining in their season. They would lose two of them – the Premier League match at Arsenal on May 1, and the Champions League final against Barca, the last match of the campaign, 27 days later at Wembley.

Fergie would be delighted, however, as his boys clinched that record 19th top-flight title with a game to spare. They had effectively won it by coming out on top in the crunch clash with their closest rivals Chelsea on 8 May. The Blues had managed a late surge but any hope they had of retaining the title they had claimed 12 months earlier was crushed by the defeat at Old Trafford.

Goals from Chicharito and Vidic, with Lampard getting a consolation for the Blues, moved United to within a single point of the title – with two games left to play. But the goals only told part of the story. United were simply better than their rivals, in terms of overall quality and mental and physical strength.

Matt Lawton, writing in the *Daily Mail*, best summed up the Red Devils' resilience and brilliance that day. He wrote, 'Take a bow, Manchester United. Sir Alex Ferguson did so before the Stretford End moments after the final whistle and rightly so given how impressive his side were. Not for the first time this season, they have proved themselves players who rise to the occasion. A team who now sit within touching distance of the 19th league title they crave because they possess a spirit too often missing in their main rivals.

'They destroyed Chelsea on every level: technically and tactically, but also mentally. They were strong where Chelsea were weak, focused where Chelsea suffered fatal lapses in concentration.'

Fergie was in triumphant spirits. He was also boldly confident – United's final two games in the league were away at Blackburn and at home to Blackpool, and he predicted they would have no problem getting the single point they needed to win the title.

He said, 'To be the most successful team is fantastic. Knowing the players they won't muck it up. They will get a point, there's no doubt about that. The minute we won that first title in 1993 the door opened, and we've been involved in the first two all throughout that period – it's a fantastic achievement.

'For the last 17 or 18 years it's been Arsenal and Chelsea as our nearest challengers, and the last few years it's been Chelsea. It took time to get the foundations of the club right and after we got the first title we improved, improved and improved.'

He was also proud that they had virtually won the league for that record 19th time by disposing of their nearest rivals. He added, 'We could have scored about six in the second half. You expect a tough game against Chelsea and we got that. We got a great start. It was a good team performance. When we gave the ball away for their goal the fans helped us by playing their part. Credit to the players because they deserved it.'

Fergie was right, as usual. His team won the title with the point they needed in the 1-1 draw at Blackburn and then tidied it all up with a 4-2 demolition of Blackpool in the final match of the league campaign at Old Trafford on Sunday May 22. A penalty converted by Rooney won Fergie his 12th league crown with the Red Devils – and that record-breaking 19th – after keeper Paul Robinson brought down Chicharito in the box. Fergie had done it: he had finally knocked Liverpool 'off their fuckin' perch'! The boss tried to play down the Liverpool angle afterwards, saying, 'It's not so much passing Liverpool. It's more important that United are the best team in the country in terms of winning titles. It's the same with the FA Cup. We have won it more times than everyone and now we have won the Premier League more times than anyone.'

And he growled when someone at the post-match press conference suggested he had won it with a United team that could not compare with his title-winning outfits of the past. He said, 'It is not fair to say it's a bad Manchester United team or a bad league. It is a tighter league, a harder league to win. Any campaign has got blips for anyone. You have got to look at the league in general.'

In between the FA Cup loss to City and the Premier League win over Chelsea, Fergie had also masterminded United's inexorable progress to another Champions League final. They beat Schalke 2-0 in Germany, with goals from Giggsy and Rooney. Then Fergie's troops completed the mission with a 4-1 triumph at Old Trafford, the goals coming from Anderson (2), Gibson and Valencia. The result was all the more commendable as the boss had given many of his regulars the night off and relied on a team made up almost entirely of reserves to win them their place at Wembley. His thinking was that the two-goal lead from the match in Germany would be enough to see them through and that he needed to rest his big guns for the all-important crunch Premier League fixture against Chelsea the following Sunday.

It was certainly a gamble – and one that had many United fans shaking their heads and biting their fingernails in tense anticipation when the team was announced. Playing a reserve team in a Champions League semi-final, with a place in the big final at Wembley at stake? But it was a calculated gamble that paid dividends as the big boys then returned fresh and saw off Chelsea after their stand-ins had done the same against the Germans. Fergie explained, 'It wasn't an easy decision. It was one of those ones I wrestled with for a few days. If it was a tight result in the last game there is no way I could have done it. With a two-goal lead there was just enough leeway to do it.'

The 6-1 aggregate win over Schalke meant they would meet old foes Barcelona in the showpiece final at Wembley.

Of course, the crack Spanish team had beaten United 2-0 in the final in Rome two years previously. But Fergie reckoned they had nothing to fear this time, even though many pundits were now openly describing Barca as 'the greatest club side in world football ever'. Fergie said, 'I don't think we should be going there lacking in confidence. We are playing a fantastic team but we can't be frightened out of our skins. Their form is there for everyone to see. Our job is to find a solution. I think we'll be quite well prepared for the final.'

Even his opposite number at Barca admitted his fear that Fergie could indeed 'find a solution' for the Wembley final. Pep Guardiola had watched from the Old Trafford stands as United's reserves demolished Schalke 4-1 and was full of plaudits afterwards. He said, 'They played a Champions League semi-final with a team full of reserves and they won 4-1 – that says everything you need to know about the quality they have. They have a great squad with two great teams and extraordinary players.'

But for once Fergie would come up short. He was powerless to halt the Barca juggernaut at Wembley. It would be the Spanish giants who – once again – gave United a footballing lesson, emerging victorious 3-1 with goals from Pedro, Lionel Messi and David Villa, with only Rooney's wonderful strike as any consolation for Fergie.

His team had proved not quite good enough, just as they had in Rome two years earlier. Fergie was honest enough to admit afterwards that they had, in all honesty, been 'given a hiding' and that they were distinctly second best to the team who notched their third Champions League success in six years.

The stats told the story of why United had been walloped: Barca had 68 per cent possession compared with United's 32 per cent; Barca had 12 attempts on goal while United had just one (Rooney's goal); Barca had six corners, United had none. It made depressing reading and Fergie would add, 'In my time as manager they are the best team I have faced. They do mesmerise you with their passing. We tried to play as near to the way we normally play but it wasn't good enough on the night and we understand that and acknowledge it.'

I was at Wembley that day and sensed a tension among United fans even before kick-off. It was as if they knew that this was going to be a struggle against a team that was simply too good. The United hordes weren't as noisy or as humorous as usual; indeed they were drowned out for much of the match by their rivals from Catalonia. An unusual state of affairs given that United supporters are among the most partisan and fanatical in the world.

Two days after the drubbing, a staunch United fan emailed me with the following fears: 'Can't really believe I'm daring to ask this, and I am feeling very low, but I will: Has Sir Alex Ferguson reached the end of the road? He is the greatest manager on these shores. But, even if he kept plugging away for the next ten years, would he overcome Barca? Even when the likes of Xavi and Iniesta have packed it in they will still have enough to shaft us (because Messi will still be there) unless the Glazers dig deep. And we know the answer to that, don't we? God, I feel gutted today. Awful, awful, awful.'

It got me thinking, too. That maybe some good would indirectly emerge from the defeat – that maybe Fergie now had the necessary carrot needed to keep him battling and inspired for another few years?

After all, it was the carrot of surpassing Liverpool's title haul that had spurred him on to those magnificent 12 top-flight title wins. Now he had a new top-notch set of rivals to snipe at: Barcelona. He would surely be aiming to knock them off their perch, too. And who would bet against him succeeding? After all, hadn't he already taken United back to the top once already?

In the dark days of 2004 and 2005 they had finished third in both seasons – behind Arsenal and Chelsea respectively. Indeed, it had appeared the Reds might never win the league again as the Abramovich era truly kicked in – and Fergie was even verbally abused by his own fans. But what happened next? Somehow the boss miraculously breathed new life into his team – and Manchester United lifted the Premier League title in 2007, 2008 and 2009...and also the Champions League in 2008!

And now the boss had the perfect incentive to round off his wonderful career with one final mission – to knock Barca off their perch. And who would bet against him achieving it? Certainly not me...

Let's now further our analysis of Fergie, the master manager, by taking a look at another side to this legend – his famous feuds. And then we'll wrap it all up by examining just why he can make a claim to be the greatest manager ever. Full stop.

CHAPTER 19

FEUD FOR THOUGHT

An enigma? Well, yes, Sir Alex could certainly lay claim to that label. He is a most complex man: on the one hand, kind, generous and unstintingly loyal if you are one of his friends or allies. On the other, stubborn, cantankerous and sometimes cruel if you happen to get on the wrong side of him. His run-ins with authority and his feuds with fellow managers, players and those involved in football in other capacities are the stuff of legend.

Let's examine some of the most famous of the (many) incidents and try to get to the bottom of the two contradictory sides of this remarkable man. Fergie was obviously moulded as a person by his Scottish upbringing on the tough streets of Govan. Life was tough when he was a boy, growing up in relative poverty in a tenement block yet with the warmth and security of a loving family. All this in a neighbourhood of south-west Glasgow where yes, you had to learn – and quickly – if you wanted to survive but where there was also a tremendous spirit of community, a togetherness that bonds neighbours and locals in those very tenements.

Govan was where Sir Alex learned the importance of family: that it came first, that it meant more than anything (yes, even football) and that loyalty to your family was vital. This would help explain his anger at the BBC many years later, when they accused one of his sons of business irregularity – they had held a red rag to a bull and would suffer as he withdrew his co-operation.

Govan also imbued the boss with a solid work ethic: a fair day's work for a fair day's pay. Or unfair, as he often saw it as he watched his father slog for a salary that was hardly commensurate with the effort and long hours put in.

When Fergie left school and embarked on a toolmaking apprenticeship, he quickly became a union rep. No way would he allow himself to be pushed around by bosses, even at an early age. This would help explain why years later he felt aggrieved at United's refusal to put him on a similar wage to his peers when he turned the club around – and why he demanded they do so (even though he wasn't always successful in the outcome).

Similarly in Scotland, he learned and was moulded by incidents in his burgeoning football career. As a player and a manager, he came to realise the importance of togetherness – the essence of teamwork rather than individual egos running wild – as he began to make his mark. He instinctively understood that the team – and sacrifice for your fellow players – was essential if you were to be successful.

Again, loyalty was a vital ingredient: Fergie was very much of the opinion that you should be willing to leap into the trenches and battle it out with the men on your side. And if you lost that loyalty and affinity, you would be better off taking your talents elsewhere. In later years, this attitude would come to flavour his relationship with players that he felt had 'got too big for their boots' and those who no longer had the interests of the team at heart – 'pop star-style footballers', as he described them, who seemed more interested in their own brand.

Extravagance did not fit in well with the Ferguson ideal of a role-model player. As he fought to make the grade, he himself had had to juggle the demands of a tool-making apprenticeship with being a part-time footballer. Certainly there was no silver spoon or Easy Street for Alex Ferguson: even when he turned professional, he would describe himself as 'an unpampered pro.'

On the other hand, if a player had an exceptional talent – and was always loyal, hard-working and committed to himself and his football club – he would move heaven and earth to keep him, Eric Cantona being the prime example.

Fergie was proud of his persona and would never apologise for the way he was. Indeed, he once described his former Aberdeen striker Steve Archibald as 'single-minded, stubborn, awkward, determined' – and then added, 'he reminded me of someone!'

In 1986, Fergie arrived at United and ironically enough, one of his first big run-ins would be with another former player at his old club Aberdeen: 'wee' Gordon Strachan. The fiery little winger fell foul of the big man at Pittodrie when he did not follow orders on the field of play. Indeed, one incident would bring about the 'throwing teacups' affair with which Fergie is often associated whenever people talk about his temper tantrums.

The situation flared up in the UEFA Cup second-round match at Arges Pitesti in 1981. Fergie had asked Strachan to play right-wing, but he constantly drifted infield and at the interval the Dons entered the dressing room 2-0 down. Fergie laid into Strachan, telling him he had not done as requested, but Strachan inadvisably answered back.

Fergie took up the story in his 1999 autobiography, *Managing My Life*: 'I swung a hand in anger at a huge tea urn that was nearby. It was made of pewter or iron and striking it nearly broke my hand. The pain caused me to flip my lid and I hurled a tray of cups filled with tea towards Strachan, hitting the wall above him.'

Sir Alex was also none too pleased when Strachan signed a pre-contract agreement with Cologne weeks before the end of the 1983/84 season. Fergie had been trying to find him a British club and was unaware he had been dealing behind his back. Fergie declared: 'Though I always felt there was a cunning streak in Strachan, I had never imagined that he could pull such a stroke on me' and claimed Strachan 'could not be trusted an inch.'

Strachan had eventually decided to join Manchester United in the summer of 1984, but he knew his number was up when Fergie followed him in November 1986. In his own autobiography, *My Life In Football*, Strachan would say: 'When Fergie moved to United, I had to endure the big stick again.' And he would also claim the feud continued when he became a manager: 'It says much about the tension in our relationship, that even as a manager I have found it difficult to discount the possibility of Fergie taking a particular interest in putting one over on me.'

Sir Alex felt Strachan was not the player he had been for him in Scotland and therefore sold him to Leeds in 1989. Revitalised with a new challenge (ironically in much the same way as Johnny Giles was when Matt Busby flogged him to the same club for a knockdown £30,000 in 1963), Strachan helped Leeds to the 1990 Second Division title and then, at Fergie's expense, the Division One crown in 1992. You might think that latter act would ensure a lifelong division between the two men, but there was a rapprochement in 2006 when Fergie accepted Strachan's invitation for a drink and a natter after United won 3-0 in a pre-season friendly at Celtic Park.

Later, when the clubs were due to meet at the same venue in a Champions League group stage clash, Strachan said: 'All the history between me and Fergie is an irrelevance to Wednesday's game. He sat in my office recently for 40 minutes and we laughed and joked and talked about football and the old days.'

Fergie would also eventually find some common ground with Arsène Wenger, the man who was to become his biggest rival in English football until José Mourinho appeared on the stage. There were certainly many fiery confrontations between Sir Alex and the Frenchman before they finally found a sort of peace in around 2008.

Wenger became manager of Arsenal in September 1996 and soon made his mark on English football. It was inevitable he and Fergie would clash, given the remarkable success the Frenchman enjoyed. In Wenger's first season, Arsenal mounted a serious title challenge for the first time since 1991 and the following year, the Gunners claimed both the Premier League title and the FA Cup.

Even before Wenger arrived, the simmering rows began. The London critics had been portraying him as a man who was an intellectual and almost professorial in his attitude to football. They pointed out that he was well travelled, spoke five languages and was unlike the typical British manager in terms of culture, upbringing and education. Wenger, they crowed, was a highly intelligent Frenchman with a degree in economics from Strasbourg University.

If all this was designed to get the backs up of the British bosses by insinuating Wenger was a far loftier, classier entity to them, then it certainly worked a treat with Fergie. He poured scorn on their claims, saying: 'They say he's an intelligent man, right? Speaks five languages? I've got a 15-year-old boy from the Ivory Coast who speaks five languages!'

In April 1997 Wenger ignited the feud when he accused the League of bending over backwards to help United, claiming the fixture list was unfair and favoured them. He said: 'It's wrong the League programme is extended so Man United can rest up and win everything.'

Fergie's response was just as cutting: 'Wenger doesn't know anything about English football. He's at a big club – well, Arsenal used to be big. He should keep his mouth shut, firmly shut. He's a novice and should keep his opinions to Japanese football.'

And it would get worse. Two years later Wenger refused to shake hands with Fergie after the FA Cup semi-final replay at Villa Park. It was the titanic match in which Keane was sent off and Giggs claimed victory from the edge of adversity with arguably the greatest individual goal ever in English football. But Fergie would say that Wenger's unsporting gesture was the biggest insult he had faced as a manager.

War in the open broke out again in 2002 when Arsenal won the double. Fergie claimed United had been the better side during the campaign and that they were certainly a much better side than the Gunners. He said: 'They are scrappers who rely on belligerence – we are the better team.' To give him his due, Wenger replied with a killer quote, probably his most famous ever: 'Everyone thinks they have the prettiest wife at home.'

The same year Fergie suggested Arsenal were getting special treatment from the FA after Patrick Vieira and Thierry Henry had their disciplinary hearings delayed for three months. He grumbled: 'They wouldn't have waited for three months if it was a United player – our disciplinary record is tremendous,

I'm very proud of it.' To which Wenger responded: 'One thing I will say is that he doesn't disturb my nights at all. We didn't do anything, but if we are clever, that's a compliment.'

It was all highly entertaining, knockabout stuff for us press scribes as the two men hurled insults at each other from their respective footballing citadels. But it did take a slightly more worrying tone in 2004, with the so-called 'Pizzagate' bust-up. In the match itself, Fergie brilliantly inspired United to a 2-0 win; a result that ended the Gunners' 49-match unbeaten run in the League. The build-up had been as tense and nerve-wracking as the action itself – the previous season, both teams were punished in what had been just the latest battle between them at Old Trafford. At the end of that match there were ugly scenes after Patrick Vieira had been sent off for aiming a kick at Ruud van Nistelrooy.

The game finished 0-0, but Arsenal allowed their frustrations to run wild after the Dutchman also missed a last-minute penalty. When the final whistle blew, they shoved and taunted Van Nistelrooy for the miss. For their part in the chaos defenders Lauren and Martin Keown were fined and hit with four- and three-game bans respectively. Ray Parlour and Vieira received one-match suspensions, Ashley Cole was fined £10,000 and Arsenal were ordered to stump up £175,000 as punishment.

Now, a year on and a week before the clash against the so-called 'Invincibles', Fergie stoked up the fires again, claiming the behaviour of the Arsenal players back then was 'the worst thing I've seen in this sport.' He added: 'Arsenal got off scot-free, really – they got away with murder. The disciplinary treatment was ridiculous when you think Eric Cantona got eight months for attacking a fan. United took their own action in suspending him for four months. I don't think Arsenal would suspend one of their own players for four months, no matter what he had done.'

Wenger told Fergie to 'calm down' when he learned of his inflammatory comments and added: 'Alex Ferguson has a good sense of humour. Maybe it would have been better to have put us all up against the wall and shot us! We have improved and learnt from last year. We are now contending for the fair-play league, so I hope we don't lower our standards.'

But they did – or more precisely, Sol Campbell did just that. The big defender was clearly resentful as he left the pitch; he had conceded a penalty after he fouled Rooney when the young forward rounded him. After missing in the previous season's encounter, Van Nistelrooy proved he had considerable bottle by dispatching the ball past Jens Lehmann.

Campbell was clearly sulking as he trudged off, while team-mates Thierry Henry and Vieira were trying to pick arguments with various United players. By the time they reached the tunnel, I am told by a United insider that Rooney was winding Campbell up – and that it took all his inner resolve to keep cool.

The first United players were back in the dressing room as Sir Alex and Van Nistelrooy brought up the rear. As the pair passed the Arsenal dressing room, slices of pizza and some soup came hurling out of the half-shut door. The volley of food missed the Dutchman, but splattered all over the boss's suit – the one in which he would have met the awaiting TV interviewers.

The United insider told me: 'There were scuffles and lots of industrial language. The stadium security staff managed to get the United men out of the corridor and into the United dressing room. It could have been a lot worse – but it looked as if one of the Arsenal contingent got a bit bruised.'

Initially, Ashley Cole had been fingered as the food thrower but I am told, on good authority, that Cesc Fabregas was the culprit. Wenger was also alleged to have headed towards Sir Alex, asking if he 'wanted some.'

In his autobiography, *My Defence*, Ashley Cole describes the bust-up in this way: 'This slice of pizza came flying over my head and hit Fergie straight in the mush ... all mouths gawped to see this pizza slip off this famous, puce face and roll down his nice black suit.'

It was certainly an unedifying spectacle, raising the stakes of the feud between the two men to a new level and particularly bad for Wenger's image. As a practising Buddhist, you would expect him to be rather more serene and calm and promoting good causes. Yet here was the great Buddha allegedly losing it, although he would later claim that 'nothing happened in the tunnel.'

Inevitably, the jokers in the press box doubled over at their own witticisms as Sir Alex quickly changed into a tracksuit for his post-match Sky TV interview. One wit suggested in a rather loud voice that Fergie had been hit by soup thrown by one Arsenal player and one United: Campbell and Heinze. The boss did not see the funny side, but commendably carried on with the interview and did not deign to lower himself by mentioning the shenanigans in the dressing rooms.

A year later, in 2005, the United boss was clearly still riled about 'Pizzagate'. He told reporters that Wenger was 'a disgrace' for not apologising for his players' behaviour after the game and rubbed salt into the wound by adding that he had not expected it anyway from 'that type of person.'

Wenger reacted by saying that Fergie should be charged with bringing the game into disrepute and that 'Ferguson does what he wants and you lot are all down at his feet.'

And then, suddenly, there seemed to be a thaw. It was

reported the two men had sat and chatted together at an international football conference and they seemed far more convivial towards each other. As far as Sir Alex was concerned, perhaps it was probably also because Arsenal were eased out at the top by Chelsea and Liverpool during the latter half of the first decade of the new century.

The Gunners simply were not the threat they had been, as reflected in the fact that as this book went to press, Arsenal had won nothing since May 2005 when they lifted the FA Cup. Their spell in the wilderness coincided with a new relationship between Fergie and the Frenchman.

Yet while Fergie would enjoy the company of Chelsea boss José Mourinho, even as the Portuguese outdid him on the trophy front, there would be no such warmth when it came to Liverpool boss Rafa Benítez.

Mourinho was a streetwise wideboy. He was clever enough and crafty enough to know that it was not in his best interests to fall out with Fergie. Instead, he cosied up to him, calling him 'gaffer' and massaging his ego by saying he was 'the greatest boss ever' (which was true, but unusual to hear from a current adversary!).

Benítez, in contrast, had no such wish to be pally with 'Meester Ferguson', as he called him. The feud between the pair simmered over the years after Benítez took charge at Liverpool in 2004, but broke out into full-scale antagonism when United and the Kop giants were both going flat out to win the League in January 2009. On 9 January, the United boss had claimed Liverpool might stutter in the run-in because of nerves: it was all part of the regular mind games he loves to play with his rivals as what he calls 'Squeaky Bum Time' (the vital business end of the season) looms each year.

Benítez bit at the rag in a big way. At his press conference following the comments, he lashed out at the United boss and produced a piece of paper from his pocket containing what he called 'facts' about 'Meester Ferguson'.

Benítez said: 'I was surprised by what has been said, but maybe they are nervous because we are at the top of the table. I want to talk about facts. I want to be clear: I do not want to play mind games too early, although they seem to want to start.

'During the Respect campaign – and this is a fact – Mr Ferguson was charged by the FA for improper conduct after comments made about Martin Atkinson and Keith Hackett. He was not punished. He is the only manager in the League that cannot be punished for these things.

'How can you talk about the Respect campaign and yet criticise the referee every single week? All managers need to know is that only Mr Ferguson can talk about the fixtures, can talk about referees – and nothing happens.

'We need to know that I am talking about facts, not my impression. There are things that everyone can see every single week. To complain and to always have an advantage is not fair.'

In an interview with the *New Statesman*, Sir Alex was asked what he thought of the 'facts' that Benítez had listed. 'Weird,' he said. 'I really don't know what he was talking about. He'd obviously worked himself up into something, because he was reading it out. I'd be amazed if his staff or his players thought it was a good idea.'

Fergie was right about that: rather than gee up his team and weigh down United, the 'facts' episode had the opposite effect. Afterwards, Liverpool's form suffered and they slowly slipped out of contention for the title they wanted so much, handing the initiative and – even worse from the Anfield club's point of view – the crown to United, who by claiming it equalled Liverpool's record of 18 top-flight titles.

That only served to send Benítez over the top again. He refused to congratulate Fergie on the achievement, simply growling: 'I will say congratulations to Manchester United. They have done well, but I do not want to say too much. I prefer just to say well done to the club, a big club, a good club.

'Normally you have to be polite and respect the other manager. During the season we have seen a lot of things that I didn't like, so that's it. I say congratulations to United because they have won. And that's it.'

As mentioned earlier in this book, Sir Alex also had run-ins with other managers, Kevin Keegan being the most prominent, back in 1996. But it wasn't just managers and players who suffered his wrath: organisations did too, if they displeased him and the BBC were the highest-profile casualties.

The feud between Fergie and the Corporation officially began in 1994 when Jimmy Hill criticised Eric Cantona after 'the King' kicked out at a Norwich player during United's 2-0 FA Cup win at Carrow Road. Told of Hill's criticism at the post-game press conference, Fergie shook his head and declared Hill was 'a prat.' The boss also claimed the BBC were anti-United and had been hoping they would crash out.

A year later, tempers frayed again when commentator John Motson quizzed Fergie about Roy Keane's poor disciplinary record. 'You've no right to ask that question, John, fucking make sure that doesn't go out!' raged the boss.

Again, the incident was smoothed over but the scars remained and when the BBC subsequently took a pop at Sir Alex's football agent son Jason in a 2003 documentary, it was game off. Since then, the boss has refused to speak to the Corporation, much to the dismay of Gary Lineker and the fans who tune in – and who are all heartily sick of hearing the likes of Carlos Queiroz and Michael Phelan drone on in his place.

Fergie has also fallen out with some of the biggest names to serve him in his quarter-decade at Old Trafford. David Beckham was the most notable of the lot: in the boss's eyes he became too big for his boots and too immersed in a pop-star lifestyle with wife 'Posh Spice' Victoria for his liking.

When the split between Becks, Fergie and United occurred in 2003, I was – as a United fan as well as a national newspaper journalist – devastated. And I must admit Sir Alex was hardly in my good books back then, and many thousands of United fans agreed. It would only be later when the man who replaced him started to shine that we realised that yes, old Fergie had been right again: Cristiano Ronaldo wasn't a bad replacement, was he? Along with George Best, Cantona, Giggs and Bobby Charlton, he was arguably one of the best footballers to play for United. Ever. But in the summer of 2003, from the outside looking in, it appeared as if Fergie had shot himself in the foot to prove a point: that he had got rid of United's best player because of his own unwillingness, some would call it immaturity, to compromise – never mind Becks'.

Surely the two men could have sat down together and thrashed out a grown-up compromise, I remember writing at the time. But no, it appeared two egos had collided and the fact that no common ground could be found meant we lost Beckham for relative peanuts. I was gutted.

Becks was the man who had certainly made the coveted No. 7 shirt his own – and who had earned the right to wear it, following in the hallowed footsteps of such greats as Bryan Robson and Cantona. That sad June day, he left for Real Madrid, having won six Premiership titles, two FA Cup winners' medals and one Champions League crown. At the same time, he would become the most famous footballer on the planet.

But Sir Alex did not take kindly to Beckham's celebrity lifestyle. To him, a footballer should be a footballer first and everything else is secondary. With hindsight, it is clear that Becks had pushed him to the limit with his contrary belief that he could be a celebrity footballer, rather than just a mere footballer.

By the end of his days at United, Becks' problem was that he seemed to get sucked into believing his own publicity. Perhaps he did listen too much to Victoria, who was much the more experienced and streetwise of the two when it came to celebrity.

David Beckham was no fool, but he did not have the vision to see that he would never get the better of Fergie. With a little more subtlety and give and take on his side, he could have surely ended his days at Old Trafford – although if that had happened, of course, we would never have witnessed the legend that was Ronaldo at the Theatre of Dreams.

But Becks did not do subtlety: he decided, for example, to take his grievance over the boot Fergie once kicked into his face into the public domain. The blow-up came about in February 2003 when, after an FA Cup defeat by Arsenal, Fergie kicked a boot across the dressing room and into Beckham's face.

Becks being Becks, he decided to wear his hair pulled back in an Alice band to show off the full glory of the stitches and the bruises – and to look hurt when the paparazzi gathered to capture the startling pictures greeting us that unforgettable morning. It probably seemed sweet revenge in the spur of the moment, yet it would be the ultimate ammunition for Fergie to now ease his player out of the exit door. He was convinced Beckham had let the pop-star lifestyle go to his head – now he knew for sure and a parting of the ways was inevitable.

David later tried to offer an olive branch by absolving his boss of blame. He said: 'I want to assure all Manchester United fans that there is complete harmony and focus as we prepare for the Juventus game [the following Wednesday in the Champions League]. The dressing-room incident was just one of those things – it's in the past now.'

But Fergie did not apologise for the incident. Instead, he tried to pour cold water on the fire, claiming it had been something or nothing. He said: 'Contrary to reports, David Beckham did not have two stitches – it was a graze which was dealt with by the doctor. It was a freakish incident. If I tried it a hundred or a million times, it couldn't happen again. If I could, I would have carried on playing! There is no problem and we move on. That is all there is to say.'

Beckham's last match for United would be the 2-1 win at Everton on 11 May 2003. The week before, the Red Devils had clinched the title with a 4-1 win over Charlton at Old Trafford.

Against Everton, he signed off his Reds career with another of his clinical free-kicks from 20-odd yards after David Unsworth brought down Solskjaer just before the interval.

On 18 June 2003, against the wishes of Fergie who had hoped to offload him to Barcelona, Beckham signed an agreement to join Real Madrid, making it clear this was his only destination. The fee, considering he was only 28 and easily the most marketable footballer in the world, was a bargain £24.5 million, with just £17 million of it upfront.

United's then chief executive Peter Kenyon claimed it was a good deal for the club – in fact, it was a disastrous one. United – and Ruud van Nistelrooy in particular – would suffer without Beckham's pinpoint deliveries. And the Red Devils would also lose out drastically off the field as Real Madrid cashed in on the Beckham name, selling an incredible one million shirts bearing his name, at £50 a pop. As the Americans say: 'Do the math'. You don't have to be a financial whiz-kid to see that Becks paid his transfer fee twice over, simply with shirt sales.

It has already been mentioned how Van Nistelrooy suffered when Becks departed – well, the big Dutchman would suffer himself when he fell out with Fergie in 2006. And he would also head the same route as Beckham: to Real Madrid, in his case for £11 million, in the summer.

Van Nistelrooy, as touched on in an earlier chapter, had initially fallen foul of the United manager when he had a bust-up with Ronaldo in January of that year. I am told by reliable sources within United that Sir Alex had to step in and restore order after the spat on the training ground. Tensions had been growing as the Dutchman voiced his anger at Ronaldo's 'showboating' over the previous couple of months. He claimed Ronaldo was too greedy and not providing him with the service he had taken for granted when Becks was at the club.

It all came to a head mid-January when United lost 3-1 to Manchester City, with Ronaldo sent off for lunging at Andy Cole. The previous month the Portuguese had been dropped by United after he was substituted in Lisbon during the Champions League defeat to Benfica.

Van Nistelrooy let it be known that he was peeved with him at that fateful training session. I am told he sneered at Ronaldo and said: 'Off you go to see your father, then' – a reference to his close relationship with assistant boss Carlos Queiroz.

Ronaldo is said to have replied, with tears rolling down his face: 'I can't, my father died a few months ago' – a reference to the sad death of José Dinis on 6 September 2005.

Naturally, Fergie was angry with Van Nistelrooy and this episode allegedly marked the beginning of the end for the big striker.

A few months later the Dutchman revealed that a four-letter blast at the boss during the Carling Cup final proved to be the final straw. He told the *News of the World*: 'It started at the

Carling Cup final, after an hour we were 4-0 ahead. I could not wait to get on as a substitute, to play half an hour and maybe score a goal and then go and lift the cup.

'It's a big trophy after all, but first Kieran Richardson was put on. After that Nemanja Vidic and Patrice Evra, and Evra had only been at the club a few weeks. I exploded and started swearing at Ferguson. That was the killing moment.

'It was both our faults, but we never made up after that. The relationship fell apart.'

Van Nistelrooy scored 150 goals in 219 games for United – and in my opinion was one of the club's greatest-ever centre forwards. But United had had his best years and once again, Fergie was proved right to move on a player eventually considered a disruptive force.

There were others, most notably Roy Keane and Paul Ince. Fergie took a dislike to Cockney Ince's self-styled image as 'The Guv'nor', labelling him a 'big-time Charlie' and flogging him to Inter Milan for £7 million in 1995. My United sources tell me that Fergie felt Ince had simply grown too big for his boots; that the boy from East London was starting to believe his own publicity. I am told the writing for Ince was firmly on the wall after one particular episode concerning him and Ferguson in 1995.

The two men had jumped out of their cars – Incey's boasting the registration GUV 8 – after parking up on the forecourt outside Old Trafford and were both heading for the entrance to the offices at the ground at the same time. As they arrived, the guard at the door nodded his head in respect and said, 'Morning, guv.' Fergie said hello back, but the man and Ince shared a sly wink as the player followed his boss through the door. No prizes for guessing the sting in the tail – the guard had been acknowledging Incey, not Fergie.

Roy Keane was another big-name casualty. As we have noted, he was a brilliant skipper and a legend in the eyes of the fans, but Keano overstepped the mark in November 2005. The Irishman forgot one of the boss's golden rules: if you have any criticisms against fellow players or staff, it stays in the dressing room. That temporary amnesia would cost him dear.

Keane had spoken out against his colleagues on the club's in-house TV channel after they were thrashed 4-1 in the Premiership at Middlesbrough. The show was subsequently pulled and just days later Keane was on his way – officially by mutual consent, though few doubted he had actually been shown the door. Even the man who had led United to seven League titles and four FA Cups was a goner.

The episode showed that in Fergie's eyes it didn't matter what you had done in the past – or how revered you were at the club. If you fell foul of the rules, you were out, simple as that. Some critics would say it was cruelty, control freakery and a sign that while Fergie could dish out criticism, he could not handle it himself. But he himself would explain that he had to rule with an iron glove at times: how else could he expect to keep in line a group of men who were multi-millionaires? He had a point – and the results would back him up – they were always the ultimate answer to those who doubted the real governor of Old Trafford.

Let's close with a final look at the extraordinary credentials that establish Fergie as being 'Simply the Best'.

CHAPTER 20

SIMPLY
THE BEST

The subtitle of this book sums it all up: 'the biography of
Britain's greatest football manager'. That's all well and good
for the modern era, some journo friends of mine carped when
they learned of the accolade – but is he the best ever? Some of
them didn't think so, arguing in the majority of cases that the
ultimate honour would go to Brian Clough or Bob Paisley.

Well, I have looked again at all the hard facts and all the
evidence and arguments – and I have to say I disagree, and that
I still stand by the big man from Govan. He has won more
major trophies than anyone else and he not only took United to
the very top, he also transformed the whole club from top to
bottom, from the youth set-up to providing the success and
entertaining football that, in turn, generated the revenues to
turn Old Trafford into one of the world's best stadiums.

Of course, there have been numerous polls over the years
asking the same question, but the majority back the case for Sir
Alex to be No. 1.

Even in 2005, when some critics had the knives out for the

United boss, a poll of League managers conducted by Tissot, a key sponsor of the League Managers' Association, confirmed Fergie's top spot. He had gained almost twice as many votes as the second-placed Clough.

The *Independent* newspaper summed up the results at the time by saying: '[Clough] famously took Nottingham Forest from the old Second Division in 1977 to become back-to-back winners of the European Cup in 1979 and 1980.

'While many fans might regard that velvet period under Clough at the City Ground as the single greatest managerial achievement, Ferguson's peers have judged his longevity and success in arguably a much more pressured era to surpass it. Clough was comfortably ahead of all other contenders, including Matt Busby, Bill Shankly, Bob Paisley and Arsène Wenger.'

Those latter comments about a 'much more pressured era' are very relevant. There's no argument that Clough worked miracles at Forest, but when he won those two European Cups, his rivals were not in the same calibre as those Fergie had to take on and beat to lift the trophy in 1999 and 2008.

In 1979, Forest overcame the minnows of Malmö, an average Swedish team, and in 1980, Hamburg, a similar outfit from Germany. Hardly the crack Barcelonas, Chelseas, Inter Milans, Juventuses and Bayern Munichs that Fergie had to get past to win the trophy.

In 2007, *The Times* entered the debate with a top 50 all-time managers from around the world. The usual suspects – Fergie, Shanks, Paisley, Busby and Cloughie – made it to the top 7, but not in the positions you might expect.

Cloughie brought up the rear in seventh, Paisley was sixth, with Shanks fifth. Fergie came in at No. 4, with Sir Matt adjudged runner-up. Sandwiched in between in third spot was

Austrian Ernst Happel, while Dutchman Rinus Michels won the coveted No. 1.

I didn't agree with the verdict at the time, and I still don't now. OK, Michels was the architect of the famed 'total football' in Holland, but he never won the World Cup, did he? And he had the most talented generation of Dutch footballers *ever* at his disposal.

As for Happel... well, that just strikes me as *The Times* playing clever buggers, trying to show they have really thought about it! No way is this relative nobody in the same league as Fergie.

At least *The Times*' assessment of the United boss came with a get-out clause to elevate him (which Fergie has since achieved): 'After knocking over the Old Firm in Scotland, he has built a modern-day monster out of Manchester United and has done so with teams of flair and adventure. A giant of football and yet his CV will always have an unmissable hole without that second European Cup. Clinch that and perhaps we can elevate him into the top three.'

In 2009, a further poll came out in favour of the United boss. Carried out by the makers of cult football management game, Football Manager 2010, it ended up with Fergie securing 26 per cent of the vote.

In second place was Sir Bobby Robson, whose credentials included Clough-like success at Ipswich Town as well as glory with bigger fish, including Barcelona and the England national team. Legendary Liverpool boss Bill Shankly came third. Like Busby at United, he built Liverpool into the club they are today, taking them from the old Second Division to the top in England. Clough was fourth, with Sir Matt fifth.

The top 10 also included legendary England boss Sir Alf Ramsey, 'Special One' José Mourinho, Arsène Wenger, Bob Paisley and Jock Stein.

Mike Jacobson, creator of the Football Manager series of games, summed up just why Fergie deserved to be top of the pile. He said: 'As the most successful domestic manager in the history of English football and with a legion of fans around the globe and scores of titles, Sir Alex clearly deserves his place at the top of this poll. The fact he can be a bit controversial – this is the man known as the 'Hairdryer' for his half-time outbursts – only makes football fans love him more.'

Also in 2009, Sir Bobby Charlton paid tribute to Fergie after United notched up the 11th Premier League win of the Scot's time at Old Trafford. Sir Bobby said he foresaw a time when Sir Alex would be immortalised at the Theatre of Dreams – just as Sir Matt was in the form of a bronze statute that now stands outside the club's megastore.

Sir Bobby said: 'You can be absolutely certain that one day there will be a permanent reminder at Old Trafford of what Alex has done for this club – in fact, he should get six statues.

'I think he is the greatest manager of all time – and not just because of what he has done at United. When he came here, he said he wanted to knock Liverpool off their perch. We have now equalled their record of 18 championships and we have the chance to win a fourth European Cup – and it's that ambition that keeps Alex going.

'But he did exactly the same to Rangers and Celtic when he was in Scotland with Aberdeen. For me, that makes him the best there has ever been.

'Matt Busby's philosophy was that you have to always play football that will please the fans – and Alex has always built his teams in the same way. It is the way we play – always adventurous. Sometimes when you play like that you can get caught out, but Alex's teams have always played in the finest traditions of Manchester United.

'You have to play attractive football at this club. It is not enough to win if you are boring. Alex has continued it after Matt Busby. Sometimes it drives you mad because the way we play means we always seem to go right to the brink.

'Even now, at my age, I kick every ball because I get so caught up in all the excitement. This is the third title in a row and that is absolutely fantastic. We have been to the other side of the world this season to play in the Club World Cup and we've had to play twice a week ever since to catch up.

'That, for me, makes this side as good as anything that has been before. In fact, I think it's the best team we've ever had at this club.'

To get the view of a United fan in the press box, I conducted an exclusive interview with Andy Bucklow, a respected national newspaper journalist and a Reds supporter since the 1960s, for his opinion on the big 'Who is the greatest of them all?' debate.

Andy, who works for the *Mail on Sunday*, told me he had no doubt about it – Fergie towered above all his rivals, but that he owed a debt to Busby, and that Fergie was similar in his approach to Sir Matt in the way he set about turning United around.

This is what Andy had to say to me: 'Sir Matt built the modern Manchester United out of rubble, Sir Alex rebuilt it out of a rabble; but the similarities between two of the greatest managers of the modern game are striking. Both took seven years to win the first League title, both had already won an FA Cup by the time they did so; both recognised the need to build for the long-term through the establishment of a strong, enduring youth set-up.

'If they are good enough, they are old enough, as it now says on the T-shirt.

'But, above all, throughout a joint tenure of 50 years at Old Trafford and 16 League titles between them, the one enduring ethos behind their respective successes, apart from an obvious knowledge of the game, has been that of man management.

'It is all too easy for dyed-in-the wool Reds who, even after the past 24 years of constant success under Fergie, still go moist-eyed at memories of the 1950s' Babes and the 1960s' joyride of the Best, Law and Charlton era. And behind it all sits the image of the genial, all-knowing, pipe-smoking Sir Matt, the kind, grandfatherly figure.

'Contrast this to the impression people still have today of Sir Alex. You can't go even a minute discussing his management style before someone mentions the "hairdryer", the term famously coined by Mark Hughes to describe a Fergie rollocking.

'But the behind-the-scenes truth is somewhat different. Busby was the first of the post-war hands-on modern managers who, in contrast to the remote figures that were his predecessors, liked nothing more than to don a tracksuit and get his ideas over to his players on the training ground. The myth, which he did little to dispel, if we're being honest, is that he used his assistant Jimmy Murphy to play the bad cop when anyone stepped out of line.

'The truth is that Matt could be as ruthless as any when he felt the need. People who cite the example of Sir Matt's tolerance of the increasingly wayward George Best as proof that he was a bit soft are muddying the waters. The Best disappearing acts and drinking sprees occurred very much at the end of Sir Matt's reign and after he had achieved his Holy Grail and lifted United's first European Cup in 1968. That triumph, and all its inevitable emotional connections back to Munich ten years earlier, drained the old man emotionally and there is no doubt that as he approached his 60s, he was never the same driven man.

'In the early days things were very different. When he arrived at the club as a demobilised sergeant major, Busby demanded an autocracy as a manager never seen before, with no interference from the boardroom.

'Harold Hardman, the chairman at the time, once said: "Our manager has asked us for advice and we will give it to him, then he'll please his bloody self." This single-mindedness was replicated, most notably in the mid-Fifties when he defied the wishes of the Football League committee to ensure United were the first English club to compete in the European Cup.

'His no-nonsense treatment of top players such as Charlie Mitten in the early Fifties and Johnny Giles in 1963, both over money, showed Busby's ruthless streak.

'Ferguson, of course, is hardly known for being a shrinking violet, but that "hairdryer" is, in reality, far more likely to be targeted at recalcitrant journalists than his players.

'Of course there have been dressing-room spats, such as the Beckham "flying boot" incident in 2003 after an FA Cup loss to Arsenal and the bawling-out of Peter Schmeichel at Anfield in 1994 after Liverpool had fought back from 3-0 down to claim a late point.

'But Ferguson hasn't won 30 trophies at OT just by playing the hard man. Ask Giggs, ask Scholes, ask Gary Neville.

'And ask Eric Cantona. Fergie showed a flexibility in his dealings with the Frenchman, which in many ways echoed Sir Matt's latter-day approach to Best. Cantona was allowed to get away with breaking club rules (apart from his kung-fu expertise, constantly flouting the club's dress code being a case in point) which was not a luxury offered to others, even the likes of hardened pros such as Hughes, Bruce or Schmeichel.

'Similarly when Eric disappeared to France soon after his seven-month ban for the kung-fu incident, Fergie tracked him all over Paris on the back of a motor scooter before persuading him, over a couple of bottles of fine red wine, that his future still lay at Old Trafford.

'The one difference in these two examples was that although both Fergie and Sir Matt were prepared to make exceptions for exceptional players, one was still at the height of his powers and riven with ambition; the other was coming to the end of the road and no longer had the energy to come up with a proper solution to the Best "problem". It was probably beyond anybody, to be fair.

'But if there hadn't been a Busby at Old Trafford, would there have been a Fergie? If Busby hadn't shown up at the bomb-strewn ground in 1945, it's entirely feasible United could well have been just one of the pack, a nearly club like Aston Villa, Spurs or, heaven forbid, Newcastle United. And would a club with such an average history have been enough to attract an Alex Ferguson in 1986?

'That's why for me, the two men will always be intertwined and we should be grateful to have had the best two club managers in British football at United for the best part of 50 years. People can throw in the likes of Brian Clough and Bob Paisley, if they want, and I admit they may have a case. Clough took two unfashionable teams to the League title and won the European Cup twice with one of them. Remarkable achievements both, but his gradual and then spectacular fall from grace, following his split from his assistant Peter Taylor, which ended in a booze-filled relegation campaign, put a dampener on that.

'As for Paisley, nobody can dispute the figures. Three European Cups, more than Sir Matt or Sir Alex. But in my view Liverpool's greatest manager has to be Shankly, who didn't win any European Cups. All credit to Paisley, but although he played his part as a member of the famous boot-room, it was

Shankly who built the foundations for those European Cup triumphs, starting with promotion from the old Division Two in 1962. Just as Sir Matt built and rebuilt three great teams and Sir Alex another three and still counting.

'On trophies alone, Ferguson has the edge over Busby if you match up League Titles (eleven to five), European Cups (two to one), FA Cups (five to two), not to mention a World Club Championship, European Cup Winners' Cup, a Super Cup, four League Cups and countless Charity Shields.

'It would be trite, however, to just do the maths. Busby operated at a time when many more clubs were capable of lifting the title, including teams such as Burnley and Wolves, not to mention Leeds, Liverpool, Everton, Arsenal and latterly Derby County and winning serial doubles, trebles and three championships on the bounce was unheard of. And despite the name of Manchester United becoming synonymous with glory and glamour throughout the world by the mid-Sixties, it has to be remembered that the club was not significantly wealthier than their rivals and, the likes of Denis Law apart, big incoming transfers were the exception rather than the rule.

'But if Sir Matt was responsible for moulding United into the force, and indeed religion, which the club was to become for millions then Fergie broke it, remoulded it, then took it a stage further. The domination of the Premier League from its inception is without precedence in the English game. And if you argue that more European Cups could – and indeed should – have been brought back to the Old Trafford trophy room, there is still time to remedy that.

'All this has been achieved with a United-style brand of thrilling brand of football Sir Matt would have approved of. There is no doubt that when Sir Alex takes one last look at his much-coveted watch, and decides he can allot no more added-on time, that Reds, and others everywhere, will be apprehensively expecting a blip.

'But his legacy is such that, barring some unforeseen Glazer-related madness, the club has the foundations and the infrastructure which he built over the past quarter of a century to expect further additions to its rich history, albeit if that means seeing off Chelsea (again) and those shopaholic, lottery-winners Manchester City.

'At the very least we will be spared the wilderness years and relegation that haunted the club after Sir Matt's professional passing. That factor alone puts Fergie out on his own.'

Provocative comments, substantiated... and certain to cause further debate, it must be said.

So, what of the future for Fergie and United? Well, when the great man eventually does retire, he will certainly have earned his statue outside Old Trafford – and if the club have any sense, a role similar to Sir Bobby Charlton. President Fergie of Manchester United... that has a nice ring about it, if Sir Bobby finally decides to step out of the limelight.

Forget the idea that Fergie staying on would somehow be detrimental to the club; that it could cause problems in the same way that Sir Matt staying on as general manager overshadowed Wilf McGuinness's elevation to manager. No, Fergie would not be asked to stay on in a supervisory capacity – he would remain in a more ambassadorial role. He would be there if the new man needed him, but distanced enough to allow him to do his job without fear of interference.

And who should that new man be? No doubt about it in my mind: the only one able to step into a giant's shadow and emerge as strong is José Mourinho.

Yes, the old Special One himself and the man that Fergie himself has said would be a fine choice. In 2009, he told CNN:

'I am glad it is not my decision but whoever it is, it needs to be someone with experience. Manchester United is a massive club. The club I joined in 1986 is nothing like the one it is today. I like José Mourinho – he is a good guy and someone I get on very well with.'

Fergie is the man who built a legend: with Mourinho, he could work from the shadows to ensure his legacy is well preserved. It would be a match made in footballing heaven. Here's to the next stage in the life of Sir Alex Ferguson, footballing genius.

CHAPTER 21

END OF AN ERA

It was the day United fans dreaded – the day the boss finally hung up his stopwatch and chewing gum, and walked away from the manager's hot-seat. 8 May, 2013 – put it in your diary for posterity. Some United fans were calling it 'United's JFK moment', as they knew they would never forget where they were and what they were doing when they heard the news that the greatest ever manager in British, and world, football was retiring.

In the sleazy corners of Fleet Street's sports desks, hacks had heard rumours that the boss was on his way the night before. They were loud and strong; the great man had only told close family and friends of his intentions, but still the news had leaked out. Fergie had made the decision at the start of 2013 but had not wanted it to be front page news until the last game of the season.

Inevitably, he was to be disappointed with that wish. Secrets are hard to keep within football and journalism at the best of times; and when they concern the most famous man in world football, it is even harder to conceal such a stunning development. A whisper here, a quiet word in a boozer there, and suddenly, with the power of the internet, the whole world is talking. Fergie was going to quit at the end of the season – and the most likely man to replace him would be an identikit of the big man himself. David Moyes, carved of the same footballing granite as Sir Alex and developed over the years in his image. Strong, respectable, a good football man, and a good human being: someone who could administer the necessary bollockings to millionaire players when needed, but also someone who, like Fergie, could offer a conciliatory, compassionate arm around the shoulder on other occasions.

Confidantes explained to Sir Alex that the news of his exit had trickled out and that the whispers would get louder and the conjecture would increase – and that it could even cause problems for United and their players and staff if the rumours were not addressed. Given the situation, the boss acted with his usual confidence.

'He told his advisers he would come clean; that he would announce his plans the following morning,' a source close to United said. 'Fergie knew the news was out on the streets and that there was no way of keeping a lid on it now. So he decided to tackle the problem head-on – just as he had done with so many other issues over the years at Old Trafford.

'Alex has never been someone who dithers and deliberates – he is an action man.'

Nice quote that: an action man. Fergie himself would surely like that as an epitaph.

Certainly the next morning, he proved just how decisive he could be as he confirmed that, yes, he was off. He released a statement in which he outlined just why he was going, how much United and the fans meant to him and how he believed he was leaving a solid, golden legacy at Old Trafford. He also revealed he was not cutting all links with the club. He would become a 'director and ambassador' – on a reported salary of £1.5million a year – which meant he would be there for the new manager, if needed.

Fergie said, 'It was important to me to leave an organisation in the strongest possible shape and I believe I have done so. The quality of this league winning squad, and the balance of ages within it, bodes well for continued success at the highest level while the structure of the youth setup will ensure that the long-term future of the club remains a bright one.

'Our training facilities are amongst the finest in global sport and our home Old Trafford is rightfully regarded as one of the leading venues in the world. Going forward, I am delighted to take on the roles of both Director and Ambassador for the club. With these activities, along with my many other interests, I am looking forward to the future.'

Sir Alex went on to pay tribute to his family, particularly wife Cathy whose support over the years has been invaluable – indeed, it was she who had persuaded him not to retire several years earlier, to the relief of United fans everywhere! He then thanked the Manchester United board for putting their faith in him and allowing him to shape the team as he had wanted, with a particular mention for Sir Bobby Charlton, before paying his respects to the Old Trafford faithful:

'To the fans, thank you. The support you have provided over the years has been truly humbling. It has been an honour and an enormous privilege to have had the opportunity to lead your club and I have treasured my time as manager of Manchester United.'

At the time, Sir Alex did not reveal exactly why he had chosen May 2013 as his retirement date. The answers would come a few days later when United played their final home match of the season – which gained extra poignancy as it became Fergie's final match as boss at Old Trafford. For the record, Fergie, then aged 71, had been in charge of United for 26 years and had won a staggering 38 trophies during his reign. That remarkable haul included 13 league titles, two Champions League crowns, five FA Cups and four League Cups.

It was a reign that would surely never be matched in world football and Fergie's resignation brought thousands of swift messages of congratulations and thanks. United chief executive David Gill led the tributes from within the club, saying he was grateful to have had such a fine manager as Fergie to work with. Gill said, 'I've had the tremendous pleasure of working very closely with Alex for 16 unforgettable years – through the Treble, the double, countless trophy wins and numerous signings.

'We knew that his retirement would come one day and we both have been planning for it by ensuring the quality of the squad and club structures are in first-class condition. Alex's vision, energy and ability have built teams – both on and off the pitch – that his successor can count on as among the best and most loyal in world sport.

'The way he cares for this club, his staff and for the football family in general is something that I admire. It is a side to him that is often hidden from public view but it is something that I have been privileged to witness in the last 16 years. What he has done for this club and for the game in general will never be forgotten. It has been the greatest experience of my working life being alongside Alex and a great honour to be able to call him a friend.'

First-team coach Rene Meulensteen said: 'He told us just this morning. He called us in his office and told us the decision he had taken. I think he is feeling a sense of relief in some ways now.'

One of Fergie's most famed – and best – buys, Ole Gunnar Solskjaer, led the tributes from outside the building. Solskjaer, now the manager of Norwegian side Molde, told MUTV: 'I will never forget the loyalty he showed me. Everything I have learnt I have learnt from the boss.'

While legendary keeper Peter Schmeichel revealed he was 'sad and bewildered' by the news: 'It's come as an absolute bombshell...I was really, really hoping he was going to stay for another couple of years.'

England manager Roy Hodgson described Ferguson's announcement as 'a sad day for English football', adding, 'It marks the end of an era in football management. No one will be able to match his achievements, his dedication, his support for colleagues in need and his team building know-how.'

While Hodgson's rugby union counterpart Stuart Lancaster said, 'His longevity and what he has achieved as a coach I think is unparalleled in world sport. I admire him hugely for what he has done.'

And golfer and loyal United fan Rory McIlroy added, 'An end of an era today. Sir Alex Ferguson, the greatest of all time! United will have a tough time trying to replace him.'

British Prime Minister David Cameron was first out of the traps from the world of 'officialdom'. He said Sir Alex's record and achievements at United were 'exceptional'. Cameron, who supports Aston Villa, then added, 'Hopefully his retirement will make life a little easier for my team!'

Labour leader Ed Miliband tweeted, 'Proud man. Great manager. Staunch Labour Party supporter. Sir Alex Ferguson will never be forgotten.'

World football's self-styled 'big two' also wanted in on the act. Fifa president Sepp Blatter tweeted: 'His achievements in the game place him without doubt as one of the greats. It was an honour to present Sir Alex with award at 2011 Ballon D'Or. Will his longevity at the top ever be repeated?'

And UEFA president Michel Platini said, 'He is a visionary who has made a massive contribution to football across Europe.'

Back in Britain, Premier League chief executive Richard Scudamore said, 'The Premier League has had the privilege to witness many great players, managers and teams. No one has made as great a contribution to the Premier League than Sir Alex Ferguson.' And League Managers Association chairman Howard Wilkinson said, 'He is the epitome of the mantra, "Survive, Win, Succeed". In private, with those he trusted, he was the very best sort of friend you could ever wish for.'

It was all very complimentary, as befitted what undoubtedly was indeed the end of an era. But United fans – and the press – remained puzzled as to why the boss had decided to go. What was the reasoning behind it all? Hadn't he said he intended to stay around and win another Champions League? Had he been nudged out of the door for some reason? Had a doctor told him he must quit for medical reasons?

All would be revealed after that final home game of the season against Swansea on Sunday 13 May. Fergie would see his troops win at Old Trafford for the final time, a perfunctory 2-1 triumph over their Welsh visitors with goals from Chicharito and Ferdinand icing the cake as they had already sewn up that record 20th top-flight title win (and the 13th under Sir Alex) with victory over Aston Villa on 22 April.

The boss revealed afterwards that he had made the decision to step down over the Christmas break. His main reason? To spend some time with his wife Cathy, after she had devoted 47 years of her life to supporting him in his footballing career. Cathy had been left heartbroken when her sister Bridget died in

October 2012 and Fergie now felt it was only right that he should devote more time to his family.

He said, 'The decision to retire is one that I have thought a great deal about and one that I have not taken lightly. It is the right time. Things changed when Cathy's sister died. She's isolated a lot now and I think I owe her a lot of my own time. For 47 years she's been the leader of the family, looked after three sons and sacrificed for me. I think she's lost her best friend, her sister Bridget, so I think I owe her time, that was important.'

He admitted he did not tell his three sons until March – and only broke the news to his brother when the news started to leak out. 'It was very difficult, there were some times when I nearly blurted it out to the family, you know, the grandchildren,' he admitted. 'I told my sons round about March and my brother didn't even know until Tuesday night because I wanted to tell the players first really, the players and my staff.'

The match against Swansea was Sir Alex's 723rd match in charge at Old Trafford. He went on to the pitch to make an emotional speech after the final whistle and was joined by his family, players and staff. He hugged his 11 grandchildren and then spoke to his adoring public, saying, 'I've got absolutely no script in my mind, I'm just going to ramble on and hope I get to the core of what this football club has meant to me. First of all, it's a thank you to Manchester United. Not just the directors, not just the medical staff, not just the coaching staff, the players or the supporters, it's all of you. You have been the most fantastic experience of my life.

'I have been very fortunate. I've been able to manage some of the greatest players in the country, let alone Manchester United. All these players here today have represented our club the proper way – they've won the championship in a fantastic fashion. Well done to the players. My retirement doesn't mean the end of my life with the club. I'll be able to now enjoy watching them rather than suffer with them.

'But, if you think about it, those last-minute goals, the comebacks, even the defeats, are all part of this great football club of ours. It's been an unbelievable experience for all of us, so thank you for that. I'd also like to remind you that when we had bad times here, the club stood by me, all my staff stood by me, the players stood by me. Your job now is to stand by our new manager. That is important.

'Before I start bubbling, I just want to pay tribute to Paul Scholes, who retires today. He's unbelievable; one of the greatest players this club has ever had and will ever have. Paul, we wish you a good retirement and I know you'll be around annoying me! Also I'd like to wish Darren Fletcher a speedy comeback to our club.

'I wish the players every success in the future. You know how good you are, you know the jersey you're wearing, you know what it means to everyone here and don't ever let yourself down. The expectation is always there.

'I'm going home, well, I'm going inside for a while, and I want to say thank you again from all the Ferguson family. They're all up there, 11 grandchildren – thank you.'

There wasn't a dry eye in the house.

Lifelong United fan Mike Gould summed up the feelings of those inside Old Trafford when he said, 'That was some end to a brilliant day. I saw grown men brought to tears in the Stretford End. Fergie got the send-off he deserved after all he had done for the club – and us supporters will always remember what he did for us. He is a legend and he deserves to have a stand at the ground named after him – and a statue of himself outside the front of the stadium. Sir Matt was the man who put us on the map in the first place – Sir Alex is the man whose work ensures we will always still there.

'We also liked the way he asked for patience and support for the new manager, David Moyes. That was never in doubt, but it was good of Fergie to do that on a day that was really all about him.'

A source close to Moyes admitted the former Everton manager was 'grateful' for Sir Alex's words of support and that he was 'contented and glad' the United legend would be there for him if needed. One of the first tasks to be dealt with in Moyes' in-tray when he officially took up his post on 1 July 2013 would be the future of Wayne Rooney – and the source admitted that David 'would take soundings from Fergie' on the matter.

Fergie had gleefully answered. 'Not my decision now!' when asked by a TV reporter if he would battle to keep Rooney at the club. The handover to Moyes had already begun – just hours after the end of the match against Swansea.

In an earlier edition of this book, I had suggested that Jose Mourinho might be the best man to follow Fergie in the hot-seat. But I could see the logic of why Sir Alex had anointed Moyes as his successor. Fergie and fellow United legend (and current president of the club) Sir Bobby Charlton were asked to find the new boss by the board, and both went for Moyes.

Sir Alex explained their thinking in this way: 'We unanimously agreed on David Moyes. David is a man of great integrity with a strong work ethic. I've admired his work for a long time and approached him as far back as 1998 to discuss the position of assistant manager here. There is no question he has all the qualities we expect of a manager at this club.'

While Mourinho would undoubtedly have continued to put trophies on the table, Moyes, who would leave Everton after 11 years in charge, had proved himself both a long-term strategist and a keen enthusiast of youth in his time at Goodison Park. He was more in the mould of Fergie; he would work his damndest to keep United at the top. What would be Everton's profound loss would, Fergie and Charlton hoped, be United's profound good fortune. Moyes would be given a six-year deal, on a salary of £5million a year, to show United's commitment to him.

He would certainly have much to live up to if he were ever to come close to emulating Sir Alex's influence and success on the club – let alone dream of having a stand named after him, or a statue built.

Since the defeat to Barcelona at Wembley in May 2011, Fergie had worked damned hard to get United back to the very top of European football. It would not be easy: Barca were still a dominant force and the likes of Bayern Munich and Real Madrid were also making their presence felt.

And even in the domestic league, the rivalry was becoming just as intense with Manchester City, under driven Italian boss Roberto Mancini, and Chelsea stepping up to the plate again. Of course, Fergie and United had achieved a record 19th league title in the 2010/11 campaign, securing the championship with a 1-1 draw at Blackburn. But after losing to Barca at Wembley a fortnight later, Fergie reacted by strengthening his squad. He admitted he was aiming to speed up the pace and craft of his team and to that extent he brought in the tricky wing skills of Ashley Young, from Aston Villa, and the dead-eyed defensive presence of the young but brilliant Phil Jones, from Blackburn.

Both would prove their worth to United over the next couple of years and Jones, in particular, would emphasise the boss's talent-spotting skills and (mostly) excellent purchases in the transfer market. None other than Sir Bobby Charlton would publicly comment on Jones – and what a buy he was, even at

£19million – when he said the boy reminded him of the late, great Duncan Edwards.

'If you talk to Bobby Charlton, Paddy Crerand, Charlton's team-mate in United's 1968 European Cup winning team confirmed, 'Phil Jones reminds him of Duncan Edwards with his power and build.'

That was some comparison – and Jones would start to build towards earning such an awesome reputation as he starred for United in the 2011/12 season. However, the season overall would be judged a failure by Fergie, as United lost their Premier League crown to bitter local rivals City, and crashed out of the Champions League at the group stage.

Sure, United had begun the season with a 3-2 Community Shield win over City at Wembley in August, 2011. But that was small change and small consolation to Fergie when Sergio Aguero smashed home the injury-time winner against QPR that took the title to the Etihad.

Just as big a disappointment to the boss was that the Red Devils went out of the Champions League at the group stage. On 7 December 2011, United lost 2-1 at Basel, which meant they finished third in their group and were demoted to the UEFA Europa League for the first time since the 1995/96 season. They then exited this second-rate tournament at the Round of 16, after losing 5-3 on aggregate to Atletico Bilbao.

Not that Fergie was that bothered about leaving the Europa League early. He had made clear his feelings about the tournament when United were parachuted into it after the 2-1 loss at Basel. He had said, 'Now we are in a competition I have never been in with Manchester United. It does mean Sundays right through and Thursday–Sunday matches. That has to be dealt with. That is our penalty for not qualifying.'

The fact he saw the competition as a punishment for failing

in the Champions League certainly riled UEFA president Michel Platini, who commented, 'The world does not revolve around England, I like England a lot, its football is fantastic, its supporters are wonderful but you shouldn't criticise the Europa League just because you've played in three Champions League finals. The Europa League is a brilliant competition, it's amazing. I know Mr Ferguson would have preferred to be in the Champions League but so would many clubs who don't have that possibility.'

The row lingered on for a few days, with Fergie admitting, 'It is a good competition, a strong competition, you only have to see some of the teams that are left in it. The point I made about it being a punishment was only in the sense of for 20 years, this club has only thought about the Champions League. We have just thought about winning that European Cup.

'The punishment is the big disappointment of not challenging for it this year, having been in three finals in the last four years. It was not a slight against the Europa League. It is a competition we want to win.'

But a source close to the United boss told me: 'Truth is, Fergie did see it as a punishment – a second-rate tournament for also-rans. That's why he shed no tears when United went out; it meant he had a clear run at the league without the complications of the Thursday night games in the Europa. And the United fans were just as blasé about it; they didn't enjoy it when other fans sang about Thursday nights on Channel 5!'

Yet the controversy with Platini could not hide the fact that the boss was downhearted that United had failed to progress beyond the group stages of the Champions League. He had set his sights on making amends for the defeat by Barca at Wembley, but his team hadn't even got beyond the starting blocks. Then, when they lost their Premier League crown to

City in the dying seconds of the 2011/12 season, his misery was complete. It had been a failure of a campaign and Sir Alex wasn't kidding himself or anyone else that it had been anything but that.

The one consolation for United fans was that Fergie would now continue in the hot-seat for at least another 12 months; no way would he walk away from Old Trafford in failure. No, he would need to at least win back the Premier League crown and, hopefully, the Champions League again before he would even contemplate retirement. That was the way he was built; the way he had always worked. Coming second meant nothing – winning was everything. Being the best was all that counted at a club like Manchester United and with a manager as ferociously competitive as Sir Alex Ferguson.

There were a couple of consolations during that barren campaign of 2011/12. The first came in November, 2011, when the club renamed the North Stand at Old Trafford the Sir Alex Ferguson Stand in honour of his 25 years at the club.

The boss told BBC Sport he had not expected such a tribute – and that club officials had done well to keep it from him. 'It was a surprise for me today, I didn't expect that. I felt really honoured and emotional when I saw my name on that stand. I must say thank you to the club for that. My assistant didn't tell me – so he's sacked!' he joked. When the BBC asked what had been the most memorable moment of those 25 years, he answered, 'I'll never forget Barcelona 1999. Never.'

The second boost for the manager came in the same month when a statue of him was unveiled on the forecourt of the stand that had been named after him. 'People normally die before they get a statue – I'm outliving death,' he quipped, clearly delighted at the unveiling ceremony.

Fergie was still joking as his wife Cathy climbed the podium to officially unveil the statue. 'Somebody has to control me and Cathy is the only one who can,' he joked. 'Mind you, I've made her promise to come here every Saturday morning and bow down in front of me!'

But he wasn't joking as he made preparations for what would be his final season as United boss; the 2012/13 campaign.

His team had lost the league to City by goal difference on the very last day of the previous season – and he was determined that would not happen again. Fergie's move to ensure that was the case? Simple: he went out and bought the top goalscorer in Britain. Yes, the deadly Robin van Persie was recruited from Arsenal for a £24million fee. OK, it was a lot of money for a player who had turned 29. But for that outlay you were getting a guaranteed goalscorer – a man who would continue to top the charts...and bring the title back to Old Trafford.

And that's exactly what Van Persie did. His goals were the essential difference between United and City. If ever there was a £24million bargain, it was Van Persie. By Christmas 2012, it was clear United were well on target for that record 20th top-flight title and the rub of the Van Persie transfer was this: his goals shot United well clear of the chasing pack and made it all the easier for the boss to push ahead with his retirement plans as 2012 turned into 2013.

For by that time, Fergie knew he would be bringing the title home – barring a shock turnaround in the club's fortunes. He could now plan his future away from United with confidence – his 'gamble' on 29-year-old Van Persie had enabled him to do that.

And the landmarks kept coming for the boss as the season progressed. On 2 September, 2012, he hit 1,000 league games as United manager in the match against Southampton. Two weeks later, he won his 100th game in the

Champions League – in the 1-0 win over Turkish outfit Galatasaray at Old Trafford.

By the middle of April 2013, it was clear that Fergie was indeed about to lead United to that 20th league title. They were so far ahead of the pack – 15 points at one stage – it was almost an embarrassing one-team procession. Confirmation of the triumph came on April 22, when they cruised to a 3-0 win over Aston Villa. And, appropriately enough, it was a Robin van Persie hat-trick that did the job that day. Fergie had been proved right once again – the Dutchman was a true winner just like his new boss.

The one blot on the copy book for the United boss was that he never did get around to winning the Champions League for a third time. He had wanted to do that to match the achievement of another legendary manager – Bob Paisley of Liverpool. But it wasn't for lack of trying, and it was certainly bad luck that cost Fergie as United lost 2-1 on aggregate to Mourinho's Real Madrid after Portuguese winger Nani was sent off. Until the dismissal, the Red Devils had been leading 1-0 and looked certain victors; after it, with ten men against one of the Continent's top teams, they simply could not compete.

It was a sad moment for Fergie: he was so distraught at the final whistle, he was unable to emerge to comment. He knew United should have won and that, in what he knew was his last stab at the trophy before retirement, they were robbed of certain victory.

But he consoled himself with the return of the league title – and with the thought that he was walking away as a winner. It was the end of an era at Old Trafford, and the end of a long, successful road for the world's best ever manager. He had achieved everything he had set out to achieve when he had arrived in 1986 – he had won everything and 'knocked Liverpool off their f****n' perch – and now he could retire from the frontline with a sense of satisfaction at his lifetime's work.

'Manchester has never seen anything like this,' Rio Ferdinand said at the city's town hall on 14 May 2013, as he and his team-mates proudly showed off the Premier League trophy. It would also double up as Fergie's final parade – and Manchester had certainly never seen anything like him...and the glut of trophies and good times he brought to the red half of the city.

And it is extremely unlikely the world of football will ever see the likes of him again.

SOURCES

The *Independent*
James Lawton
Eric Harrison
George Switzer
Steve Brenner
The *Sun*
The *Daily Mail*
Sweet FA – Graham Kelly
Steven Haywood
Terry Graham
Lee Clayton
Key 103
IMUSA
MUTV

Kevin McCarra
The *Guardian*
Sky TV
manutd.com
Dave Moore
ITN Sport
Sir Bobby Charlton
Bryan Robson
Daily Telegraph
My Life In Football – Gordon Strachan
My Defence – Ashley Cole
New Statesman
News of the World